THE STORY OF THE NEGRO

VOLUME I

BOOKER T. WASHINGTON

The Story of the Negro

The
Rise of the Race from Slavery

By

BOOKER T. WASHINGTON

VOLUME I

NEGRO UNIVERSITIES PRESS
NEW YORK

Originally published in 1909
by Doubleday, Page & Company

Reprinted 1969 by
Negro Universities Press
A Division of Greenwood Publishing Corp.
New York

Library of Congress Catalogue Card Number 69-16564

PRINTED IN UNITED STATES OF AMERICA

PREFACE

IN WRITING this volume it has been my object to show what the Negro himself has accomplished in constructive directions. I have not undertaken to discuss the many problems which have arisen through the contact of the Negro with other races, but to tell a simple, straight story of what the Negro himself has accomplished in the way of attaining to a higher civilisation.

It ought to be explained, too, that I have not undertaken to write any formal or detailed history of the entire Negro race. In many cases names of worthy and successful individuals have been omitted for want of space. In other cases I have used names merely as illustrations of what the race has been able to accomplish.

I want to make grateful mention, also, of the service which Dr. Robert E. Park has rendered in the preparation of this volume. Without his constant and painstaking assistance I could not have accomplished the object which I have had in view. I am deeply grateful, also, to Mr. Monroe N. Work for valuable assistance.

If the reading of these chapters shall in any degree inspire any Negro to make himself useful and successful in the world, and if in any degree what I have written will cause any individuals, not members of my own race, to take a more generous and hopeful view of the condition and prospects of the Negro, I shall feel that I have accomplished what I started out to do in the writing of these pages.

BOOKER T. WASHINGTON.

Tuskegee Institute, Alabama.

CONTENTS—Volume I

PART I

THE NEGRO IN AFRICA

PART II

THE NEGRO AS A SLAVE

THE STORY OF THE NEGRO

VOLUME I

Part I

THE NEGRO IN AFRICA

The Story of the Negro

CHAPTER I

FIRST NOTIONS OF AFRICA

SOME years ago, in a book called "Up From Slavery," I tried to tell the story of my own life. While I was at work upon that book the thought frequently occurred to me that nearly all that I was writing about myself might just as well have been written of hundreds of others, who began their life, as I did mine, in slavery. The difficulties I had experienced and the opportunities I had discovered, all that I had learned, felt and done, others likewise had experienced and others had done. In short, it seemed to me, that what I had put into the book, "Up From Slavery," was, in a very definite way, an epitome of the history of my race, at least in the early stages of its awakening and in the evolution through which it is now passing.

This thought suggested another, and I asked myself why it would not be possible to sketch the history of the Negro people in America in much the same way that I had tried to write the story of my own life, telling mostly the things that I knew of my own personal knowledge or through my acquaintance with persons and events, and adding to that what I have been able to learn from tradition and from books. In a certain way the second book, if I were able to carry out my design, might be regarded as the sequel of the first, telling the story of a struggle through two and one-half centuries of slavery, and during a period of something more than forty years of freedom, which had elsewhere been condensed into the limits of a single lifetime. This is, then, the task which I have set myself in the pages which follow.

There comes a time, I imagine, in the life of every boy and every girl, no matter to what race they belong, when they feel a desire to learn something about their ancestors; to know where and how they lived, what they suffered and what they achieved, how they dressed, what religion they professed and what position they occupied in the larger world about them. The girl who grows up in the slums of a large city, the Indian out in the wide prairie, the "poor white" boy in the mountains of the Southern states, and the ignorant Negro boy on a Southern plantation, no matter how obscure their origin, each will feel a special interest in the people whose fortunes he or she has shared, and a special sympathy with all that people have lived, and suffered and achieved.

The desire to know something of the country from which my race sprang and of the history of my mother and her people came to me when I was still a child. I can remember, as a slave, hearing snatches of conversation from the people at the "Big House" from which I learned that the great white race in America had come from a distant country, from which the white people and their forefathers had travelled in ships across a great water, called the ocean. As I grew older I used to hear them talk with pride about the history of their people, of the discovery of America, and of the struggles and heroism of the early days when they, or their ancestors, were fighting the Indians and settling up the country. All this helped to increase, as time went on, my desire to know what was back of me, where I came from, and what, if anything, there was in the life of my people in Africa and America to which I might point with pride and think about with satisfaction.

My curiosity in regard to the origin and history of the dark-skinned people to which I belong, led me at first to listen and observe and then, later, as I got some schooling and a wider knowledge of the world, to inquire and read. What I learned in this way only served, however, to increase my desire to go farther and deeper into the life of my people, and to find out for myself what they had been in Africa as well as in America.

What I was first able to hear and to learn did not,

I confess, take me very far or give me very much satisfaction. In the part of the country in which I lived there were very few of my people who pretended to know very much about Africa. I learned, however, that my mother's people had come, like the white people, from across the water, but from a more distant and more mysterious land, where people lived a different life from ours, had different customs and spoke a different language from that I had learned to speak. Of the long and terrible journey by which my ancestors came from their native home in Africa to take up their life again beside the white man and Indian in the New World, I used to hear many and sinister references, but not until I was a man did I meet any one, among my people who knew anything definite, either through personal knowledge or through tradition, of the country or the people from whom my people sprang. To most of the slaves the "middle passage," as the journey from the shore of Africa to the shore of America was called, was merely a tradition of a confused and bewildering experience, concerning whose horrors they had never heard any definite details. Nothing but the vaguest notions remained, at the time I was a boy, even among the older people in regard to the mother country of my race.

In slavery days the traditions of the people who lived in the cabins centred almost entirely about the lives and fortunes of the people who lived in the

"Big House." The favourite stories around the cabin fireside related to what this or that one had seen on some distant journey with "old master," or perhaps to the adventures they had when master and they were boys together.

It has often occurred to me that people who talk of removing the Negro from the Southern states and colonising him in some distant part of the world do not reflect how deeply he is rooted in the soil. In most that the white man has done on this continent, from the time Columbus landed at San Salvador until Peary penetrated farthest North, the Negro has been his constant companion and helper. Any one who considers what the Negro has done, for example, in the Southern states alone, in cutting down the forests, clearing the land, tilling the soil and building up the farms and the cities, will recognise that, directly and indirectly, his labour has been an enormous contribution to the civilisation of the Western world. Any one, on the other hand, who will listen to the songs that we sing, and the anecdotes that are told by the Negro and concerning him; any one who will read the literature and the history of the Southern states, will see that the Negro has contributed, not merely his labour, but something also of his inner life and temperament to the character and quality of the South.

Until freedom came the life of the Negro was so intimately interwoven with that of the white man that it is almost true to say that he had no separate history. To the slave on the plantation the "Big House," where the master lived, was the centre of the only world he knew. It was after freedom came that the masses of the Negro people began to think of themselves as having a past or a future in any way separate and distinct from the white race. There were always some among them, like Frederick Douglass, who were different in this respect from the masses. They became the fugitive slaves.

After I began to go to school I had my first opportunity to learn from books something further and more definite about my race in Africa. I cannot say that I received very much encouragement or inspiration from what I learned in this way while I was in school. The books I read told me of a people who roamed naked through the forest like wild beasts, of a people without houses or laws, without chastity or morality, with no family life and fixed habits of industry.

It seems to me now, as I recall my first definite impressions of my race in Africa, that the books I read when I was a boy always put the pictures of Africa and African life in an unnecessarily cruel contrast with the pictures of the civilised and highly cultured Europeans and Americans. One picture I recall vividly was in the first geography I studied. It was the picture of George Washington placed side by side with a naked African, having a ring in his nose and a dagger in his hand. Here; as elsewhere, in order to put the lofty position to which the white race has attained in sharper contrast with the lowly condition of a more primitive people, the best among the white people was contrasted with the worst among the black.

Naturally all this made a deep and painful impression upon me. At this time I had the feeling, which most of us are likely to have when we are young and inexperienced, that there must be something wrong with any person who was in any way, whether in dress or manners, markedly different from the persons and things to which I was accustomed. It seemed to me at that time a mark of degradation that people should go about with almost no clothes upon their backs. It did not occur to me that, possibly, the difference in the customs of wearing clothes in Africa and in America, and the difference in the feeling that people in Europe and in Africa have about clothes, was largely a matter of climate. It seemed to me that a human creature who would willingly go about with a ring in his nose must be a very fierce and terrible sort of human animal, but it never occurred to me to have any such feelings in regard to the persons whom I had seen wearing ornaments in their ears. In spite of all this, I still held fast to the notion that a race which could produce as good and gentle and loving a woman as my mother must have some good in it that the geographers had failed to discover.

It is hard for one who is a member of another race and who has not had a like experience to appreciate the impression that has often been made upon me, and upon other members of my race as they have listened, as inexperienced boys and girls, to public speeches in which the whole Negro race was denounced in a reckless and wholesale manner, or as they have read newspapers and books in which the Negro race has been described as the lowest and most hopeless of God's creation. Sometimes, when I was a young man, I was driven almost to despair by the hard and bitter, and frequently, as it seemed to me, unjust statements about my race. It was difficult for me to reconcile the ruthless denunciations which men, with whom I was acquainted, would make in their public speeches, with the uniform courtesy and kindness which they had shown to me and others of my race in all their private relations. Even now it is difficult for me to understand why so many Southern white men will allow themselves, for the purpose of enforcing an argument or in the heat of a political discussion, to go so far in the denunciation of the Negro as to do injustice to their own better natures and to their actual feelings toward coloured people whom they meet, perhaps, in business, or toward the servants employed in their own household, the woman who cooks their food, looks after their house and cares for their children. I mention these facts because they serve to illustrate the singular relations of interdependence and opposition in which the white and black people of the South stand to each other to-day, all of which has had and is having a very definite influence upon the development of my people in the South.

The hard and discouraging statements which I was compelled to hear in regard to my race when I was a boy, had, at different times, two very different effects upon me. At first they sometimes made me feel as if I wanted to go away to some distant part of the earth and bury myself where I might be a stranger to all my people, or at least where the thing that we call race prejudice did not exist in the way it does in the Southern states. Sometimes I thought of doing something desperate which would compel the world, in some way or other, to recognise what seemed to me the wrongs of my race. But afterward, and on second thought, the effect was to drive me closer to my own people, to make me sympathise with them more intimately and more deeply, to feel toward them as I did toward my own dear mother who had brought me into the world when she and they were slaves.

In the end there grew up within me, as a result of both these feelings, a determination to spend my life in helping and strengthening the people of my race, in order to prove to the world that whatever had been its feelings for them in the past it should learn to respect them in the future, both for what they were and what they should be able to do. I made up my mind, also, that in the end the world must come to respect the Negro for just those virtues for which some people say he is despised, namely because of his patience, his kindliness, and his lack of resentment toward those who do him wrong and injustice.

The feelings that divided my mind and confused my purposes when I was a young man, have also divided the members of my race. The continual adverse criticism has led some of us to disavow our racial identity, to seek rest and try our successes as members of another race than that to which we were born. It has led others of us to seek to get away as far as possible from association with our own race, and to keep as far away from Africa, from its history and from its traditions as it was possible for us to do.

My attention was first called to this disposition of members of certain section of my race to get away from themselves, so to speak; to be ashamed, in other words, of their history and traditions, when I found them bashful or lukewarm in regard to singing the old songs which are the peculiar and unique product of Negro life and civilisation in this country. I have heard musical critics, whose judgment the world respects, say that the old plantation hymns and songs were among the most original contributions that

America has made, not only to music but to any one of the so-called fine arts, and this not merely for their intrinsic charm and beauty but for their qualities, which make it possible for the trained musician to develop out of them more elaborate and refined musical forms, such as have been given to them recently by the Negro composer, Coleridge-Taylor. For myself, though it has been my privilege to hear some of the best music both in Europe and America, I would rather hear the jubilee or plantation songs of my race than the finest chorus from the works of Handel or any other of the great composers that I have heard. Besides, this music is the form in which the sorrows and aspirations of the Negro people, all that they suffered, loved, and hoped for, in short their whole spiritual life, found its first adequate and satisfying expression. For that reason, if for no other, it should be preserved.

What I have said here of my own feelings in regard to my race is representative of the feelings of thousands of others of the black people of this country. Adverse criticism has driven them to think deeper than they otherwise would about the problems which confront them as a race, to cling closer than they otherwise would have done to their own people, to value more highly than they once did, the songs and the records of their past life in slavery. The effect has been to give them, in short, that sort of race pride and race consciousness which, it seems to me, they need to bring out and develop the best that is in them.

So it was that, thinking and studying about the origin and the destiny of my people, and of all of the forces that were working for and against them in my own country and elsewhere, the desire to know more about the history of my own people steadily increased and I tried, as well as I was able, to understand the Negro thoroughly, intimately, in those qualities in which, as a race, he is weak, as well as in those qualities in which he is strong.

This habit of observation and study of my own race, in the way I have described, led me to inquire into the personal histories of the men and women of my own race whom I have met in all parts of the United States. I sought to make myself acquainted with their difficulties and their successes, to understand their feelings and their habits of thought, to discover the inner drift and deeper currents of their lives; for any one who knows to any extent the character of the Negro people, knows that they have, just as other people, an outside and inside, and one cannot always tell what is going on deep down in their hearts merely from looking in their faces. Sometimes the Negro laughs when he is angry and cries when he is happy. Very often, has it seemed to me, the Negro himself does not know or fully understand what is going on in the depth of his own mind and heart.

Perhaps it will not be out of place for me to say here, at the beginning of this book, that the more I have studied the masses of the race to which I belong, the more I have learned not only to sympathise but to respect them. I am proud and happy to be identified with their struggle for a higher and better life.

Now and then I have read or heard it said that, in consequence of the inconveniences, the hardships and the injustices that members of my race frequently suffer, because of the colour of their skins, there was something exceptional and tragic about the situation of the Negro in America, "the tragedy of colour," as one writer has called it. No doubt there is much that is exceptional in the situation of the Negro, not only in America, but in Africa. No one is more willing than I to admit this to be true. But hardships and even injustice, when they concern the relations of people who are divided by creed, by class, or by race, are not exceptional. On the contrary, they are common, and every race that has struggled up from a lower to a higher civilisation has had to face these things. They have been part of its education. Neither is there, as far as my experience goes, anything peculiarly tragic connected with the life of the Negro, except in the situation of those members of my race who, for one reason or another, have yielded to the temptation to make a secret of their lowly birth and appear before the world as something other than they are. Every coloured man knows, or has heard, of such cases, and in the whole history of the Negro race there are few sadder stories than some of these lives. I should say it was only when an individual suffers from his own folly, rather than the mistakes of others, that he is likely to become the hero of a tragedy. This is just as true of a race. The Negro race has suffered much because of conditions for which others were responsible. As a rule Negroes have had very little chance thus far, to make mistakes of their own. We have not been free long enough. While the world hears a great deal about "the tragedy of colour" and other phrases of the so-called Negro problem, I have observed that the world hears little, and knows, perhaps, less about the Negro himself. This is true of white people but it is also true of coloured people.

Some time ago, I had the privilege of meeting at Cambridge, Mass., a group of about twenty-five young coloured men who were studying at Harvard University. I found that most of these young men had a high standing in the University, were respected by their professors and, upon inquiring in regard to the subjects of their studies, I learned that several of them had taken extended courses in history. They seemed to know in detail, the story of Greek and Roman and English civilisations, and prided themselves upon their knowledge of the languages and history of the French and German peoples. They knew a great deal about the local history of New England and were perfectly familiar with the story of Plymouth Rock and the settlement of Jamestown, and of all that concerned the white man's civilisation both in America and out of America. But I found that through their entire course of training, neither in the public schools, nor in the fitting schools, nor in Harvard, had any of them had an opportunity to study the history of their own race. In regard to the people with which they themselves were most closely identified, they were more ignorant than they were in regard to the history of the Germans, the French, or the English. It occurred to me that this should not be so. The Negro boy and girl should have an opportunity to learn something in school about his own race. The Negro boy should study Negro history just as the Japanese boy studies Japanese history and the German boy studies German history.

Let me add that my knowledge of the Negro has led me to believe that there is much in the story of his struggle, if one were able to tell it as it deserves to be told, that it is likely to be both instructive and helpful, not merely to the black man but also to the white man with whom he is now almost everywhere, in Africa as well as America, so closely associated. In the last analysis I suppose this is the best excuse I can give for undertaking to tell "The Story of the Negro."

CHAPTER II

THE AMERICAN NEGRO AND THE NATIVE AFRICAN

THE stories which I heard as a child were what the average American Negro boy is likely to hear in regard to his African ancestors, and my chief reasons for repeating them is that they were very largely mistaken and need to be corrected.

I had always heard Africa referred to as the "Dark Continent"; I pictured it to myself as a black, sunless region, with muddy rivers and gloomy forests, inhabited by a people, who, like everything else about them, were black. I supposed that the nearer I got to the original African, the blacker I would find him, and that all lighter coloured Negroes I had seen were a spurious sort, whose blood had been adulterated by mixture with some of the lighter races. I was much surprised, therefore, to learn, when I came to study the native races of Africa, that the man, whom scientists believed to be the original African, namely, the Bushman — and with him I include his near relatives, the Dwarfs of Central Africa — was not black but yellow; that the Negro, the real black man, is after all merely one of the earliest settlers of the continent, coming from somewhere else, probably Asia, no one knows exactly where or how.

In a recent volume upon "The Native Races of South Africa," George W. Stow says in regard to relations of the Bushmen and the other Negro people of South Africa:

> It seems somewhat surprising that so many writers have continued to class these people [Bushmen] with the Negroes and other dark-skinned species of men; whereas, if we are to judge from the physical appearance, with a solitary exception of the hair, no two sections of the human race could be more divergent. Their closest affinities in this respect are certainly more frequently to be found among those inhabiting the Northern Hemisphere than any other portion of the world.*

On the other hand it appears from native traditions that, with the exception of the Bushmen, all the native peoples emigrated from the North to the South. Other traditions state that, "when their forefathers migrated to the South, they found the land without inhabitants, and that only the game and the Bushmen were living in it."

It is an indication of the low estimate which the other South African tribes put upon the Bushmen that they did not count them as "inhabitants."

One who studies the books about Africa will read a great deal about the true Negro who lives, as the books tell us, in the Soudan, a part of Africa that is

* "The Native Races of South Africa," George W. Stow, p. 6.

often referred to as Negroland. After I had learned that the original African was not a black man and not a Negro, in the strict scientific sense of the word, I was led to explore, as well as I was able by the aid of books and maps, that part of Africa where the Negro is supposed to be at home. I wanted to find more about the real black man.

The true Negro, I learned, is only one section of what is ordinarily known as the Negro race; the other is the Bantu, a mixed people, generally brown in colour, who were the first invaders of South Africa, driving out the original Bushmen, and gradually extending themselves over most of that part of the continent below the equator.

Negroland, stretching clear across the country, or at least from the Atlantic to the Nile, as far north as the Desert of Sahara and as far south as the equator, is a wide region, and there are many different tribes and many different types of people inhabiting it. From the North Arab invaders and merchantmen have entered the country and mingled with the earlier and darker races. Wave after wave of conquest has poured itself out over the rich lands between the desert and the mountains that divide these inland regions from the coast and hundreds of years of slave-raiding have so broken up and intermingled the different racial stocks that it is as hard for one, not an expert, to find the "true Negro" in Africa — that is without any mixture of foreign blood — as it is to find the colour line in the United States.

How difficult this sometimes is I may, perhaps, illustrate by an experience of my own a few years ago in Alabama. I was travelling at this time with one of our students at Tuskegee, who was very light in colour, when we had some distance to go in a carriage. At the end of our journey, the owner of the carriage, who was a white man, collected fifty cents from me but called upon the student who was with me for a dollar. After considerable argument and some inquiry, we discovered that it was the rule to charge white men a dollar for the same service for which Negroes paid only fifty cents, and my companion had been taken for a white man. But even after this the student was not inclined to pay the extra price. He seemed to think fifty cents was too much pay for being a white man, at least for so short a time.

Upon another occasion, when an important exposition was being held in one of our Southern states, I recall that, in order to encourage Negroes to attend, the exposition authorities decided that on certain days of the week coloured people could be admitted at half price. The white people were to pay the regular price, fifty cents. The notion of the managers was that many coloured people were staying away from the exposition because they were too poor to pay the regular entrance fee, and that if the price were lowered on certain days large numbers, who could not otherwise afford it, would go. The event proved that the calculations of the managers were correct. Large numbers of coloured people crowded into the exposition on Negro day, but at the end of two weeks the doorkeepers had become desperate. They wanted to throw up their jobs because, as they said, it was too embarrassing work to pick out, by their colour, the black people from the white.

As an illustration of the way in which the intermingling of the racial stocks has come about in Africa, I may mention the fact that, when Dr. Barth, in 1850, first visited the Negro city of Kano, which is the most important trading centre of Western Soudan, he found it, a place of thirty to forty thousand inhabitants, which at certain seasons of the year was increased to sixty thousand, divided into numerous quarters, each of which was inhabited by a different type of people. One quarter was devoted almost exclusively to Arab merchants; a second was inhabited by Fellani, the ruling class; still other quarters were taken up by different tribes of the subject people, among them the merchant and manufacturing people, the Hausas. In addition to these, there were the slaves — gathered from all portions of the country but principally from the tribes living near the coast — who made up nearly half the population.*

* "Discoveries in North and Central Africa," Henry Barth, P.H.D., Vol. I, p. 507.

I cannot now remember where I first got the idea that a man who was dark in colour was necessarily more ignorant and in a lower stage of civilisation than one who was lighter. At any rate there seemed to be a general understanding to that effect, when I was a boy — at least among most people. Perhaps it was due to the fact that on the plantations, as a rule, lighter coloured slaves were more often employed as house servants, and, because of their more intimate association with their masters, were held in higher esteem and had more opportunities for advancement than the field hands. Perhaps it was merely a reflection of the general opinion, which slaves somehow imbibed, that everything white was good and everything black was bad. I recall that in the matter of religion, although, it may never have been directly referred to, we, always understood that God was white and the Devil was black.

In any case I grew up with the idea that in Africa the lowest and most degraded type of man was black, and the blacker he was the further down in the scale of civilisation I expected him to be. The fact seems to be that this is nowhere true in Africa. For instance, the Hausas, the great trading people of the Soudan, who live in walled cities and carry on a trade extending over the whole region between the West Coast and the Nile, are, according to Dr. Charles Henry Robinson, "as black as any people in the world." The Bushmen, on the other hand, who, as I have already said, are yellow, have nowhere risen above the hunting stage of civilisation.

No one question, I may say right here, is more frequently asked me than this: "What is the relative ability of the Negro of mixed and unmixed blood?" I usually answer that my experience and observation convince me that, where the environment has been equally favourable, there is no difference in ability.

As an illustration I may say that at Tuskegee it has been customary to award the honour of delivering the valedictory address to the student making the highest average in scholarship, industrial work and deportment, and during a period of about twenty years, ten of those who gained this honour were Negroes of pure blood. I understand that at Hampton Institute, in Virginia, where they have had an experience covering a considerably longer period, the same thing has been found to be true. I might add that the late J. C. Price, during his lifetime by all odds the leading and most prominent man of his race in North Carolina and one of the most eloquent men in the country, was pure black. The two leading and most progressive men, in commercial and business directions, in the State of Mississippi, Isaiah T. Montgomery and Charles Banks, have no mixture of blood. W. W. Brown, who founded the largest and most successful fraternal organisation that has ever existed among the black people in America, was a pure black. It would not be difficult to multiply examples of this kind, but there is one other name that should not be omitted — Major R. R. Moten, Commandant at the Hampton Institute, Hampton, Va., who is one of the few Negroes in this country who can trace his ancestry, in an unbroken chain, back to his people in Africa. The most conspicuous example of a success in literature is, perhaps, Paul Lawrence Dunbar, the poet, who was a man of unmixed blood.

Let me add that, as my observation and experience of human life have widened, I have learned to doubt the wisdom of laying down any general rules that fix for all times the status of any people, or determine in advance the progress they are able or likely to make under conditions different from those in which they happened, at the present time, to be found.

I had a lesson in this respect a few years ago at Tuskegee. It happened that in one of the geography classes, which at that time were studying Africa, the students came one day upon a passage in which the Bushmen were described as the lowest type of human being to be found in Africa. The writer went on to describe this people in a way which made our students feel that the Bushmen were about as low, degraded and hopeless a type of human nature as could well be imagined.

While the class was discussing this passage, a boy in the back of the room raised his hand and indicated that he had something to say. It turned out that he had recently come from South Africa and knew something of the natives, and he did not agree with the statements in the geography. He went on to say that his mother was a Bushwoman and that his father was a Hottentot, a tribe which is generally supposed to be closely related to the Bushmen. He had been born in the bush. Afterward, while he was still a small boy, his father and mother had moved into town and he had been enabled in this way to get something of an education. As the young Bushman happened to stand near the head of his class and spoke with personal knowledge of both his father's and mother's people, as well as of the other tribes of South Africa, what he had to say was listened to with the greatest interest and attention. When he followed it up by going to his room and bringing back photographs with which to illustrate his statement, both the class and the teachers were convinced that, however much truth there might be in the general description given in geographies, the Bushmen who, for a hundred years or more, had been hunted like wild beasts by the other stronger tribes of South Africa, were to a very large extent, the victims of circumstances.*

*" Every race of man, savage or civilised, that came in contact with them [the Bushmen] appropriated their land without a single pretext of justification, and waged a war of extermination against them as soon as they resisted or resented the wrong that was done them. The pastoral tribes of natives and colonial flock-owners could not appreciate the feelings of attachment which those who lived by the chase alone had to their hunting-grounds, while the constant encroachments which were made upon them impressed the untutored minds of the hunter race with the idea

This incident helped to confirm me in the belief that in our efforts to help the weaker peoples of the earth, we should not despair even in the case of the most humble and backward of the human family. In mathematics and in physical sciences it is possible to make exact statements and lay down laws that are universal and unchanging, but in what concerns human life and history we cannot be so precise and definite. Human beings are constantly doing unprecedented things and it is usually, I suspect, the unexpected and unprecedented things that men do that are the most important.

As a boy I had been accustomed to hear Africa referred to as one hears of Mexico, as if it were a place where a comparatively homogeneous people lives, having much the same customs, language, and civilisation; in short, as if it were a country instead of a continent. It was some time before I was able to realise the vast extent and variety of the territory over which the dark races of Africa are spread. Africa is larger and considerably more varied in its geographical structure than North America. The territory occupied by the dark races of Africa, for example is more than two times that occupied by the United States.

---

that the whole world was arrayed against them. Their almost fierce love of independence, their almost equally unalterable determination to maintain and die in their primitive modes of life, utter contempt — at least of the majority of them — for all pastoral or agricultural pursuits, made them to be looked upon by all the larger and more robust of the African races as a species of wild animal, which it was praiseworthy to exterminate whenever an opportunity offered."—"Discoveries in North and Central Africa," Henry Barth, Ph. D., Vol. I, p. 215.

I found also that I had only the vaguest notion of the multitude of different peoples that inhabit Africa and the variety of civilisations represented among its inhabitants, not only among the more advanced races along the Mediterranean but also among the Negro peoples who still hold possession of nearly seven-eighths of the continent. For instance, Sir Harry H. Johnston says of the people inhabiting the English protectorate of Uganda, where a careful study has been made of the native peoples:

> Within the limits of the Protectorate are to be found specimens of nearly all the more marked types of African man — Congo Pygmies, and the low types of the Elgon and Semliki forests, the handsome Bahima, who are negroids and are as much related to the ancient Egyptians as to the average Negro, the gigantic Turkana and the wiry and stunted Andorobo, the Apollo-like Masai, the naked Nile tribes, and the scrupulous clothed Baganda. These last again are enthusiastic, casuistic Christians, while other tribes of the Nile provinces are fanatical Mohammedans. The Bahima are burdened with a multiplicity of minor deities, while the Masai and kindred races have practically no religion at all. Cannibalism lingers in the western corners of the protectorate; while natives of the other provinces are importing tinned apricots or are printing and publishing in their own language summaries of their history.*

Speaking of the popular notion of the African people to which I have referred, Professor Jerome Dowd, a Southern white man who resides in Charlotte, N. C., author of a recent sociological study of the African races, says:

---

*" The Uganda Protectorate," Sir Harry H. Johnston, Vol. I, preface.

When the average European or American white man thinks or writes of the Negroes he considers them as one race and attributes to them certain traits which are supposed to be equally common to all groups and to all localities. This is a mistaken view and may be likened to an attempt to class all of the Aryan peoples as a homogeneous race, having common features and traits. In fact the Negroes of the world, just as the Aryans, are scattered over a great area, live in different environments and have varied and opposite mental and physical peculiarities. Indeed, the Negro races of the world differ from each other even more widely than the different branches of the Aryan stock. In Africa, for example, the Negroes are distributed over the territory of much greater extent and of greater physical diversity than is true of the Aryan races of Europe. They also differ more than the Aryan races in general appearance, in stature, physiognomy, and mental and moral constitution. Hence, to speak of all Negroes in Africa as one race, having common characteristics, is as misleading and is as unscientific as if we should consider all Europeans and Americans as of one race, and attribute to all of them the same traits.*

Another statement which one frequently hears, made indiscriminately of the dark races of Africa, is that they are constitutionally lazy and cannot be induced to work. I shall have something to say about the Negro as a labourer later in this work; here it is, perhaps, sufficient to recall the fact that in the greater portion of Africa the black man is still almost the only labourer. It is he who builds the railways and the bridges, digs the gold in the South African mines, and collects the rubber in the Congo forests. Miss Mary Kingsley, in her volume, "Travels in West Africa," says of the Kruboys,

* *Southern Workman*, May, 1908.

"that they are the most important people of West Africa; for without their help the working of the Coast would cost more lives than it already does, and would be in fact practically impossible." In his book on Tropical Africa, Henry Drummond, describing the way in which the natives come from far and near to try the sensation of methodical work on the building of the Cape to Cairo railway, says:

> The severest test to which the Native of Central Africa has yet been put is in the construction of the Stevenson Road between Lakes Nyassa and Tanganyika. Forty-six miles of this road have already been made, entirely by native labour, and the work could not have been better done had it been executed by English navvies. I have watched by the day a party of seventy Natives working upon the road. Till three or four years ago, none had ever looked upon a white man, nor till a few months previously had one of them ever seen a spade, a pick-axe or a crow-bar. Yet these savages handle these tools to such purpose that with only a single European superintendent they have made a road full of difficult cuttings and gradients, which would not disgrace a railway contractor at home. The workmen keep regular hours, six in the morning till five at night, with a rest at midday — work steadily, continuously, willingly and, above all, merrily. This goes on in the heart of the tropics, almost under the equator itself, where the white man's energy evaporates and leaves him so limp that he cannot be an example to his men.*

The fact is, very little comes out of Africa, from an elephant's tusk to a diamond, that is not the result of the labour of the African. This does not mean that the native labourer is always as persistent and intelligent as he should be, nor that native labour is,

* "Tropical Africa," Henry Drummond, p. 64.

everywhere and for all purposes, of the same value. Experience has shown that one tribe is more useful in one form of labour and another tribe in some other form. What the African has needed most to make him a better labourer has been the same incentive to work which the white man had. Where one stick sharpened forms a spear, two sticks make a fire, and fifty sticks a place to live, there is little incentive to systematic and persistent work. This completeness and modesty of wants is, in my opinion, at the bottom of the difficulty in Africa. The truth is that the Negro in Africa or out of it develops in industrial efficiency, as other human beings do, in response to his needs and his opportunities.

I had this fact impressed upon me in a very striking way during a recent visit to Cleveland, Ohio, when I went to see a little brass foundry run by a coloured man who is engaged in the manufacture of those little brass wheels that run along the trolley wires of our electric railways and, by means of the trolley pole connect the cars with the electric current.

The operation of casting these wheels, as I was informed, requires unusual skill and experience, because it is necessary to secure just the right degree of hardness and toughness in the metal, and I was the more interested in noticing the way in which this man and his assistants did their work because I recall that the art of working in iron was one of the crafts that had been the special property, from time immemorial, of the people of my race.

Dr. Franz Boas, Professor of Anthropology at Columbia University, says that, "while much of the history of early invention is shrouded in darkness, it seems likely that at the time when the European was still satisfied with rude stone tools, the African had invented or adapted the art of smelting ore."

I had been reading a few days before a description of the rude methods by which, with little more than a simple bellows and a charcoal fire, native Africans reduced the ores and forged the implements, many of them of great beauty as well as usefulness, which one may still meet with in many parts of Africa.

I am not sufficiently familiar with the detailed methods of smelting ores and casting metals to be able to even suggest the vast distance between the primitive methods of the Native African and the infinitely more intricate and complicated technique of the modern industry. The thought, the study and the invention of thousands, perhaps of millions of minds, have contributed to create the very conditions of the modern iron industry. The contrast between the Native African, working laboriously in the solitude of the African forests, with his primitive tools, after a traditional method, and the American Negro, in his own foundry, with the advantage of all the machinery, knowledge, and the skill that modern science and modern invention have contributed to the improvement of iron industry, is impressive enough. But this contrast does not represent the difference in innate qualities in the men themselves, but rather the difference in the civilisations that surround them.

It probably requires just as much skill and just as much patience to make one of those long and graceful spearheads you may see on the end of an African lance as it does to make the trolley wheel; but it takes all our civilisation to make the trolley wheel possible.

In what I have written thus far in regard to Africa and African peoples I have sought to emphasise the vastness of the territories which they inhabit; the distances which divide them from one another; the variety of physical types in which they are represented; the complicated social relations that sometimes exist among them, and the difficulty of making general statements, laying down general laws that hold good at all times and all places for all of the African peoples.

There is, however, a tie which few white men can understand, which binds the American Negro to the African Negro; which unites the black man of Brazil and the black man of Liberia; which is constantly drawing into closer relations all the scattered African peoples whether they are in the old world or the new.

There is not only the tie of race, which is strong in

any case, but there is the bond of colour, which is specially important in the case of the black man. It is this common badge of colour, for instance, which is responsible for the fact that whatever contributes, in any degree to the progress of the American Negro, contributes to the progress of the African Negro, and to the Negro in South America and the West Indies. When the African Negro succeeds, it helps the American Negro. When the African Negro fails, it hurts the reputation and the standing of the Negro in every other part of the world.

I have rarely met in America any one of my race who did not, in one way or another, show a deep interest in everything connected with Africa. The millions of Negroes in America are almost as much interested, for example, in the future of Liberia and Abyssinia, as they are in their own country. There is always a peculiar and scarcely definable bond that binds one black man to another black man, whether in Africa, Jamaica, Haiti, or the United States. One evidence of this interest of the Negro in America in the Negro in Africa is the work that the American Negro churches are doing in Africa to help civilise and Christianise their brethren there. There is scarcely any branch of the Negro church in America that does not have an organisation through which it is sending men and women and money into some portion of Africa. The readiness with which some of the strongest and brightest men and women in

America, who have had superior opportunities, are ready to return to Africa and give their lives in an effort to uplift their fellows, indicates the strong racial tie that binds the black people of the world together.

On the other hand, it is true that Negroes in other parts of the world are beginning to interest themselves more and more in the fortunes of the Negro in America. In a very marked degree the one hundred and thirty millions of black people outside of America are looking to the ten millions of Negroes in the United States for guidance and for inspiration. They are watching closely the progress of these American Negroes. They are beginning to realise that if it is possible for the ten million black men in America, surrounded by modern machinery and all the other forces of civilisation, to get into line and march with the procession, that it is also possible for them, in time, to follow, somewhat more slowly, perhaps, but in the same direction.

CHAPTER III

THE AFRICAN AT HOME

SOME time during the latter part of 1899, or the early part of 1900, I received through the German Embassy, in Washington, a letter saying that the German Colonial Society wanted a number of students from Tuskegee to go out to German West Africa to teach the natives how to produce cotton by American methods.

While I had been a student at Hampton Institute, Virginia, it was one of my ambitions, as it has been the ambition of a great many other Negro students before and since, to go out some day to Africa as a missionary. I believed that I had got hold at Hampton of a kind of knowledge that would be peculiarly helpful to the Native Africans and I felt that my interest in the people out there, vague and indefinite as it was, would in some way or other help and inspire me in the task of lifting them to a higher plane of civilisation.

After I went to Tuskegee I gave up my ambition of going to Africa. I had not been long there, however, before I was convinced that I could, perhaps, be of larger usefulness through the work I was able to do in this country, by fitting, for the same service I wanted to perform, Africans who came as students to America, and by sending from Tuskegee men and women trained in our methods, as teachers and workers among the native peoples. The request I received through the German Embassy was, therefore, particularly welcome to me, for it gave me an opportunity to realise, in a direct way, the ambition I had never wholly lost sight of.

A group of our best students was selected for this African mission. They went out to Togoland, West Africa, and began to establish stations in different points in that colony, and then started in to grow cotton, using the native labour as far as they were able, but necessarily, at first, doing a large part of the work themselves.

They met all sorts of difficulties. They found the American cotton was not suited to African soil, and were compelled to cross it with native varieties in order to produce an hybrid type that possessed the valuable qualities of both. They had considerable difficulty, at first, with the native labourers. I remember that John Robinson, one of the party who remained to carry out the work after the others had returned home, told me of an incident, which made me see, in a way in which I had not been able to see before, that the education of the native African in the white man's civilisation must begin much farther back and with much simpler matters than most of us are likely to imagine.

Among the other things this party had taken out to Africa was a wagon, which had been manufactured by the students at Tuskegee. While this wagon was being unloaded and put together, the native porters looked on with interest, never having seen anything that went on wheels before. After the wagon had been loaded ready to start the attention of members of the party was turned for a time in another direction. When they came back to the wagon they were greatly surprised to see that the natives had unloaded and taken it apart, and were busily engaged in fastening its wheels and other parts on their heads, preparatory to carrying them, along with the other goods, to their destination in the interior. Mr. Robinson explained to them, through an interpreter, the use of the wagon, and tried to show them the advantage of it. They were interested in seeing this curious machine of the white man work, but they were quite positive in their conviction that the good old-fashioned way of carrying everything on their heads was the better. Now that roads have been opened up and the natives have actually seen a wagon worked, Mr. Robinson tells me they take it as a hardship if they are asked to carry anything.

During the time this experiment in educating the Native African was going on, I followed its progress, through the accounts I received from students on the ground and from the reports of the German Colonial Society, with close attention and intense interest. It was the nearest I had come, up to that time, to anything like a practical and intimate acquaintance with the African at home.

Among the first thing the Tuskegee students did in Africa was to build for themselves comfortable houses, to supply them with well made but simple furniture, to put in these houses not only the necessities, but some of the comforts of life. I was interested to note that, within a few months the Natives and, especially the women, had gotten the notion that they wanted the same kind of houses and some of the same kind of furniture. The women naturally made their wants known to the men, and before these students had been in Africa half a dozen years the Natives in their vicinity had reached the point where, with the training they had received and with the desire they had gained for better homes to live in, better tools to work with, and for all the other advantages which the black man in America seemed to possess over the black man in Africa, they were performing about as satisfactory service as the same class of human beings would have performed in any other part of the world.

Native Africans have been sent from Africa to Tuskegee. Our Tuskegee students have returned from time to time and made their reports of successes. Thus in a very vital and practical manner has our institution become connected with the progress and civilisation of our brethren in the darker continent.

Some time ago in looking through the pages of some magazine or book of science, I ran across a statement that, when men first began to study the stars systematically and with telescopes, they discovered a certain class of errors in their calculations which were due to the personality of the observers. One man's brain, acting quicker, would record the stars as moving more rapidly; another would record them as moving more slowly than their actual movements. It became necessary, therefore, in order to make the calculations correct, to study and take account of these personal aberrations.

It has occurred to me, in the course of my reading about the African peoples, that it would contribute much to the accuracy of our knowledge, if some study were made of the sort of errors that creep into our observations of human beings. Important as it is that we should have a correct knowledge of the stars, it is more important that we should have an accurate knowledge of men. For instance, I have noticed that a man born and reared in the Southern states invariably looks upon the Negro with different eyes from the man born and reared in the Northern states. In their reports and interpretations of the simplest facts they are often widely divergent in their views. Even when they agree with each other about the Negro, for instance, it has often seemed to me that their agreement was due to a misunderstanding.

Frequently amusing situations occur in the discussion of the Negro. Many of these have occurred in my presence. It seldom occurs, for instance, when I am travelling on a train that the discussion does not turn on the question as to what is the physical, moral, and mental effect on the individual when he is of mixed blood. One man will argue very seriously that there should be no mixture of blood, for the reason that he is quite sure that wherever there is a mixture it results in a weakened individual, bodily, mentally, morally. Within ten or fifteen minutes another man will begin, in the absence of the first, to discuss the same subject and will, in an equally serious and positive manner, state that wherever in all history the Negro has been able to accomplish anything of value to the world it had been because he had some tincture of white blood in his veins.

During these discussions I am sometimes reminded of an incident that occurred during my early boyhood, which, because it illustrates a phase in the development of the Negro in America, I may be permitted to mention it here. Very soon after the days of slavery and even before the public school system had been organised, there arose in the community a discussion among our people as to whether the world was round or flat. It lasted for several days, and divided the community into two pretty stubborn factions. During the discussion a coloured man came along, a school teacher, who had very little actual learning, and made application to open a school. The question as to whether the world was flat or round was submitted to him, or rather he was asked how he would treat the question in the schoolroom, and he replied that he was prepared to teach either "flat," "round," or just as the individual family requested.

The continual discussion of the Negro often reminds me, as I have stated, of this story. The Negro question or the Negro himself seems able to be accommodated to almost any and every shade of opinion. That explains how two men with diametrically opposite views sometimes come to an agreement about the Negro; one thinks he should be flat and not round, the other thinks he should be round and not flat; but both agree that there is something wrong with him.

If it is difficult for people of the same race to understand one another when they are talking about things in regard to which their experience has been different, it is still more difficult for one race to pass judgment upon another, particularly when these races differ so widely from one another as the white man and the Negro. Dr. Franz Boas has called attention to this difficulty in a paper before the American Association of Science. "As the white race is the civilised race," he says, "every deviation from the white type is considered as the characteristic feature of a lower type; . . . the greater the difference between the intellectual, emotional and moral processes and those found in our civilisation, the harsher the judgment of the people."*

Under these circumstances it is natural enough that the black man, who is furthest removed physically from the white man, should suffer more than others from the sort of prejudice Professor Boas describes. With the possible exception of the Jew, no race has ever been subjected to criticisms so searching and candid, to state it mildly, as the Negro. And yet I have found that those who have known and understood the Negro best, have usually been kindest in their judgment of him and most hopeful of his future.

For instance, the late Miss Kingsley, an Englishwoman, who seems to have entered deeper into the mind of the West African than most others, says of the West Coast Negro:

> The true Negro is, I believe, by far the better man than the Asiatic; he is physically superior, and he is more like an Englishman than the Asiatic; he is a logical, practical man, with feelings that are a credit to him, and are particularly strong in the direction of property. He has a way of thinking he has rights whether he likes to use them or no, and he will fight for them when he is driven to it. Fight you for a religious idea the African will not; he is not the stuff you make martyrs out of, nor does he desire to shake off the shackels of the flesh and swoon into Nirvana. . . .

---

*"Proceedings of the American Association for the Advancement of Science," Vol. XLIII., 1894.

His make of mind is exceedingly like the make of mind that thousands of Englishmen of the stand-no-nonsense, Englishman's-house-is-his-castle type. Yet, withal, a law-abiding man, loving a live Lord, holding loudly that women should be kept in their place, yet often grievously henpecked by his wives, and little better than a slave to his mother whom he loves with the love he gives to none other.*

Concerning the affection which the African has for his mother, Miss Kingsley quotes the Rev. Leighton Wilson.

Mr. Wilson was born and educated in South Carolina. In 1834 he went to Africa as a missionary and remained there for eighteen years, in close contact with the civilisation of the forefathers of the present American Negroes. He was among the first missionaries to Africa. He remained in the active service of the Southern Presbyterian Church until his death in 1886. While in Africa he studied the languages and reduced the native tongue of some of the tribes to writing. He says:

Whatever other estimate we may form of the African, we may not doubt his love for his mother. Her name, whether dead or alive, is always on his lips and in his heart. She is the first thing he thinks of when awakening from his slumbers and the last thing he remembers when closing his eyes in sleep; to her he confides secrets which he would reveal to no other human being on the face of the earth. He cares for no one else in time of sickness, she alone must prepare his food, administer his medicine, perform his ablutions, and spread his mat for him. He flies to her in the hour of his distress, for he well knows if all the rest of the world turn against him, she will be steadfast in her love, whether he be right or wrong.

* "West African Studies," p. 373.

If there be any cause which justifies a man using violence towards one of his fellowmen it would be to resent an insult offered to his mother. More fights are occasioned among boys by hearing something said in disparagement of their mothers than all other causes put together. It is a common saying among them, if a man's mother and his wife are both on the point of being drowned, and he can save only one of them, he must save his mother, for the avowed reason if the wife is lost he may marry another, but he will never find a second mother. . . .*

Mr. Wilson points out that the Africans of the Grain Coast have long since risen above the hunting life; they have fixed habitations, cultivate the soil for means of subsistence, have herds of domestic animals, construct for themselves houses which are sufficient to protect them alike from the scorching heat of the sun and the chilly damps of the night; they show a turn for the mechanical arts, and in the fabrication of implements of warfare and articles of ornament they display surprising skill.

"As we see them in their native country," he continues, "they show none of that improvidence or want of foresight for which they have almost become proverbial in this country, which shows that circumstances have made them what they are in this respect. They plant their crops with particular reference to the seasons of the year, and they store away provisions for their future wants with as much regularity as any people in the world, so that times of scarcity and want are less frequent among them

*"Western Africa," pp. 116, 117.

than among others who pretend to a much higher degree of civilisation."

Referring to the farms of the Kru people, the tribes from which the seamen of the West Coast are drawn, Mr. Wilson says:

> The Natives of the Kru country cultivate the soil to some considerable extent. Their farms are generally two or three miles distant from the villages, and are made at this distance to keep them out of the reach of their cattle. Nearer to the villages they have inclosed gardens in which they raise small quantities of plantains, corn, bananas, peas, beans, and a few other vegetables.

Of the mechanical skill of the neighbouring Ashanti people, whose territory is in the English Gold Coast colony, Mr. Wilson tells us, "that they manufacture gold ornaments of various kinds and many of them of much real taste. They fabricate swords, agricultural implements, wooden stools, and cotton cloths of beautiful figures and very substantial texture."*

From time to time, as Tuskegee graduates have returned from the various stations in Africa in which they have been at work, they have brought back with them specimens of native workmanship in iron, wood and leather. I have frequently been impressed with the beauty of some of the designs that native craftsmen have worked out upon their spears and in their homespun cotton cloth. The leather tanned by some of these native tanners is often surprisingly

* "Western Africa," p. 187.

beautiful in colour, design and finish. Some of the specimens of the native handicrafts have been placed on exhibition in the museum at Tuskegee, and in one or two cases we have been able to reproduce in our classes in basketry the shapes and designs of some of these native articles.

"Nothing, perhaps," says Professor Franz Boas, "is more encouraging than a glimpse of the artistic industries of the native African. A walk through the African museums of Paris and London and Berlin is a revelation. I wish you could see the sceptres of African kings, carved of hardwood and representing artistic form; or the dainty basketry made by the people of the Kongo River and of the region of the Great Lakes of the Nile, or the grass mats of their beautiful patterns.

"Even more worthy of our admiration," he continues, "is the work of the blacksmith who manufactures symmetrical lance heads, almost a yard long, or axes inlaid with copper and decorated with filligree. Let me also mention in passing the bronze castings of Benin and the West Coast of Africa, which, although perhaps due to Portuguese influences, have so far excelled in technique any European work, that they are even now almost inimitable."*

The blacksmith seems to occupy a very important place in the social life of Africa. Travellers have

* Atlanta University Leaflet, No. 19.

found these smiths at work in the most remote and inaccessible parts of the continent, where they may be seen collecting the native iron and copper ores; smelting and reducing them, and then working them in their primitive forges, into hoes, knives, spear and arrow heads, battle-axes, wood-working tools, rings and hatchets.

Just as everywhere in the Southern states to-day, especially in the country districts, at the crossroads, or near the country store, one finds the Negro blacksmith, so, in some of the remote regions in Africa, every village has, according to its size, from one to three blacksmiths. Each smith has an apprentice and his art is a craft secret most zealously guarded.

Samuel P. Verner, like the Rev. Leighton Wilson, a Southern white man and missionary of the Southern Presbyterian church, says in his book, "Pioneering in Central Africa," of these African blacksmiths:

> The proficiency of some of these men is astonishing. I frequently have my work done by them and their skill amazed me. They have the art of tempering copper as well as of making soft steel. Some of the objects of their craft which I placed in the National Museum at Washington are revelations to the uninitiated in their remarkable complexity and variety.

Mr. Verner's mission station was in the Kongo Free State, on the upper courses of the Kasai, in the heart of savage Africa where the people have never been touched by the influences of either the European or Mohammedan civilisations. Speaking of the carving and wood working of some of these tribes, Mr. Verner says:

> Some of these Africans are wonderfully adept. They can produce a geometrical figure whose perfection is amazing. Their tools are of the simplest, yet they can carve figures of men and animals, pipes, bowls, cups, platters, tables, and fantastic images. I saw a chair carved out of a solid block of ebony. Their work in ivory is also rare and valuable and I believe their talent in those lines ought to be developed.

Throughout West Africa, wherever the European has not established his trading factory, the native market is an institution which is a constant source of surprise to travellers. These markets are the native clearing houses for the produce of the soil and the fabricated articles of the land. They are generally the centre of the trading operations of a district ranging from ten to thirty miles. Here will be seen vegetables and fruit, poultry, eggs, live pigs, goats, salt of their manufacture, pottery of their own make, strips of cloth, grass-woven mats, baskets and specimens of embroidery and art work, besides numberless other articles of various sorts and kinds which are essential to African comfort and well being. From the small group of native merchants who travel with their wares within a radius of thirty or fifty miles, to the large caravans of the Hausa traders who cross the Desert of Sahara, and at times reach the Eastern and Western confines of the continent, everywhere in Africa the black man is a trader.

Among the more primitive tribes the village markets are confined to two or three hundred buyers or sellers, but in the greater markets like that of Kano and Upper Nigeria, twenty or thirty thousand traders will be gathered together at certain seasons of the year. It is an interesting fact, as indicating the African's interest in trade, that in many tribes the market place is considered sacred ground, and, in order that trade may be carried on there without interruption, no strife is permitted within its precincts.

Professor Boas, writing in 1904, said:

> The Negro all over the African continent is either a tiller of the soil or the owner of large herds; only the Bushmen and a few of the dwarf tribes of Central Africa are hunters. Owing to the high development of agriculture, the density of population of Africa is much greater than that of primitive America and consequently the economic conditions of life are more stable.
>
> It may be safely said that the primitive Negro community with its fields that are tilled with iron and wooden implements, with its domestic animals, with its smithies, with its expert wood-carvers, is a model of thrift and industry, and compares favourably with the conditions of life among our own ancestors.*

It is just as true in America, as it is in Africa, that those who know the Negro intimately and best have been, as a rule, kindest and most hopeful in their judgments of him. This may seem strange to those who get their notion of the Southern white man's opinion of the Negro, from what they see in the press and hear from the platform, during the heat of a

* *Ethnical Record*, March 1904.

political campaign, or from the utterances of men who, for one reason or another, have allowed themselves to become embittered. Southern opinion of the Negro, particularly as it finds expression in the press and on the platform, is largely controversial. It has been influenced by the fact that for nearly a hundred years the Negro has been the football in a bitter political contest, and there are a good many Southern politicians who have acquired the habit of berating him. The Negro, in the South, has had very little part in this controversy, either before or since the war, but he has had a chance to hear it all, and it has often seemed to me, if, after all that has taken place, the Negro is still able to discuss his situation calmly, the white man should be able to do so also. But that is another matter.

Nineteen times out of twenty, I suppose, a stranger coming South, who inquires concerning the Negro from people he meets on the train or on the highways, will get from these men pretty nearly the same opinion he has read in the newspapers or heard in political speeches. These criticisms of the Negro have been repeated so often that people have come to accept and repeat them again without reflection. The thing that shows this to be true is, that the very men who denounced all Negroes will very likely before the conversation is ended tell of one, and perhaps, half a dozen individual Negroes in whom they have the greatest confidence.

A Southern white man may tell you, with the utmost positiveness, that he never knew a single Negro who would not steal — except one. Every white man knows one Negro who is all right — a model of honesty, industry, and thrift — and if he tries to remember, he will think of other Negroes in whom he has the greatest confidence, and for whom he has a very genuine respect. Considering that there are a good many more white people in the South than there are Negroes, it seems to follow, logically, that in spite of what one hears about the Negro in general, there are a good many individual Negroes who are pretty well thought of by their white neighbours.

It is well to take into consideration, also, that when Southern people express their confidence and their respect for an individual black man, they are speaking of one whom they know: on the contrary, when they denounce in general terms the weakness and the failure of the Negro race, they have in mind a large number of whom they know a great deal less.

I do not mean to suggest that there is no justification for the criticism of the Negro that one often hears in the South. I have never thought or said that the Negro in America was all that he should be. It does seem to me, however, that the Negro in the United States has done, on the whole, as well as he was able, and as well as, under all the circumstances, could be reasonably expected.

It was not unusual, particularly in the early part of the last century, to find among the slaves men who could read and write Arabic and were learned in the lore of the Koran. W. B. Hodgson, a Southern slave holder, published in 1857 a paper in which he gave an account of a Negro slave who had translated the gospel of John into Negro dialect, using "the letters of the Koran, the book of his first religious instruction, in transcribing the gospel, the book of his second instruction and conversion, and in the adopted dialect of his land of captivity." Most of the slaves came from what were known as the pagan tribes of the coast. In spite of the fact that so large a proportion of the slaves came from these interior tribes it was not until Mungo Park made his famous first journey to the interior of the Soudan in 1795 that the Western world knew anything definite about that region. The eminent German traveller and scholar, Dr. Henry Barth, first reached the famous commercial city of Kano in 1850, and until 1900 it was said not more than five Europeans had ever visited that city. The accounts that travellers give of the region and the people present a picture of African life so different from that of the coast cities that I am tempted to quote at some length from these descriptions.

Several peoples, of strikingly different characteristics, contributed to form the several loosely connected states which now form the British Colony of Northern Nigeria, of which Kano is the principal city. The most important and interesting of these are the Hausas and the Fulahs or Fellani, as they are sometimes called. The Fulahs are noted for their military spirit; the Hausas for their commercial enterprise. One has a light complexion and the other is dark.

The Fulahs are an equestrian people, with a cavalry armed with lances and swords. They are zealous Mohammedans with a knowledge how to "divide and govern." Their independent character is described by the proverbial saying that "a Fulah man slave will escape or kill his master, and that a Fulah girl slave will rule the harem or die." The Hausas are superior to the Fulahs in the arts of peace. They are possessed of unusual industry, judgment and intelligence and have a considerable degree of literary taste. The Hausas carry on the internal trade of the North and Central Soudan. They are well clothed and have many well built cities with population sometimes of from twenty to sixty thousand. Barth, in describing Kano, which is, perhaps, to West Africa, what Chicago is to the United States, tells us that he mounted on horseback, "rode for several hours round all the inhabited quarters, enjoying at his leisure from the saddle the manifold scenes of public and private life, of comfort and happiness, of luxury and misery, of industry and indolence, which were exhibited in the streets, the market places, and in the interior of the courtyards." Here he saw "a row of shops filled with articles of native and foreign produce with buyers and sellers in every variety of figure, complexion, and dress." Now an "open terrace of clay with a number of dye-pots and people busily employed in various processes of their handicraft; here a man stirring the juice and mixing with indigo some colouring wood in order to give it the desired tint, there another drawing a shirt from the dye-pot, there two men beating a well-dyed shirt"; further on, "a blacksmith busy with his tools in making a dagger, a spear or the more useful ornaments of husbandry," and, in another place, "men and women hanging up their cotton thread for weaving."

The market of Kano, said to be the largest in Africa, is celebrated for its cotton cloth and leather goods. Traditions of Kano go back over a thousand years. It is surrounded by walls of sun-dried clay from twenty to thirty feet high and fifteen miles in circumference.

The greatest chieftain that ever ruled in West Africa, Mohammed Askia, lived in Kano. He became ruler in 1492 and held sway over a region probably as large as the German Empire. Barth tells us that Mohammed Askia was an example of the highest degree to which Negroes have attained in the way of political administration and control. His dynasty, which was entirely of native descent, is the more remarkable if we consider that this Negro king was held in the highest esteem and veneration by the most learned and rigid Mohammedans. Not only did he consolidate and even extend his empire, but went in 1495 on a pilgrimage to Mecca accompanied by 1,500 armed men, 1,000 on foot and 500 on horseback, and founded there a charitable institution. He extended his conquests far and wide from what is now the centre of Nigeria, westward almost to the borders of the Atlantic Ocean and northward to the south of Morocco. Askia governed the subjected tribes with justice and equity. Everywhere within the borders of his extensive dominions his rule spread well-being and comfort.*

The career of Mohammed Askia is possibly the best example of the influence of Mohammedanism on that portion of Africa from which our American slaves were taken.

* "Discoveries in North and Central Africa," Henry Barth. See also, "A Tropical Dependency": an outline of the ancient history of the Western Soudan with an account of the modern settlement of northern Nigeria," Thora L. Shaw, (Lady Lugard.)

CHAPTER IV

THE WEST COAST BACKGROUND OF THE AMERICAN NEGRO

SLAVES were probably brought to America from every part of Africa, for the slave trade seems to have penetrated, before it ended, to every corner of the continent. But the larger number of them came, undoubtedly, from the West Coast. It is said that, at one time, 200,000 slaves sailed annually from the West Coast of Africa, and during a period of two hundred years, it is estimated that 3,200,000 slaves were shipped to America from a single point in the Niger Delta.* These people of the West Coast were, for the most part, the broken fragments of races that had been driven to the sea by the stronger races of the interior. They did not represent the highest to which the black man had attained in Africa, and their contact with the white man of the slave-trading class during the four hundred years or more that the foreign slave trade was in existence, did not improve them.

The African slave trade was not the source of all that was evil in the native life of the West Coast,

* "West African Studies," Mary H. Kingsley, p. 510.

but it is responsible for a great deal of it. The slave trade did not, for instance, cause the destructive tribal wars among the Natives, but it incensed them. It added the motive of gain and gave the savage warfare the character of a commercial enterprise. The evils of the traffic did not end, however, with the immediate and tangible destruction that it wrought. It corrupted the native customs and destroyed the native industries. It substituted the cheap machine-made European goods for the more artistic native manufactures, which take a great deal more time and energy to produce.

"At the present time," says Professor Boas, "the distribution of Negro culture in Africa is such that in all the regions where the whites have come in contact with the Negro, his own industries have disappeared or have been degraded. As a consequence, all the tribes that live near the coast of Africa are, comparatively speaking, on a low level of industrial culture. It is but natural that the blacksmith, who can exchange a small lump of rubber picked up in the woods for a steel knife, prefers this method of obtaining a fine implement to the more laborious one of making a rather inefficient knife of soft iron with his primitive tools. It is not surprising that the cheap cotton goods replace the fine grass-cloth and the bark-cloth which the African women prepare. The European trader carries to the coast of Africa only the cheap products of European factories, but nothing that would give to the Negro the white man's method of work."*

Of course the degradation of the native industries, in the way Professor Boas has described it, is not confined to Africa nor to the slave trade; it goes on wherever machine-made goods come in contact with native and home-made products. Much the same thing may be seen among the Negro farmers in the Southern states where they have yielded to the temptation to raise nothing but cotton — what is called the "money crop." For example, the Tuskegee Institute is located in the midst of one of the finest sweet potato growing soils in the world. Notwithstanding this, canned sweet potatoes used to be shipped into this part of Alabama. It requires less work to use the canned sweet potatoes which have been dug, cleaned, and cooked, than it does to prepare the land, produce the sweet potato crop, clean them, and cook them. But it makes the farmer dependent upon the store-keeper or more frequently on the money-lender.

One of my favourite ways of emphasising this mistake, in my talks to the Negro farmers, is to get a basket of canned vegetables from the store, show them what they are buying, calculate what they are paying for them, and make clear to them how much they could save and how much more independent they would be if they raised these things at home.

---

* *Ethnical Record*, March, 1904, p. 107.

It may be interesting to note here exactly what it was the white man gave the black man for those cargoes of human beings that were shipped from Africa to America. The list of trade goods was somewhat different at different periods of the slave traffic and for different parts of the coast. The following is a list of trade goods as used in the latter part of the seventeenth century for the region about Sierra Leone:

French brandy or rum
Iron bars
White calicoes
Sleysiger linen
Brass kettles
Earthen cans
All sorts of glass buttons
Brass rings or bracelets
Bangles and glass beads of sundry colours
Brass medals
Gunpowder
Musket balls and shot
Old sheets
Paper
Red caps
Men's shirts
Earrings
Dutch knives
Hedging bills and axes
Coarse laces
Crystal beads
Painted calicoes (red), called chintz
Oil of olive
Small duffels
Ordinary guns
Muskets and fuzils
All sorts of counterfeit pearls
Red cotton
Narrow bands of silk stuffs or worsted, about half a yard broad for women, used about their waists

In those early days it was customary to reckon the value of slaves in hides and in bars or iron. A slave was worth at Gambia from twelve to fourteen bars of iron, which is equal in value to about one-half a hogshead of brandy.

The slave trade brought to the surface the worst in

both the white and the black races. In the slave marts of the coast towns it was usually the worst elements of both races that met, but it was here that the African got his first notion of the white man's civilisation, and it was here also that the white man gained his first and most intimate acquaintance with the African.

There is, I understand, a very natural and a very widespread distrust among the Natives of the coast towns and of the civilisation they represent.

One hears so little from the Natives themselves in regard to this subject, or any other for that matter, that I am tempted to quote here a statement of Miss Kingsley which gives an insight into the way the African mother looks upon these matters:

> It is to the mass of African women, untouched by white culture, but with an enormous influence over their sons and brothers, that I am now referring as a factor in the dislike to the advance of white civilisation; and I have said they do not like it because, for one thing, they do not know it; that is to say, they do not know it from the inside and at its best, but only from the outside. Viewed from the outside in West Africa white civilisation, to a shrewd mind like hers, is an evil thing for her boys and girls. She sees it taking away from them the restraints of their native culture, and in all too many cases leading them into a life of dissipation, disgrace, and decay; or, if it does not do this, yet separating the men from their people. . . . Then again both the native and his mother see the fearful effects of white culture on the young women, who cannot be prevented in districts under white control from going down to the coast towns and to the devil. It is this that causes your West African bush chief to listen to the old woman whom you may see crouching behind him, or you may not

see at all, but who is with him all the same, when he says, "Do not listen to the white man, it is bad for you."*

The Negro people of the country districts in the Southern states are, I suspect, much more like the masses of the Africans, who live beyond the influences of the coast towns, than any other portion of any race in the United States. As often as I can find the time to do so, I get out into the country among this class of people. I like to sleep in their houses, eat their food, attend their churches, talk with them as they plant and harvest their crops. In this way I have gotten the inspiration and material for much that I have written and much that I have had to say from time to time about the Negro in America.

In recent years I have noticed among the people, in what I have called "the country districts," a growing distrust for the city, not unlike that distrust of the Africans in the bush for the coast towns. Among the debating societies that are frequently formed among the country people, and in the churches and in the school houses, wherever the people get together, as they are fond of doing, to talk over their local affairs or discuss some abstract question, one of the favourite topics of discussion is the relative merits of the town and country. In the absence of other forms of excitement it frequently happens that a whole community will divide on some purely abstract question of this kind, and the debate

* "West African Studies," p. 376 et seq.

will continue for months at a time. Usually the younger people are for the city and its opportunities, but the older people are for the country and its independence.

The most self-reliant and substantial characters among my race that I know in the South are those who have been so surrounded as not to get hold of the vices and superficialities of towns and cities, but remained in the country where they lead an independent life. I have seen many of these characters who have come to our Tuskegee Negro conferences. I have in mind one man in particular, J. M. Sanifer, a farmer from Pickins County, Alabama, who comes to our Negro conference every year. The first thing that he usually exhibits when he begins to speak is a new suit of clothes. The history of this suit of clothes is interesting. The wool out of which it has been made has been grown upon the backs of sheep owned by himself and pastured on his land. The wool has been woven into cloth by his wife. The garments have been made entirely by his wife and daughters. This man takes great pride in explaining to his fellow members of the conference how he produces his own clothes, his own food, and I remember on one occasion he mentioned that during the previous twelve months he had had, except coffee, nothing in his home in the way of food that had not been produced on his farm. Mr. Sanifer has had very little of what we sometimes call "book learning," but there are some things that one learns from the study of things as well as from the study of books. There were some things that the African learned in American slavery; there are some other and quite different things the American Negro is now beginning to learn in freedom. None of these more fundamental matters are ordinarily taught from books; but if they are to be counted as part of what we call education, then Mr. Sanifer is educated.

I have suggested in what I have already written some of the reasons why the white man has not found the black man at his best on the West Coast and particularly in the West Coast towns. To judge the African by what one may see in these coast towns or by what one may see in South Africa, or in the Nile regions of the Soudan, or wherever the native African has come in close contact with white civilisation, is much the same as if one were to judge the civilisation of America by what one can see in the slums of great cities. The people who live in these slums are, for the most part, uneducated, and have lost many of the habits and customs that make life decent and dignified. But few people, I dare say, would wish to pass judgment, either on the future of America or of the people who live in the city slums merely from what they were able to see there during a hurried or casual visit.

The descriptions of travellers often give one the impression that the moral, religious, and intellectual life of the African is a mere jumble of cruel and fantastic superstitions. But the African religion is not a mere superstition.

"After more than forty years' residence among these tribes," says Rev. R. H. Nassau, "fluently using their language, conversant with their customs, dwelling intimately in their huts, associating with them in the varied relations of teacher, pastor, friend, master, fellow-traveller and guest, and in my special office as missionary, searching after their religious thought (and therefore being allowed a deeper entrance into their soul life than would be accorded to a passing explorer) I am able unhesitatingly to say that among all the multitude with whom I have met, I have seen or heard of none whose religious thought was only a superstition."*

In reading Dr. Nassau's book, I was impressed with the fact that Fetishism, as he defines it, is not merely a West African religion, but a West African system of thought, a general point of view and way of looking at things which enters into all the Native's ideas, and gives its colour to most of the affairs of his daily life.

This way of looking at and interpreting things so thoroughly pervades everything West African, is so different from our way of looking at things and is, as it seems to me, so important to any one who wants to get at the back of the African's mind, and find

---

* "Fetishism in West Africa," R. H. Nassau, p. 36.

something consistent in his institutions and behaviour that I am tempted to quote again here at some length from Miss Kingsley on this subject. She says:

> One of the fundamental doctrines of Fetish is that the connection, of a certain spirit with a certain mass of matter, a material object, is not permanent; the African will point out to you a lightning-stricken tree and tell you that its spirit has been killed; he will tell you when the cooking pot has gone to bits that it has lost its spirit; if his weapon fails it is because some one has stolen or made sick its spirit by means of witchcraft. In every action of his daily life he shows you how he lives with a great, powerful spirit-world around him. You will see him before starting out to hunt or fight rubbing medicine into his weapons to strengthen the spirits within them, talking to them the while; telling them what care he has taken of them, reminding them of the gifts he has given them, though those gifts were hard for him to give, and begging them in the hour of his dire necessity not to fail him. You will see him bending over the face of a river talking to its spirit with proper incantations, asking it when it meets a man who is an enemy of his to upset his canoe or drown him, or asking it to carry down with it some curse to the village below which has angered him, and in a thousand other ways he shows you what he believes if you will watch him patiently.*

The fundamental difference between the African and the European way of thinking seems to be that for the African there is no such thing as dead matter in the world. Everything is alive, and for that reason there is no such thing as a machine, at least in the sense that we think of it. We are inclined to look at the physical world about us as if everything that happened was turned out relentlessly by some

* "West African Studies," p. 130.

great passionless machine. But the African thinks that the world is alive in every part; it is a world of spirits and persons like ourselves.

Miss Kingsley continues:

> The more you know the African the more you study his laws and institutions, the more you must recognise that the main characteristic of his intellect is logical, and you see how in all things he uses this absolutely sound but narrow thought-form. He is not a dreamer or a doubter; everything is real, very real, horridly real to him. It is impossible for me to describe it clearly, but the quality of the African mind is strangely uniform. This may seem strange to those who read accounts of wild and awful ceremonials, or of the African's terror at the white man's things; but I believe you will find all people experienced in dealing with uncultured Africans will tell you that this alarm and brief wave of curiosity is merely external, for the African knows, the moment he has time to think it over, what the white man's thing really is, namely, either a white man's Juju or a devil.
>
> It is this power of being able logically to account for everything that is, I believe, at the back of the tremendous permanency of Fetish in Africa, and the cause of many of the relapses into it by Africans converted to other religions; it is also the explanation of the fact that white men living in districts where death and danger are every-day affairs, under a grim pall of boredom, are liable to believe in Fetish, though ashamed of so doing.*

African medicine, so far as it has any system at all, is based on Fetish. The African believes that diseases are caused by an evil spirit, and the efficacy of drugs depends on the benevolent spirits, which, being put into the body, drive away the malevolent disease-causing spirits.

"There is," says Miss Kingsley, "as in all things

* *Ibid.*, p. 124.

West African, a great deal of Fetish ceremonial mixed up with West African medical methods. Underlying them throughout there is the Fetish form of thought, but it is erroneous to believe that all West African native doctors are witch doctors, because they are not. One of my Efik friends, for example, would no more think of calling in a witch doctor for a simple case of rheumatism than you would think of calling in a curate or a barrister; he would just call in the equivalent to our consulting physician, the country doctor, the *Abiadiong*. But if he started being ill with something exhibiting cerebral symptoms he would have in the witch doctor at once."

What Miss Kingsley calls the *Abiabok* is really the village apothecary, who is also a sort of country doctor whose practice extends over a fair-sized district, wherein he travels from village to village. Big towns have resident apothecaries, and these apothecaries are learned in the properties of herbs, and they are surgeons as far as surgery is ventured upon. "A witch doctor," says Miss Kingsley, "would not dream of performing an operation."

Ex-President G. W. Gibson of Liberia, with whom I have talked, who went out to Africa as a boy, shortly after the colony was founded, speaks the native language fluently and has a long and intimate acquaintance with the native peoples, says that certain of the African methods of dealing with disease are very effective. For instance, the people in Liberia are frequently troubled with rheumatism and dropsy. For these diseases, he says, no medicines have been found equal to those of the Native doctor.

Like all the other crafts in Africa the use of drugs is a trade secret, and the native doctor has to go through a long apprenticeship before he is allowed to practise. It is not unusual, Mr. Gibson says, for some one living in the settlements, white men as well as black, to go out to those Bush doctors to obtain relief from certain kinds of disease.

Sometimes the coloured people in America, particularly those of the older generation, have had very quaint notions about medicine, but many of them, even those most ignorant of books, seem to be natural doctors or nurses. Frequently at Tuskegee a boy or girl having after been given the best care by our resident physician has remained sick for several months with few signs of recovery. Then the mother of this student would come to the institution and ask permission to take her child home for a few weeks. Notwithstanding the fact that the mother lived a long way in the country, miles from any doctor, the student would return within a few weeks in an apparently sound and healthy condition.

The methods of the witch doctor, as distinguished from the methods of the ordinary village doctor, seem to me, to a certain extent, like those of the Christian Scientist, at least in so far as he seeks to work directly on the soul and to drive out the disease by driving the idea of it out of the patient's mind. The witch doctor has to do with malevolent spirits, but as some of these malevolent spirits are human beings, his methods often take the form of a criminal proceeding, he being called in to assist in the conviction of the persons who are responsible for the disease. It is these criminal proceedings that have given the witch doctor his present bad reputation. And yet it is admitted that the witch doctors, as a rule, are very skilful in ferreting out crime.

One of the most interesting books in regard to Africa which I have been able to lay my hands on is Sarbah's "Fanti Customary Laws," a collection made by a native lawyer and member of the English bar, from cases tried under English jurisdiction in native courts. This customary law corresponds, in the life of the Fanti people, a tribe inhabiting what is known as the Gold Coast, to the common law of England, and Mr. Sarbah, in collecting it in a permanent form has performed a service for his people not unlike that of Blackstone for the English common law. Everywhere in Africa where the life of the people has not been disturbed by outside influences, the people are governed by law. There is law relating to property, to morality, to the protection of life, in fact, in many portions of Africa law is more strictly regarded than in many civilised countries.*

"No other race on a similar level of culture," says Professor Boas, "has developed as strict methods of legal procedure as the Negro has. Many of his legal forms remind us strongly of those of mediæval Europe. For instance, it is hardly a coincidence that the ordeal as a means of deciding legal cases when all other evidence fails, has been used in Europe as well as throughout Africa, while it seems to be entirely unknown in ancient America."

In looking at the social institutions of the African we must not ignore his popular assemblies that are generally held in the palaver house or in the open air. Here matters legislative as well as judicial are settled. Though there are no written laws, certain ancient customs and usages form the precedent for discussion and settlement. When a law has been agreed upon, it is customary in some of the coast tribes for a public crier to proclaim it through the town. This is repeated at dusk when all the people are supposed to be at home so that no one can plead ignorance in case the law is violated. In

*"Fanti Customary Laws, a brief introduction to Principles of the Native Laws and Customs of the Fanti and Akan Sections of the Gold Coast, with a Selection of Cases thereon Decided in the Law Courts," John Mensah Sarbah.

trial cases the witness takes an oath of which the following is an example:

O God! come down, thou givest me food.
In this case I come as a witness and I will speak.
If I tell lies, I will go in the bush and serpent bite me;
If I go in a canoe, the canoe will sink and I drown;
If I climb a palm-tree I must fall and die.
You (God) let the thunder fall and kill me.
If I tell the truth, then I am safe in Thee.

The native African tribes, which have never been touched by the Mohammedan civilisation have, as is generally known, no written literature. Only one tribe, the Vei people who live in the hinterland of Sierra Leone and Liberia, have invented an alphabet.* But Africans are great story-tellers and, according to Leighton Wilson, they have almost any amount of "unwritten lore, in the form of fables, allegories, traditionary stories and proverbial sayings, in which is displayed no small share of close observation, lively imagination and extraordinary shrewdness of character." He describes one famous African story-teller, Toko, by name, who might have been an ancestor of Joel Chandler Harris's "Uncle Remus."

"Toko," he says, "has a very remarkable and intelligent countenance, strongly marked with the

* It [the Vei language] possesses a syllabic alphabet of over two hundred characters, invented in 1834 by Doalu Bukerè, a powerful member of the tribe. This writing system is even still used in correspondence and for recording family events, and in it the inventor wrote a history of his nation and a treatise on ethics.—*Africa, Élisée Reclus, Vol. III, p.* 218.

deep vein of natural humour which pervades his whole composition. He is careless in dress, unpretending in his manners, but his shrewdness and unbounded humour, almost in spite of himself, peer out at every turn in conversation. When he sets out to rehearse one of his favourite fables, all his humour is at once stirred up, and he yields himself to the spirit of the story. He is all glee himself, the hearer cannot for his life avoid being carried along with him. The wild animals of the woods are summoned before his audience, they are endowed with all the cunning and shrewdness of man and before you are aware of it, you have before your imagination a perfect drama."

Heli Chatelain, who has collected some of this unwritten literature in a volume entitled "Folk Tales of Angola," says that those who "think the Negro is deficient in philosophical faculties ignore their proverbs which both in direction and depth of meaning, equal those of any other race."

"At the bottom of patience," says one of these proverbs, "there is heaven." "Hold a true friend with both hands," says another. "Hope is the pillar of the world," and, "He is a heathen who bears malice," are others.

Perhaps the Native African, except under Mohammedan influences, has been less successful in building up and maintaining permanent and lasting governments than in other directions, but he has been more successful in this respect than is generally supposed.

Professor Boas, speaking of some Negro Central African tribes that have never come under Mohammedan influence, says:

The power of organisation that manifests itself in Negro communities is quite striking. Travellers who have visited Central Africa tell of extended kingdoms, ruled by monarchs, whose power, however, is restricted by a number of advisers. The constitution of all such states is, of course, based on the general characteristics of the social organisations of the Negro tribes, which, however, have become exceedingly complex with the extension of the domain of a single tribe over neighbouring peoples.

The Lunda empire, for instance, is a feudal state governed by a monarch. It includes a number of subordinate states, the chiefs of which are independent in all internal affairs, but who pay tribute to the emperor. The chiefs of the more distant parts of the country send caravans carrying tribute once a year, while those near by have to pay more frequently. The tribute depends upon the character of the produce of the country. It consists of ivory, salt, copper, slaves, and even, to a certain extent, of European manufactures. In case of war the subordinate chiefs have to send contingents to the army of the emperor. The succession in each of the subordinate states is regulated by local usage. Sons and other relatives of the subordinate chiefs are kept at the court of the emperor as a means of preventing disintegrations of the empire.

A female dignitary occupies an important position in the government of the state. She is considered the mother of the emperor. She has a separate court, and certain districts pay tribute to her. Both the emperor and female dignitary must be children of one of the two head wives of the preceding emperor. The emperor is elected by the four highest counsellors of the state, and his election must be confirmed by the female dignitary; while her election takes place in the same way, and she must be confirmed by the emperor. The office of counsellors of the state is hereditary. Their power is important, because four among them have the privilege of electing the emperor and the female dignitary, as described before. Besides this, there is a nobility, consisting, as it would seem, of the wealthy inhabitants, who have the privilege of expressing their opinion in regard to the affairs of the state. This empire is known to have existed since the end of the sixteenth century, although its extent and importance have probably undergone many changes. It would seem that sometimes the boundaries of the state were limited, and that at other times many tribes were subject to it. In 1880 the state was about as large as the Middle Atlantic states.

One reason for the instability of the kingdoms that have grown up and flourished from time to time on the Western Coast is, as Mr. Dowd has pointed out, that the forests and rivers cut the population into fragments and prevent cooperation.

It is interesting to note that Negro freedmen have not only established governments in Haiti in America, Liberia in Africa, but from 1630 to 1700 fugitive slaves maintained the Negro State of Palmares in what is now Brazil, against all the other slave-holding provinces of that colony. Negro slaves, imported from East Africa to become guards of palaces and fighting seamen for the Indian princes, became so powerful that they carved out states for themselves, one or more of which are still ruled by Negro princes, as dependencies of the government of India.*

Of the native states of Central Africa none have been more studied, or better known than the

* "The Colonisation of Africa," Sir Harry H. Johnston.

Kingdom of Uganda. In a recent article Mr. Winston Churchill, M. P., writes concerning the country and the people:

> The Kingdom of Uganda is a fairy tale. You climb up a railway instead of a bean stalk, and at the end there is a wonderful new world. The scenery is different, the vegetation is different, and, most of all the people are different from anything elsewhere to be seen in the whole range of Africa. Instead of the breezy uplands we enter a tropical garden: in place of naked painted savages clashing their spears and gibbering in chorus to their tribal chiefs, a complete and elaborate policy is presented. Under a dynastic King, a parliament, and a powerful feudal system, an amiable, clothed, polite, and intelligent race dwell together in an organised monarchy upon the rich domain between the Victoria and Albert Lakes. More than two hundred thousand natives are able to read and write. More than one hundred thousand have embraced the Christian faith. There is a court, there are regents and ministers and nobles, there is a regular system of native law and tribunals; there is discipline, there is industry, there is culture, there is peace.

This description of conditions in Uganda strikes me as the more interesting because this progress has been made in a land where the white man cannot live. "Every white man," says Mr. Churchill, "seems to feel a sense of indefinable depression. A cut will not heal, a scratch festers. In the third year of residence even a small wound becomes a running sore. One day a man feels perfectly well; the next, for no apparent cause, he is prostrated with malaria, and with malaria of a peculiarly persistent kind, turning often in the third or fourth attack to blackwater fever. In the small European community at Entebbe there have been quite recently two suicides. Whether, as I have suggested in East Africa, it be the altitude, or the downward ray of the Equatorial sun, or the insects, or some more subtle cause there seems to be a solemn veto placed upon the white man's permanent residence in these beautiful abodes."

It has often seemed to me that, in estimating the possibilities of the Negro race, one should not overlook the extraordinary capacity of the Negro for adapting himself, whether in Africa or in America, to the conditions in which he finds himself. It is this power of fitting himself into, and adapting himself to, new conditions, which has enabled him to survive under conditions in which other peoples have perished. The Indian in the West Indies, in South America and North America, the Sandwich Islanders, the Australians and the New Zealanders have steadily receded before the advance of the white civilisation. The Negro is the only primitive people, as I have said elsewhere, which has looked the white man in the face and lived.

The Natives of South Africa are an illustration of the quality I refer to. The changes which the white man has made, during the last fifty years in South Africa, have brought enormous hardship to the native peoples. Against these changes they have frequently rebelled, but in the end, as they saw they were facing the inevitable, they have sought to adapt themselves to it. And they have not become discouraged; and they have not died out. On the contrary, they have steadily increased in numbers as the inter-tribal wars died out.

I remember some years ago meeting a young African who had come to Tuskegee as a student from the region around Johannesburg, South Africa. He had managed to save a considerable sum of money at the time of the late Boer war in South Africa, and he had made use of that money to come to America to get an education. He had not learned, at this time, to speak our language fluently, and it was with some difficulty that he expressed himself in English. I managed to get from him, however, a vivid impression of the change that had come over him and his people since the white men first invaded their country. He had grown up, he said, in the kraal, with no thought and no ambition to do otherwise, than his father had done before him — to till a little strip of land, to tend the cattle, and, as he said, "to play." In the simplicity of this life there was no thought and no care for the future, no notion that life could ever be other than it was. Looking back upon it, this seemed one long, unbroken holiday. He very well understood how crude and how aimless this savage life was likely to seem to people who lived in a higher stage of civilisation, but he made no apologies for it. He said it was "glorious"; that was his word.

But the white man came, and soon all was changed.

At first his people welcomed the strangers, for they had long been acquainted with the missionaries and liked them. But after the discovery of gold and diamonds the white man came in ever increasing numbers, bringing with him strange customs and wonderful machinery.

At the same time came the drought and pestilence and a great war. For the first time within his memory people began to die of hunger. Many of the young men left their villages and went into the mines and then wandered away into the cities and never came back. The old men were much troubled and began to sit long in council considering what was to be the future of the people and what was the best thing to do.

Out of all this unrest there has grown up among the Natives an ardent desire for education. It is pathetic to note the earnestness with which, at the present time, these people are seeking the white man's education in order that they may fit themselves and their people for the white man's civilisation. And this desire for education, so far as I can learn, is not confined to those who live in the settlements but it has taken hold, also, of the people living in the remote regions, wherever a Christian missionary has penetrated.

Some of the African chiefs have sent their sons as students to Tuskegee and I have frequently been touched by the appeals for assistance in the way of teachers that have come to us through these students and from other sources.*

An incident quoted by Archibald Colquhoun in a recent book on South African affairs, gives some idea of the earnestness of this desire of the Natives for education.

A Native family, squatting on a Dutch Africander farm, earned between them a small sum weekly for rooting up prickly pear, the farmer's pest. Not being near any school, they paid the whole sum,

---

* As showing the widespread desire for education among these people a report of an educational meeting, which I ran across some time ago, struck me as significant. As a result of a general invitation 160 natives of note assembled December 28, 1905, at Lovedale, the seat of the first important industrial school for Natives in Africa. They came from the most populous districts of Cape Colony, from Bechuanaland, from the Orange Free State and from Basutoland. There were pastors of all denominations, chiefs of tribes sent by their headchiefs, men of influence representing no special part of the country, among them two editors of native newspapers.

This meeting was called at the instance of Dr. James Stewart, who for forty years had been the director of the Lovedale school. The commission appointed after the Boer war to investigate the condition of the natives had recommended, after two years investigation, the establishment of a university for blacks. The purpose of this meeting was to secure the carrying out of this project. Unfortunately, five days before the assembly convened Dr. Stewart died. He did not live to see the realisation of his plan, but the meeting was a success. It was announced at this meeting that if the Natives would raise $200,000 among their own people the Government would give the school an annual grant of $50,000. After two days of discussion the proposition was unanimously endorsed by the convention.

The report of this meeting makes the following comment upon the proceedings:

"A remarkable fact in regard to the action of this convention was the spirit of union that reigned. The Natives who had come together from all points of the compass, laid wholly aside their tribal jealousies and their bloody quarrels of former times. More than that the ordinary barriers which divide the sects seemed no longer to exist; the Lutherans voted with the Presbyterians, the Anglicans with the Wesleyans and the Congregationalists. Finally the Native chiefs put off their dignities and surrendered for the time being their prerogatives in order to discuss and to vote in the ranks with their subjects. The blacks who had never been able to unite for war, when the whites were killing and robbing them of their lands, were all now of one mind and purpose for establishing a great center of higher education for all the natives of South Africa."

their entire income, to a Native teacher (a half educated man from the nearest kraal) to act as tutor to their children, and they subsisted on what they could glean, or (it is to be feared) steal. When they were questioned on the subject these people were perfectly clear as to their motive, which was to give their children a better chance in the world. "In the face of such a strong demand," says Mr. Colquhoun, "it is useless to make any attempt to stop the tide of progress. If Natives cannot get the education they demand in South Africa, they can and will go to America for it."*

* "Africander Land," p. 51.

Part II

THE NEGRO AS A SLAVE

CHAPTER V

THE FIRST AND LAST SLAVE-SHIP

SOME time in August of the year 1619 a strange vessel entered the mouth of the James River, in what is now the State of Virginia, and, coming in with the tide, dropped anchor opposite the little settlement at Jamestown. This ship, which carried the Dutch flag, had the appearance of a man-of-war, but its mission, as it turned out, was peaceful enough, for its purpose was trade, and among other merchandise it carried twenty Negro slaves.

This Dutch man-of-war, which brought the first slaves to the first permanent English settlement in the new world, is, so far as the United States is concerned, the first slave-ship, for it was probably the first slave-trader to visit the North American continent.

But the twenty Africans were not the first slaves to reach what is now the territory of the United States, and the oversea African slave-trade had been in existence for a century before this time. In fact, Negro slaves were known in ancient Greece and Rome and regular accounts of the African slave trade with Europe are in existence since 990 A. D. In 1442 Portuguese ships brought back Moorish prisoners from a voyage to the Coast of Africa. As ransom the Portuguese accepted a certain amount of gold and a number of "black Moors," with curled hair. About this same time the Spanish merchants of Seville began to import gold and slaves from Western Africa. As witness to the extent of this traffic, there is still preserved an interesting letter, written in 1474 to the celebrated Negro, Juan de Valladolid, also called the "Negro Count," which not only shows that the number of these dark-skinned aliens in Spain was at that time considerable, but gives some idea, also, of the manner in which they were treated.

"For the many good, loyal, and signal services which you have done us, and do each day," the letter begins, "and because we know your sufficiency, ability, and good disposition, we constitute you mayoral and judge of all the Negroes and mulattoes, free or slaves, which are in the very loyal and noble city of Seville, and throughout the whole archbishopric thereof, and that the said Negroes and mulattoes may not hold any festivals, nor pleadings among themselves except before you, Juan de Valladolid, Negro, our judge and mayoral of the said Negroes and mulattoes.

"And we command," the letter continues, "that you, and you only, take cognisance of the disputes, pleadings, marriages, and other things which may take place among them, for as much as you are a person sufficient for that office and deserving of your power, and you know the laws and ordinances which ought to be kept, and we are informed that you are of noble lineage among the said Negroes."* The letter is signed Ferdinand and Isabella, King and Queen of Spain.

When the Spanish explorers and adventurers came to America they brought many of these Spanish Negroes with them as servants and as slaves. It is probable that a few Negroes were sent out to the West Indies as early as 1501. Soon after this date, as shown by a letter of King Ferdinand, dated September 15, 1505, a considerable number of slaves were introduced into Santo Domingo. In this letter the following sentence occurs: "I will send you more Negro slaves as you request. I think there may be a hundred." Here we have the beginning of African slavery in America, over a century before its introduction into Jamestown, Va.

The records show that Negroes in 1516 worked with Balboa on the Isthmus of Panama; that Pizarro,

---

*The organization of a quasi-independent Negro state within the limits of a larger controlling white state, the existence of which is suggested in this letter, has a parallel, I may say in passing, in Connecticut, where a state organisation with governor, judge and other officers formerly existed with jurisdiction over the minor offences of slaves. In this way the slaves of Connecticut, long before emancipation was seriously considered in the United States, were given a form of self-government. The plan seems to have been conceived by some of the older Negroes who exercised their office, with the consent of their masters, but also with the authority which their age and experience exercised over the younger members of the community.—" Economic Co-operation Among Negro Americans," Atlanta University Publications, No. 12, p. 19.

the conqueror of Peru, and Las Casas, the Dominican Bishop and missionary, had Negro bodyguards.

Negroes also accompanied the expeditions of Vasquez de Ayllon, Narvaez, Coronado and De Soto. With the ill-fated expedition of Narvaez was the Negro Estevan, in English, Stephen. For eleven years, from 1528 to the year of his death, 1539, this Negro Stephen was with the Spanish explorers on the mainland of North America. He wandered hundreds of miles across what is now the southwestern part of the United States, two centuries or more before our western frontier touched that section of the country. He was a slave of one of the survivors of the Narvaez expedition and must have been a man far above the average type. In one of the folk-tales of the Zuni Indians he lives to-day, after a lapse of more than three and a half centuries, and one well-known writer of American history has called him the discoverer of Arizona.

According to the Spanish historian, Oviedo, Negroes were among the settlers of the Spanish colony of Chicora, in 1526, on what is now the coast of South Carolina, and this, so far as known, was the earliest appearance of the black man on the soil of the United States. In 1526, when, under Vasques de Ayllon, eighty-one years before the English, the Spaniards tried to found a settlement on the James River near the present sight of Jamestown, Virginia. Negro slaves were employed in the work. An insurrection of the Negro labourer and the death of Ayllon were among the causes for the failure of the venture. African slaves accompanied the expedition of De Soto to Florida in 1539. Negro slaves were settled at St. Augustine, Florida, by Pedro Menendez, in 1565. These, however, were Spanish slaves who had been trained as artisans and cultivators of the soil and were of a different character from those fresh levies of labourers who were brought direct to America from Africa.*

Almost nothing is known of the history of the ship that brought the first slaves, in 1619, to the settlement of Jamestown; not even its name is remembered. The coincidence has often been noted, however, that the *Mayflower*, which is said to have brought to America the first seeds of civil and religious liberty, reached Plymouth a year later, 1620, so that Negro slavery is older than Anglo-Saxon liberty on the soil of the United States.

In reading the early history of the United States, I have been impressed with the fact that religious animosities among European people were largely responsible for the settlement of America.

The original thirteen states of the Union were very generally settled by refugees from the religious wars and religious persecutions of Europe, and three of them at least, Massachusetts, Pennsylvania, and Maryland, were settled by religious sects who

* Magazine of American History, Vol. 26, pp. 349-366.

had crossed the ocean in order to secure freedom of religious worship.

The Scotch-Irish, who so widely settled the southern colonies, left their homes in Ireland to a large degree because of the oppression that they suffered in consequence of their religious faith.

North Carolina, which was one of the first of the English colonies to grant religious liberty to the persecuted sects of Europe, was frequently referred to as a "Quaker Colony," because of the number of those persecuted people who settled there.

South Carolina was also a refuge for a large number of Huguenots, who were the Calvinists of France. As an illustration of some of the milder forms of persecution to which these people were subjected in their homes, in France, because of their religious opinions, I may quote the following paragraph, from Bancroft's History of the United States:

> Huguenots were, therefore, to be employed no longer in public office; they were, as far as possible, excluded from the guilds of tradesmen and mechanics; and a Calvinist might not marry a Roman Catholic wife.*

It is a very curious fact that, at the very same time ships were leaving Europe with people who were seeking in America a solution and an escape from the religious controversies that had for centuries torn Europe asunder, other ships were leaving

* Bancroft's History of the United States, Vol. 11, p. 176.

Africa bearing to this continent other people who were to be the seeds of new conflicts and leave, as a heritage, a new problem; a problem in many ways as difficult and perplexing as that which faced Europe at the beginning of the Protestant Reformation.

Religious prejudice, transplanted to American soil, did not at once die out. A study of some of the older colonial codes will show that Quakers, who were nonconformists, and Catholics, who were not always counted as Christians, were subjected to restrictions which were frequently quite as severe as those imposed upon the free Negroes before the war. Under the law of Virginia in existence in 1705, for instance, Catholics, Indians and Negro slaves were denied the right to appear "as witnesses in any case whatsoever, not being Christians," but this was modified somewhat in 1732, when Negroes, Indians, and mulattoes were admitted as witnesses in the trial of slaves.*

In one particular instance religious prejudice against the Catholics was curiously associated with prejudice, on account of race, against the Negro. I refer to what is known in the history of New York as the "Negro Plot of 1741."

In this year the city of New York was thrown into convulsions of excitement by the rumours of a conspiracy among some of the lower class of Negroes,

* History of the Negro Race, Williams, Vol. I., p. 129.

supposed to have been instigated by Spanish Catholics, to burn the city and destroy the inhabitants. These rumours were confirmed by a letter, received about this time from General Oglethorpe of Georgia, which reported that Spain had employed a number of Catholic priests, who were to go through the country pretending to be physicians, dancing masters, "and other such kinds of occupations," who were to get the confidence of families and so further the plans "to burn all the considerable cities in English North America."

Shortly before this time a Spanish vessel, manned in part by Spanish Negroes, had been captured and the Negroes, although they claimed to be free, sold into slavery in the colony. Suspicion directed to one of these slaves added to the excitement. Among other persons arrested was a man supposed to be a Catholic priest. Circumstances seemed to connect certain other Catholics in the colony with the supposed conspiracy. As usual, in such instances of intense social commotion, fresh rumours and fresh suspicions added fuel to the excitement and before it had died away one hundred and seventy-eight persons were arrested, thirty-six were executed and seventy-one transported. Among those executed was the supposed Catholic priest to whom I have referred. Eighteen Negroes were hanged and fourteen were burned. They were executed in sight of the spot where the United States Custom

House now stands in the square that still has the name of Bowling Green. It occurs to me, as I am writing this, as an illustration of the progress of the Negro, that Charles W. Anderson, the United States Collector of Internal Revenue, who occupies a suite of offices in this building is a Negro.

In spite of the numerous "confessions" of white people and black, arrested during the period that the excitement lasted, there does not seem to have been any sufficient evidence that any conspiracy to burn the city existed. The explanation seems to be that the community was for the time labouring under one of those strange social delusions, like that which seized upon the people of New England during the period of the Salem witchcraft panic. The situation, as it existed at the height of the excitement, as well as the circumstances that finally brought the prosecutions to an end, are summed up in the following paragraph from Smith's "History of New York":

> The whole summer was spent in the prosecutions; every new trial led to further prosecutions: a coincidence of slight circumstances was magnified by the general terror into violent presumptions; tales collected without doors, mingling with the proofs given at the bar poisoned the minds of the jurors; and the sanguinary spirit of the day suffered no check till Mary, the capital informer, bewildered by frequent examinations and suggestions, lost her first impressions, and began to touch characters which malice itself did not dare to suspect.*

---

* Quoted in Williams, "History of the Negro Race," Vol. I., p. 169.

I have referred here at some length to these circumstances because they show that in times past religious prejudice, like racial prejudice, has often been the source of those wild fears and vague suspicions by which one class of people in the community is sometimes incited to violence against another and weaker class.

In spite, however, of the bitter animosities that once divided them, the people of the different religious creeds have since learned to live side by side in peace. Is there any sound reason why the white man and the black man, who, after all, understand one another here in America pretty well, should not do as much? I do not believe there is.

In 1741, at the time of the "Negro Plot," the population of New York City numbered 10,000, of which 2,000 were Negroes. At this time the number of slaves in the whole colony of Massachusetts did not amount to more than 3,000. The number in Pennsylvania had reached 11,000 in 1754, but in some of the more southerly colonies the number of slaves, particularly in proportion to the number of inhabitants was considerably larger. In South Carolina, for instance, the Negroes were at one time in the proportion of 22 to 12 of the white population.* In 1740 this state had 40,000 slaves.

* Bancroft's "History of the United States," Vol. II., p. 171.

In spite of restrictions that were put upon it from time to time the slave-trade continued to flourish down to the time of the American Revolution, when for a time it ceased, only to leap into more vigorous life at the close of the war. At the beginning of the nineteenth century England held in all her colonies in the new world 800,000 slaves. France had 250,000; Denmark 27,000; Spain and Portugal 600,000; Holland 50,000; Sweden 600. There were about 900,000 slaves in the United States and about 2,000,000 in Brazil.*

I was much impressed in reading some years ago Mungo Park's travels with his account of slavery as he found it in those parts of Africa which he visited. His description enabled me, as I thought, to see how easily and naturally the milder form of domestic slavery, which seems to have existed in those countries from the earliest times, had grown, under the influence of contact and commerce with European people, into foreign slave-trade. In other ways, also, it seems to me I have learned something about African slavery in America, from what I read of African slavery in Africa.

At the time of Park's famous journey he estimated that the proportion of slaves to the free population, in the regions through which he travelled, was about three to one. These slaves were of two descriptions: those who were born slaves and those

* "Suppression of the Slave Trade," DuBois, p. 131.

who had become slaves either through capture in war, insolvency, or as punishment for crime.

There existed at that time in Africa regular markets for the purchase and sale of slaves, just as they afterward existed at Alexandria, at Natchez, and New Orleans in America. Mungo Park noted, also, the interesting fact that in the eye of an African purchaser the value of a slave increased in proportion to his distance from his native kingdom, for the reason that when slaves were only a few days' journey from their homes they frequently succeeded in making their escape. On the other hand, when several kingdoms intervened, making escape more difficult, they were more easily reconciled to their situation.

The same thing was true, and for the same reason, during the existence of slavery in America. For instance, from 1820 to 1830, slaves were selling at from $150 to $300 each in Virginia, while during the same time the same slaves in New Orleans would be worth from $800 to $1,200. The difference was due, in large part, to the agricultural conditions, since at that time an able-bodied Negro could earn $200 a year for his master on a sugar plantation in Louisiana, over and above the cost of his keep. But the difference was due in a considerable degree, also, to the fact that in Louisiana the slave was, under ordinary conditions, beyond all hope of freedom.*

* "The Domestic Slave Trade of the Southern States," Winfield N. Collins, pp. 28 and 29.

"The slaves which are purchased by Europeans on the coast," Mungo Park continues, "are chiefly of this description" (i.e., from the interior). "A few of them are collected in petty wars, which take place near the coast, but by far the greater number are brought down in large caravans from the inland countries, of which many are unknown, even by name, to Europeans."

It was true in Africa, as it was afterward in America, that slaves of mild disposition and such as were not disposed to run away were retained by their masters, while others who showed signs of discontent or appeared in other ways intractable, were disposed of in some distant state. Thus the domestic slave-trade merged easily and naturally nto the foreign slave-trade and the intractable slaves from the interior were sent to America.

On his way back to the coast, after his long journey to the interior, Mungo Park joined company with a party of merchants on their way to the coast, having among other merchandise a coffle of slaves, which they exchanged later for European rum and tobacco.

These long marches of the slave-caravans and the methods of caring for and confining the slaves in the part of the country through which Mungo Park travelled were not unlike those which one might have seen fifty years ago on one of the old slave-roads, from Alexandria, Virginia, to Natchez, Mississippi, although the African journey was in many respects more difficult.*

In the course of this long and tedious journey from the interior of Africa to the coast, Mungo Park had an opportunity to become thoroughly acquainted with all phases of the slave-traffic, as it then existed, and he has given many intimate and interesting glimpses into the life, thoughts, and feelings of the unfortunate captives, whom he seemed to have an unusual ability to understand and sympathise with. Of one party of captives which, at one point in his journey, were added to the caravan, he said:

> Eleven of them confessed to me that they had been slaves from their infancy, but the other two refused to give any account of their former condition. They were all very inquisitive, but they viewed me at first with looks of horror, and repeatedly asked if my countrymen were cannibals. They were very desirous to know what became of the slaves after they had crossed the salt water. I told them they were employed in cultivating the land; but they would not believe me, and one of them, putting his hand upon the ground, said, with great simplicity: "Have you really got

* In his history, "The Domestic Slave Trade of the Southern States," pp. 52, 101, Prof. Winfield N. Collins, of Claremont College, N. C., says:

"The number of slaves currently estimated to have been transported to the South and Southwest during 1835 and 1836 almost staggers belief. The Maryville, Tenn., *Intelligencer* made the statement in 1836 that, in 1835, 60,000 slaves passed through a Western town on their way to the Southern market. Also, in 1836 the Virginia (Wheeling) *Times* says, intelligent men estimated the number of slaves exported from Virginia during the preceding twelve months as 120,000, of whom about two-thirds were carried there by their masters, leaving 40,000 to have been sold. . . . In the transportation of slaves the utmost precautions were necessary to prevent revolt or escape. When a 'coffle' or 'drove' was formed to undertake its march of seven or eight weeks to the South the men would be chained — two by two, and a chain passing through the double file and fastening from the right and left hands of those on either side of the chain."

such ground as this to set your feet upon?" A deeply rooted idea that the whites purchase slaves for the purpose of eating them, or of selling them to others that they may be devoured hereafter, naturally makes the slave contemplate a journey toward the coast with great terror, insomuch that the 'slatees' are forced to keep them constantly in irons and watch them very closely to prevent their escape.

At another part of the journey one of the slaves belonging to the coffle, who had travelled for several days with great difficulty, was unable to travel farther and his master therefore determined to exchange him for a young girl belonging to the townspeople with whom they were stopping. "The poor girl," Park continues, "was ignorant of her fate until the bundles were all tied up in the morning, and the coffle ready to depart, when, coming with some other young women to see the coffle set out, her master took her by the hand and delivered her to the singing man. Never was a face of serenity more suddenly changed into deepest distress; the terror she manifested on having the load put upon her head and the rope fastened round her neck, and the sorrow with which she bade adieu to her companions were truly affecting."

This dread of the African slave of being sent down to the slave-markets of the coast towns is like the fear that constantly haunted the slaves in Maryland, Virginia, and the other border states, that some day they might be sold into the Far South. The most heartrending scenes of slave-life in the South occurred when owners, on account of debt or some other misfortune, were compelled to separate families and sell them to the traders. It was not alone the parting of children from parents, husbands from wives, that made these scenes sad and memorable, but frequently it was just as hard for the slaves to part from their owners and members of his family, to which, through years of association, they had become deeply attached. This feeling of sorrow has found expression in the words of an old plantation song that originated in Virginia, the words of which are in part as follows:

Mother is Massa goi'n to sell, sell us to-morrow?
Yes, my child! Yes, my child! Yes, my child!
Going to sell us down in Georgia?
  Yes, yes, yes,
Going to sell us way down in Georgia.
    Yes, yes, yes!
    Oh! Watch and pray!
      Fare you well mother,
      I must leave you.
      Fare you well,
      Fare you well, Mother,
      I must leave you.
      Fare you well.
      Oh! Watch and pray!

The slave-caravan, to which Mungo Park was attached, finally reached the river Gambia, where the slaves were set on board a ship and brought down to the coast. At Goree one hundred and thirty, of whom about twenty-five had been of free condition and were able to read and write Arabic, were shipped to America. There being no other vessel at hand, Park took passage on the slaver and followed the slaves, whom he had accompanied from the interior to their destination in America.

"My conversation with the slaves," he said, "gave them great comfort and, in truth they had need of every consolation in my power to bestow; not that I observed any wanton acts of cruelty practised either by the master or seamen toward them, but the mode of confining and securing Negroes in the American slave-ships made these poor creatures suffer greatly and a general sickness prevailed among them. Besides the three who died at Gambia, and six or eight while we remained at Goree, eleven perished at sea, and many of the survivors were reduced to a very weak and emaciated condition."

After 1808, when it became a crime to bring slaves from Africa to the United States, the conditions under which the trade was carried on grew worse. In the course of the next forty years, before the trade with the United States finally ended in 1862, it seems that every possibility of cruelty and of suffering, inherent in the traffic, was exhausted by the experience of those who were merchants and those who were merchandise in this iniquitous traffic. Of the slaves imported from the region at the mouth of the Niger it was estimated that one-third and often more perished before they reached the coast, 15 to 20 per cent. more were lost in the voyage on the middle passage or while they were going under the process of seasoning, so that the number of slaves that finally found their way to the plantations did not, in many cases, represent more than one-third of those who were originally torn from their homes by slave-raiders in order to meet the demand for labour in America.*

Sometimes people, enticed down to the coast by showing them strips of bright coloured calico, were seized and put on board the slave-ships. In other cases, after the slave-traders had successfully got on board a party of slaves, they seized the native slave-merchants themselves and carried them off, in turn, into slavery. I have often heard Major R. R. Moton, of Hampton, relate the story, which was told him by his grandmother, of the manner in

*A writer quoted by Miss Kingsley (West African Studies, p. 511), says that a moderate allowance for loss of life between the interior and the slave-ship would be at least 40 per cent. This was in the region of the lower Niger, whence, according to Mr. Clarkson, the historian of the abolition of the slave trade, more slaves were taken than from all the other slave-dealing centres of the West and Southwest Coast of Africa.

"Death hovered always over the slave-ship," says the historian Bancroft. "The Negroes, as they came from the higher level to the seaside — poorly fed on the sad pilgrimage, sleeping at night on the damp earth without covering, and often reaching the coast at unfavourable seasons — imbibed the seeds of disease, which confinement on board ship quickened into feverish activity. There have been examples where one-half of them — it has been said, even, where two-thirds of them — perished on the passage. The total loss of life on the voyage is computed to have been, on the average, fifteen, certainly full twelve and one-half, in the hundred: the harbors of the West Indies proved fatal to four and one-half more out of every hundred. No scene of wretchedness could surpass a crowded slave-ship during a storm at sea, unless it were the same ship dismasted or suffering from a protracted voyage and want of food, its miserable inmates tossed helplessly to and fro under the rays of a vertical sun, vainly gasping for a drop of water.— "History of the United States," Vol. III, p. 405.

which his great-grandfather, at that time a young African chief, was enticed on board a slave-ship and brought to America. He had successfully brought down to the coast and sold a party of slaves which he had taken as captives in one of the tribal wars. The trade concluded he was himself invited to dinner on board the slave-ship. He was given something to drink which put him to sleep. When he awoke he found himself far out at sea, no longer a prince but merely one among the number of slaves he himself the day before had sold.

Some few years ago during a stay of a few days at Mobile, Alabama, I visited a little colony of Africans, who local tradition says are the remnants of the last cargo of the last slave-ship which was landed in the United States.

Mobile Bay during the latter days of the slave-trade was a favourite entrance for slave-smugglers to the United States. At the upper entrance of the bay, where the Alabama and Tombigbee rivers pour their waters into it through a number of different channels, there are many places in which it was possible to hide a slave-ship. It was in one of these ships, smuggled in through these channels, by which the majority of the people in the "African Colony" were brought to America.

In this community I met native Africans who still speak the old tribal language and still retain to some extent, I was told, their ancient tribal customs. I talked with one of these men who still passes by his African name. He is called Ossie Keebe. He told me his were a hill people. They lived in the uplands of Dahomey, seven days from the sea. There had been a war — there was always war in those slave-raiding days, he said — and one night their village had been captured and all who were not killed were marched down to the sea and sold.

When I asked this old man if he ever thought of returning to Africa, he replied: "Yes, I goes back to Africa every night, in my dreams." Meeting this old man whose dreams carry him back to Africa, I felt as if I had discovered the link by which the old life in Africa was connected with the new life in America.

The people I met in the African colony were not, however, the last slaves brought to the United States. The famous yacht, Wanderer, which carried 500 slaves into Georgia in 1858, is supposed to have brought 420 slaves more in 1860. But as late as 1862 a ship ran the blockade of Federal ships and landed slaves in Mobile. Far up the river in some remote part of that wilderness of swamp and water there still may be seen, I have been told, above the surface of the water portions of the iron work of the *Lawrence*, which was possibly the last ship to bring slaves into the United States. The ship was burned to keep it from falling into the hands of the

"Yankees" during the war, but there are young men in the African colony who still remember to have played about the hull when they were boys. There are still people living in Mobile who were brought over as slaves upon it in 1862.

No one will ever know how many thousands of Africans, during the progress of the slave-trade, were carried from their homes in Africa to be used as labourers in the opening up of the new and wild country in North and South America. It has been estimated that 270,000 slaves were brought into the United States between the years 1808 and 1860, from the time that the slave-trade was legally abolished to the time when it practically ceased. In view of the fact that other estimates indicate that fifteen thousand slaves were smuggled into the United States in 1858; that at another time fifteen thousand slaves were brought into Texas alone in one year, this may be taken as a low estimate.

Even this is no indication of the number of slaves that were imported during this time and before into the West Indies and into South America. South America and the West Indies, like some of the states of the Far South, were slave-consuming countries, and it was necessary to constantly bring in new levies to keep up the supply.

I have taken some pains to examine the different estimates made by different writers at different periods of the slave-trade and for different portions of North and South America, and I have reached the conclusion that the total number of slaves landed in the western world from the beginning to the end of the slave-trade cannot have been less than twelve millions, and was probably much more.

Perhaps twelve millions more were taken in the slave-raids, perished on the way to the coast or in the "middle passage," or in the process of seasoning, so that no less than twenty-four million human beings were either brought to America as slaves or perished on the way hither. I have not examined carefully the figures of European emigration, but I venture to say that from the time America was discovered down to 1860, the number of white people that have immigrated from Europe to North and South America is less than the number of black people who were brought over in slave-ships during the same period.

CHAPTER VI

THE FIRST SLAVES

DURING a recent visit to Baltimore, Maryland, chance threw in my way a facsimile copy of an old Baltimore newspaper, the *Maryland Journal*, the first number of which was published August 20, 1773. This paper contained one or two items of news, and several advertisements that were peculiarly interesting to me. One of these advertisements, which attracted my attention, was about as follows:

TEN POUNDS REWARD

RAN away, on the 6th of July laſt, from the ſubscriber, living in Bond's forest, within eight miles of Joppa, in Baltimore County, an Irish Servant Man, named OWEN M'CARTY, about 45 years old, 5 feet 8 inches high, of a swarthy complexion, has long black hair, which is growing a little grey, and a remarkable ſcar under the right eye. He had on and took with him when he went away, a ſhort brown coat, made of country manufactured cloth, lined with red flannel, with metal buttons, oznabrigs trowſers patched on both knees, a white ſhirt, an old pair of ſhoes, and an old felt hat. He was a ſoldier in ſome part of America about the time of Braddock's defeat, and can give a good deſcription of the country. Whoever takes up the ſaid Servant and brings him to Alexander Cowan, or John Clayton, Merchants, in Joppa, or to the ſubſcriber, if he is taken in the County, ſhall receive FIVE POUNDS, and if out of the County, the abovementioned TEN POUNDS, as a reward and conſideration for his trouble and expenſe. BARNARD REILLY.

Until a short time ago the condition of bondage had always been associated in my mind, as in the minds of most coloured people in this country, with a black skin. I had heard, as most schoolboys have heard, that centuries ago there had been white slaves in England and that in other parts of Europe slavery and serfdom had lasted to a much later period than in England. I remember reading somewhere the story of Pope Gregory who, seeing some beautiful English slaves exposed for sale in the Forum at Rome, was so impressed by their sad condition that he determined to undertake the conversion of Britain. These events, however, all belong to a remote past. I never had the least idea until I began to investigate the subject that any human being except the Indian and the Negro had ever been bought and sold, and in other respects treated as property in America. The fact is, however, that, although Negro slaves were brought to Jamestown, only twelve years after the first settlement there, the system of white servitude had preceded black slavery in both the Plymouth and Virginia colony. Most of the work on the plantations and elsewhere was performed at first by white servants who were imported from England and sold like other merchandise in the markets of the colony. The historian, Bancroft, says of this matter:

Conditional servitude, under indentures or covenants, had from the first existed in Virginia. The servant stood to his master in the relation of a debtor, bound to discharge the cost of emigration by the entire employment of his powers for the benefit of his creditors. Oppression early ensued: men who had been transported into Virginia at the expense of eight or ten pounds, were sometimes sold for forty, fifty, or even threescore pounds. The supply of white servants became a regular business, and a class of men, nicknamed "spirits," used to delude young persons, servants, and idlers, into embarking for America, as to a land of spontaneous plenty. White servants came to be an article of traffic. They were sold in England to be transported, and in Virginia were sold to the highest bidder; like Negroes they were to be purchased on shipboard, as men buy horses at a fair. In 1672 the average price in colonies where five years of service were due, was ten pounds while a Negro was worth twenty or twenty-five pounds.*

It has often been said that the almshouses and the prisons were emptied to furnish labourers for the colonies of Virginia, South Carolina, and Georgia. But it was not merely the destitute and the outcast that were sold into servitude in the English colonies in America. Many of these persons were political prisoners and persons of quality.

"So usual," according to the same historian, "was this manner of dealing in Englishmen that not the Scots only, who were taken in the field of Dunbar, were sent into involuntary servitude in New England, but the Royalist prisoners of the battle of Worcester; the leaders in the insurrection of Penruddock were shipped to America."

At other times large numbers of Irishmen were sold into servitude in different parts of America. Because the number of slaves brought to America

* Bancroft's "History of the United States," Vol. I, p. 175.

was so immense, the sufferings which they underwent has made a profound impression upon the world, but from all that I have been able to learn, the sufferings endured by these unfortunate Irish bond-servants during the course of the long voyages to America were frequently as hard as those of the slaves. "The crowded exportation of Irish Catholics," Bancroft remarks, "was a frequent event, and was attended by aggravations hardly inferior to the usual atrocities of the African slave-trade."

In 1685, when nearly a thousand prisoners were condemned to transportation for taking part in the insurrection of Monmouth, "men of influence at court scrambled for the convicted insurgents as a merchantable commodity."

Bond-servitude as it existed in the English colonies was in many respects peculiar and unlike any form of servitude which had existed among English people.

The first bond-servants were sent out by the London company, the company by which the Virginia colony was founded. It was not intended that servants should be transferred from one master to another. But the depressed condition of agriculture following the massacre of 1622, according to James Ballagh, compelled planters to sell their servants and thereafter "made the sale of servants a very common practice among both officers and planters."

For instance, in 1623, George Sandys, the treasurer of Virginia, was forced to sell the only remaining servants of the company, the seven men on his plantation, for one hundred and fifty pounds of tobacco.

"Gradually," says Mr. Ballagh, "the legal personality of the servant was lost sight of in the disposition to regard him as a chattel and a part of the personal estate of the master, which might be treated and disposed of very much in the same way as the rest of the estate. He became thus rated in inventories of estates, and was disposed of both by will and deed along with the rest of the property."*

At the same time there grew up a systematic speculation in servants both in England and in Virginia. A servant could be transported to America for from six to eight pounds and sold for from forty to sixty pounds. London and Bristol were the chief markets for young men and women who were sold to shipowners who transported them to America and sold them.† The number of servants imported who were obtained in this and other ways was, from 1650 to 1675, when the trade began to decline, considerable. The number

---

* "White Servitude in the Colony of Virginia," Johns Hopkins University Studies, p. 44.

† Bristol, which was the last to give up the practice of selling bond-servants to the English colonies in America, had been six hundred years before, at the time of the Norman Conquest, the chief stronghold of the slave-trade. At that time any one who had more children or more servants than he could keep, took them to the market-place at Bristol. A historian of that time, William of Malmesbury, says that it was no uncommon thing to behold young girls exposed for sale in the Bristol market, in the days when Ireland was the greatest mart for English slaves.—Greene's "Short History of the English People," Vol. I., p. 110. "History for Ready Reference," Larned, Vol. I., p. 317.

of such white servants imported into Virginia alone from 1664 amounted to 1,500 a year. And it is said that the number sent from England to the colonies and the West Indies amounted to 15,000 a year.

It was surprising to me to learn that a little more than two hundred years ago Englishmen sold the prisoners taken in their civil wars in much the same way that the African people captured and sold people of their own race. But the knowledge of these facts has helped me to understand that when Negro slavery began in this country the condition of the African slaves was not so exceptional as it afterward became and as it now seems.

Under the conditions I have referred to, the gradual transition from white servitude to Negro slavery, which took place during the seventeenth and eighteenth centuries, came about naturally and easily. At first the condition of the Negro slave was in most respects like that of the white servant, except that one was a servant for a fixed period of years and the other was a servant for life. As time went on, however, the two things, black slavery and white servitude, began to grow apart. The condition of the white servant was continually improved, and the condition of the black slave grew steadily worse. The same thing which took place in Virginia took place in other Southern colonies. Finally, at the close of the eighteenth century Negro slavery had almost entirely replaced white servitude in all the Southern colonies.*

Speaking of the causes which brought white servitude to an end in North Carolina, Dr. John Spencer Bassett, formerly Professor of History and Political Science in Trinity College, N. C., says:

> The incoming of Negro slaves, who, when the experimental stage was passed, were seen to be cheaper than the white servants, was probably the most powerful of all the causes of the decreased importation of bond-servants. The rivalry was between the whites and the blacks. The blacks won. It is impossible not to see in this an analogous process to that by which Negro slavery supplanted Indian slavery in the West Indies. The abuses connected with Indian slavery touched the conscience of the people, and the Negroes who could better stand slavery were introduced to replace it. The abuses connected with white slavery touched the hearts of the British people, and again the Negro was called in to bear the burden of the necessary labour. In each case it was a survival of the fittest. Both Indian slavery and white servitude were to go down before the black man's superior endurance, docility, and labour capacity.†

I have referred at some length to conditions of white servitude in the English colonies before the introduction of the Negro slaves in order to illustrate how easily and naturally the transition was

* The condition of the apprenticed servants in Virginia differed from that of slaves chiefly in the duration of their bondage, and the laws of the colony favoured their early enfranchisement. . . . Had no other form of servitude been known in Virginia than such as had been tolerated in Europe, every difficulty would have been promptly obviated by the benevolent spirit of colonial legislation. But a new problem in the history was now to be solved. For the first time the Ethiopian and the Caucasian races were to meet together in nearly equal numbers beneath a temperate zone.— Bancroft, "History of the United States," Vol. I., pp. 176, 177.

† "Slavery and Servitude in the Colony of North Carolina," Johns Hopkins University Studies, p. 77.

made from slavery in Africa to slavery in America. But I confess these facts have for me another and a different interest. It is important that the people of my race should not gain the idea that, because they were once in slavery, their situation is wholly exceptional. It is important that we should bear in mind, when we are disposed to become discouraged, that other races have had to face, at some time in their history, difficulties quite as great as ours. In America Negro slavery succeeded white servitude and it seems probable if the Negro had not been discovered and brought to this country as a labourer the system of white servitude would have lasted in this country a great deal longer than it actually did.

I was interested in noting in what I have read concerning the relations of the races at this early period that the first distinctions made between the black man and the white man were not on the ground of race and colour, but on that of religion. That is no doubt characteristic of a time when people were divided by religion rather than by race. The Negroes were "heathen," and the law distinguished between those who were Christians and those who were not. For instance, the law declared that no Christian could be made a slave for life. The white bondmen were usually referred to as "servants," or "Christian servants," and were in this way distinguished from slaves. "The right to enslave a Negro," says Professor Bassett, "seems to have been based on the fact that he was a pagan." There was a general notion throughout all Christendom that it was wrong for one Christian to enslave another, and that as soon as a pagan was baptised he could be no longer held as a slave. This prevented, for many years, the work of Christianising the Negroes. So strong was this feeling that it was necessary in several of the colonies to pass laws expressly stating that the condition of the slave was not changed when he was taken into church.*

On the other hand, as the white servant was a Christian, the principle was gradually established that he could only be held in servitude by Christians, or those "who were sure to give him Christian usage!" "Thus free Negroes, mulattoes, or Indians," says Mr. Ballagh, "although Christians, were incapacitated from holding white servants, as also were infidels, 'such as Jews, Moors, and Mohammedans.' Where a white servant was sold to them, or his owner had intermarried with them, the servant became *ipso facto* free."†

It is a curious fact that one of the first laws passed discriminating against the Negro because of his race took away from him the right to hold a white man in bondage.

In Virginia and Maryland it was one hundred and

* "Slavery and Servitude in the Colony of North Carolina," Johns Hopkins University Studies, p. 45 *et seq.*

† "White Servitude in the Colony of Virginia," Johns Hopkins University Studies, p. 63.

fifty years before white servitude finally gave way to Negro slavery. In other Southern colonies, Negro slavery, introduced from the West Indies, was almost from the first the only form of labour known on the plantations.

In South Carolina an effort was made to re-establish serfdom, as it had existed one hundred years before in England, and as it still existed in Europe. In Georgia it was hoped, by prohibiting slavery, to establish a system of free labour. But in both cases the effort failed.

General Oglethorpe, the founder of Georgia, declared that slavery was "contrary to the teachings of the gospel and opposed to the fundamental law of England," and when it was proposed to introduce slavery into the colony he declared that "he declined to permit so horrid a crime." But within fifteen years from the founding of the colony slavery was fully established there and the law against it had been repealed.

The fact seems to be that the white "servants," such as the company was able to obtain from England, were not fitted to withstand the climate. Rev. William B. Stevens, formerly Professor of History in the University of Georgia, says that strenuous efforts were made to import white servants but "many escaped to Carolina. . . . Even the German servants so often pointed to as patterns of industry and sobriety were complained of as being 'refractory, filled with ideas of liberty and clandestinely quitting their masters', who 'were compelled to resort to corporal punishment or other summary means to bring them to obedience.'"

In one of the several documents prepared at that time, setting forth "the true state of the colony," it is said that so general was the sickness during the summer months that "hardly one-half of the servants or working people were even able to do their masters or themselves the least service; and the yearly sickness of each servant, generally speaking, cost his master as much as would have maintained a Negro for four years."

With the introduction of the rice planting the necessity of employing Africans was doubled. So difficult did the first settlers find the task of clearing the land and planting and harvesting the rice that one writer declares the "white servants would have exhausted their strength in clearing a spot for their own graves, and every plantation would have served no other purpose than a burying ground to its European cultivators."*

No doubt the black man withstood the climate, particularly in the states of the Lower South and the West Indies, and did the rough pioneer work that was required at that time better than the white man did or could. Even to-day in most of the West Indies, in many parts of South America, and in some

* "A True and Historical Narrative of the Colony of Georgia," p. 120.

parts of the United States, as for instance in the rich lands of the Yazoo Delta, the Negro is almost the only man who labours with his hands. But even with Negro labour the work of clearing the forests and planting the crops was carried on in those early days with great loss of life. During the whole period of slavery plantations in the West Indies, in South America, and in some parts of the United States the plantations had to be constantly recruited with fresh levies from Africa to carry on the cultivation of the soil.

After doing all this pioneer work, making it possible for other human beings to live and prosper there, one cannot wonder that the Negro thinks it a little strange that Italians and people from other parts of Europe and even Asia are invited into the South and granted privileges that even the Negro himself does not enjoy. Having performed a service so necessary and so important for the white man at a time and under circumstances such as other persons could not or would not have performed it, it is not strange if the Negro feels that, at least, the Southern people ought to deal more kindly with him than with any foreign race which, after nearly three hundred years of occupation by the white man and the black man, has just begun to enter this country.

Among the early colonists of the Carolinas were the Moravians and the Salzburgers, who were opposed to slavery upon religious grounds. These people withstood for some time the temptation to employ Negro slaves. At length, however, they received a message from the head of the church of Europe to the effect that if they took slaves with the purpose of receiving them into the church and leading them to Christ, not only was this not a sin, but it might prove a blessing.*

It is an interesting fact which I learned when I visited their community a few years ago, that the first person baptised among the Moravians of Salem, N. C., was a Negro. The Moravians of Salem are still among the black man's warmest friends. I might add that, so far as I know, the Moravian is the only religious sect whose missionaries ever voluntarily sold themselves into bondage, as did Leonard Dober and Tobias Leupoldt at San Crux in the West Indies, that they might evangelise their fellow slaves.

This desire to Christianise the African and give him the benefit of a higher civilisation was frequently, during slavery, offered as an excuse for importing African labourers to this country and holding them in slavery.

People differ, and will always differ no doubt, as to whether the desire to civilise the African was a sufficient excuse for bringing him to America, at the cost of so much suffering and expense. For my own part, I am disposed to believe that it was worth all

* "History of Georgia," Stevens, p. 312. Bancroft, Vol. III., p. 448.

that it had cost. At any rate, now that the black man is here and permanently settled in the midst of the white man's civilisation, there can be no good reason for depriving him of the benefits of being here. If any race other than the Anglo-Saxon has earned a right to live in this country and to enjoy the opportunities of American civilisation, it seems to me the Negro has earned that right.

One who has not studied the economic conditions under which the first slaves lived and laboured cannot understand the enormous service that the Negro performed for the civilisation of America during these early and pioneer days.

The Indian, both in North and South America, was pressed into the service of the white man, but he was not equal to the task and perished under the hard conditions in which he was compelled to labour.

Concerning the value of the Negro in Brazil, Heinrich Handlemann, the German historian of that country, says: "The service of the African under conditions as they then existed was, in fact, indispensable. On the other hand, the Indians, either as slaves or as free labourers, were always poor labourers, without industry and without persistence."

In Brazil, in Cuba, and in other portions of the West Indies, one Negro as a labourer was counted equal to four Indians.*

---

*"History of Slavery in Cuba, 1511–1868," Herbert H. S. Aimes.

It seems to be equally true that no part of the white race was equal to the task which the Negro performed in the forests and in the sugar, rice, and cotton fields of the far South. Repeated attempts were made to bring in white labourers to perform the work of the Negro, but without success.

In his history of Louisiana, Gayarré mentions the fact that about 1718 John Law, the author of the great speculation in Louisiana lands, agreed to bring 1,600 Germans to Louisiana and settle them on a concession of twelve miles square granted to him on the Arkansas River. Other grants were made upon the same terms. In accordance with the terms of the grant the Mississippi Company, of which Law was the head, sent out a number of German peasants, but they were soon swept away by the climate. Several different attempts of this kind were made and when they failed it was determined to bring Negroes direct from Africa. Vessels were accordingly sent out and brought back cargoes of Negro slaves, who were distributed among the inhabitants. By 1728 there were 2,600 Negroes in the colony and lands were rising in value.

Early attempts were made to introduce German labourers into some of the more tropical states of Brazil, but they "perished wholesale of famine and hardships of all kinds." In 1764, 400 exiled Acadians were settled in the region known as St. Nicholas, Haiti, but they were unable to stand the climate and were transferred to Louisiana. About the same time 2,400 Germans founded there the state of Bombardopolis, but they met the same fate. Some of them accompanied the Acadians to Louisiana, where traces of them still remain. The others who survived were soon absorbed by the black population about them and it is said that some of their descendants of mixed blood may still be found inhabiting the district.*

The history of the first attempt to settle German peasants in Louisiana reminds me of an interesting story told by George W. Cable in his book of "Strange True Stories of Louisiana." The incidents to which I refer occurred in connection with another and later German immigration, when some poor people were sent over, not as settlers, but as labourers, to Louisiana.

Some time early in the last century a shipload of these Germans arrived in New Orleans. Many of them were respectable people who had paid their own way to America. Others had been sent over with the understanding that they were to work out their passage after they reached this country. The journey was a hard one; there had been a great deal of sickness, and, as was often the case among those early immigrants, many of them had died. When they arrived in port they were sold, much after the fashion of the bond-servants of Virginia, for a period

* "North America," Reclus, Vol. II, p. 411.

of service. In the confusion, it is said, many of those who had paid their way and were entitled to their freedom were sold with the rest. Among these was a little girl, who had lost both her father and mother on the journey to America. She was sold as a servant, upon the landing of the ship, and years passed before her friends again got any trace of her. She was at this time a slave. She had no memory of her parents, nor of a time when she had been free. She believed herself to be a Negro and called herself a "yellow gal." Her resemblance to her mother was, however, so great that her friends began proceedings to secure her freedom, and after a long trial, lasting years, her identity was finally established and she was freed.

One thing that made it difficult to prove that she was free was the fact that at this time so many others of the slaves in Louisiana were as white as she. It was testified that the man who owned her had several other slaves upon his plantation who were white.

I mention this story here because it is one of the curious facts that have happened in connection with African slavery and because it illustrates how close the servitude of the white man brought him to the condition of the Negro slave. To a very large extent the curse of slavery rested not merely upon the African but upon every man who worked with his hands.

In the same way and to the same extent the uplifting of the Negro in the South means the uplifting of labour there; for the cause of the Negro is the cause of the man who is farthest down everywhere in the world. Educate him, give him character, and make him efficient as a labourer, and every other portion of the community will be lifted higher. Degrade the Negro, hold him in peonage, ignorance, or any other form of slavery and the great mass of the people in the community will be held down with him. It is not possible for one man to hold another man down in the ditch without staying down there with him.

VII

THE INDIAN AND THE NEGRO

SHORTLY after I went back to Hampton Institute, in 1879, to take a further course of study, General Armstrong, the head of that institution, decided to try the experiment of bringing some Indian boys from the Western states and giving them an opportunity, along with the Negro, to get the benefits of the kind of education that Hampton Institute was giving. He secured from the reservations something over one hundred wild, and for the most part entirely unlettered, Indians, and then he appointed me to take charge of these young men. I was to live in the same building with them, look after the discipline, take charge of their rooms, and in general act as a sort of "house father" to them.

This was my first acquaintance with the Indians. I do not know that I had ever seen an Indian previous to this time, although I had read something of them and had become greatly interested in their history. During the few years that I was in charge of these Indian boys I had an opportunity to study them close at hand, and to get an insight into their characters. At the same time I had an opportunity to compare them, in their studies, in their deportment, and in their conduct generally, with the Negro boys by whom they were surrounded. Within a short time I noticed that, in spite of the great differences between them, each race seemed to have acquired a genuine regard and respect for the other. This is the more remarkable from the fact that the Indian, as he comes from the reservations, is very proud; feels himself superior to the white man, and is very doubtful about the value of the white man's civilisation that he has been sent to study. Of course, he naturally feels very much superior to the Negro, for one reason because he knows that the Negro has been at one time held in slavery by the white man.

At this time I had no idea of the close and intimate relations into which the Indian and the Negro had been brought at various times and in various places during the history of their life together in the Western world. The association of the Negro with the Indian has been so intimate and varied on this continent, and the similarities as well as the differences of their fortunes and character are so striking, that I am tempted to enter at some length into a discussion of the relations of each to the other, and to the white man in this country.

Recently I heard a story which illustrates to a certain extent what these relations of the three races are at the present time. The story was told me by a teacher who had in his class a certain number of Indians and an equal number of Negroes. They had been together for some time, and had managed to get pretty well acquainted with one another. One day, while the teacher was discussing with them some facts in their history in which he referred to the contribution that each of the races had made to the civilisation in this country, he called upon one of the Indians to tell the class what seemed to him the good qualities of the Negroes, as he understood them. This young Indian seemed to have discovered a number of valuable qualities in the Negro. He referred to his patience, to his aptitude for music, to his desire to learn, etc. Then the teacher called upon one of the Negro students to tell what qualities he had discovered in the Indian that he regarded as admirable and worth cultivating. He referred to his courage, to his high sense of honour, and to his pride of race. After this, the teacher called upon any one in the class to stand up and tell them in what respects he thought the white man was superior. The teacher waited for a few moments, but no member of the class rose. Then he spoke again to the class, asking them if there was no one there who was willing and able to say a word for the white race. But, to his surprise, not one of the class had a word to say.

This comparatively trivial incident illustrates, I suspect, pretty well the relations that now exist in this country between the three races — the Indian, the Negro, and the white man. One of the first things that a student of another race learns, when he begins to study the history, the literature, and the traditions of the Anglo-Saxon, is the superiority which that race has, or feels it has, over all others. No doubt these boys, both the Indian and the Negro, had been made to feel this superiority. It had led them, perhaps, to have a special interest in one another, and given each a desire to discover and note the qualities that were rare and valuable in the other. They had never learned to note the valuable qualities in the white race, because they had been made to feel that the white race did not need, and perhaps did not deserve, their sympathy. It was to me an interesting illustration of the way in which all the dark-coloured people of this country, no matter how different in disposition or in temperament they may be, are being drawn together in sympathy and interest in the presence of the prejudice of the white man against all other people of a different colour from his own.

As a matter of fact, the Negro and the Indian have been in very close and very intimate association in America from the first. The Negro was introduced as a labourer in the West Indies, in the first instance, to take the place of the native Indian, who was the first slave in America. But Indian slavery in the West Indies, South America and in North America did not by any means cease upon the first appearance of Negro slavery. After the Spaniards had used up nearly all the native population of the islands of Cuba and Haiti, in working the mines, they sent out slave-raiders to the coasts of Florida, to the other West Indies, and to the coast of South America to get Indian slaves, particularly from the stronger Carib tribes. During the long wars between the Spanish in Florida and the English in the Carolinas, in which Indians took part on both sides, many hundreds of Indian prisoners were shipped as slaves to the West Indies.

For a long time a price was fixed on every Indian prisoner that should be brought into Charleston and the enslavement of the Indians, according to an early historian of the colony, "was made a profitable branch of trade." Not only were Indian slaves shipped to the West Indies but large numbers of them were sold into the New England colonies from South Carolina. For instance, in 1708 an Indian boy brought thirty five pounds, and an Indian girl brought fifteen pounds at Salem, Massachusetts, in 1710. So large, in fact, was, at one time, this traffic in Indian slaves between the southern and the northern provinces that in 1712 a law was passed in Massachusetts prohibiting the importation of Indian servants or slaves; the reason given for this measure in the preamble to the law is the bad character of the Indian: "being of malicious, surley, and very ungovernable." This law was directed especially against the Southern Indians, the Tuscaroras and others, of whom 800 were made prisoners as a result of a war which expelled that tribe from the Carolinas. Similar laws were passed by Pennsylvania in 1712, New Hampshire in 1714, and Connecticut and Rhode Island in 1715.*

When the French troops fought and destroyed the Natchez Indians, under Governor Perier, in 1731, forty male Indians and four hundred and fifty women and children were sent to San Domingo, where they were sold as slaves. At the close of the Pequot War in New England something like two hundred of the Indians that remained were sent to the Bermuda Islands and exchanged for Negro slaves. An extensive trade in Indian slaves was carried on for many years with the coast of Venezuela.

During all this time, for a hundred years or more, the Indian and the Negro worked side by side as slaves. In all the laws and regulations of the Colonial days the same rule which was applied to the Indian was also applied to the Negro slaves. For instance, in Bishop Spangenberg's "Journal of Travel in North Carolina," written in 1752, it is stated that the law declared "whoever marries a Negro, Indian, mulatto, or any other person of mixed blood, must pay a fine of fifty pounds." In all other regulations that were made in the earlier days for the control of the slaves, mention

*History of Slavery in Massachusetts, G. H. Moore, pp. 61, 62.

is invariably made of the Indian as well as the Negro.

Gradually, however, as the number of Negro slaves increased the Indians and their descendants who were held in slavery were absorbed into and counted with the body of the Negro slaves. I venture to say that the amount of Indian blood in the American Negro is very much larger than anyone who has not investigated the subject would be inclined to believe. Very frequently I have noticed Indian features very distinctly marked in the students who have come to us, not only from the Southern states, but also from Cuba, Porto Rico, and the other West Indian islands. In some parts of South America this amalgamation of the two dark-skinned races has gone very much further than it has elsewhere. The Negro maroons of Dutch and British Guiana, who have established little republics of their own back in the mountainous parts of those two states are very largely mixed with Indians. Most of the inhabitants of Panama, I understand, like some of their Central American neighbours, are of mixed blood, the various elements being the Spanish, Indian, and the Negro. In some of the villages of the Atlantic coast side of the Isthmus of Panama Negroes largely outnumber the natives with whom they have intermingled to form the present population. In several of the other islands of the West Indies, where Negroes make up nearly the whole population, there are still distinct traces among them, of remnants of the Indian race that formerly inhabited these islands, as, for instance, in the islands of St. Vincent and Dominica.

A number of the Negroes of the United States, I might add, who have become prominent in one direction or another, are known to have Indian blood in their veins. I have heard it said, for instance, though I do not know it to be true, that Frederick Douglass had some Indian blood. It is pretty well known that Crispus Attucks, the leader of the Boston Massacre, was a runaway slave with considerable Indian blood in his veins. Paul Cuffe, the noted Negro skipper, who took the first shipload of Africans back to Africa, and who therefore deserves the honour of being the first actual coloniser of Africa by American Negroes, was a man of Indian ancestry. Among the Negroes in our day who are of Indian ancestry I might mention T. Thomas Fortune, who always speaks with pride of the fact that he has in his veins the fighting blood of his Seminole ancestors.

I remember hearing Mr. Fortune say that he had in his veins Negro, Indian, and Irish blood, and that sometimes these antagonistic strains fell to warring with each other, with very interesting results.

In many other ways besides their connection with slavery, the Indian and the Negro have been brought together in this country. In Louisiana, at different times, the Negroes fought with the white man against the Indians. At other times, the Indians conspired with the Negro slaves against the white man in an effort to throw off the yoke of slavery. In 1730 the Chickasaw Indians conspired with some of the slaves of New Orleans to destroy the whole white population. The conspiracy was discovered, however, and the leader, Samba, and seven other Negro leaders were broken on the wheel to pay the penalty for their crime. In Alabama the Negroes fought with the whites against the Indians.

One of the most interesting and picturesque chapters in the history of the warfare of the white man and the Indian is that which relates the long struggle of the Seminoles, who were mixed with and supported by runaway Negroes from the plantations of Georgia and the Carolinas, to maintain their independence and preserve their territory. There is a pretty well established tradition that the famous Seminole chief Osceola, who, for a long time, had been their faithful friend, finally turned against the whites, because his Negro wife, who was the daughter of a fugitive slave, was captured and sold across the border into slavery.

In a recent account of the last of the unconquered Seminoles, who are still living in the Everglades of Florida, I noticed reference to an Afro-Indian, who apparently holds a position among these people corresponding to that of a sheriff, since he is described as executioner of the tribe.

The Cherokee Indians of Georgia were large slave-owners, as were also the Creek Indians of Alabama.

When, in 1838, these Indians were compelled to move westward to the Indian Territory they took a great many of their Negro slaves with them. During the Civil War the Indians of the Territory along with the white people of the South, defended their right to hold slave property, but the terms of peace freed these slaves of the Indians as they did those of the other Southern slave-holders, and since that time the freedmen have been incorporated in the different Indian nations of Indian Territory to which they belonged as slaves.

So thoroughly have the Negroes and the Indians intermingled in some of the Indian nations that in travelling through the country nearly every Indian you meet seems to be, if I may judge by my own experience, either a Negro, or a white man.

A few years ago I visited that part of Oklahoma that was formerly known as Indian Territory, and I recall my feeling of disappointment and surprise when I saw almost no Indians either at the railway stations or in the towns that I visited, whereas I had expected to see the streets thronged with them. When I asked a man I met quite casually on the street where the Indians had all gone, he replied that they "were back in the hills."

"You know," he continued, "as soon as the Indian sees a whitewashed fence he thinks it is time for him to get out. He is afraid if he stays he will get civilised."

Now this is one respect in which the Negro, largely,

I believe, because he has passed through the condition of slavery, differs from the Indian. The Negro has learned, during his contact with the white man in slavery, not to be afraid of civilisation. The result is that as soon as he sees a whitewashed fence he tries to get next to it.

The two races, the Indian and the Negro, have often been compared to the disadvantage of the Negro. I have frequently heard it stated that the Indian proved himself the superior race by not submitting to slavery. As I have already pointed out, it is not exactly true that the Indian never submitted to slavery. What is nearer the truth is that no race which has not at some time or other submitted to slavery of some kind never succeeded in reaching a higher form of civilisation. It is just as true of the Bushmen of South Africa, as it is of the Indian, that they never submitted to slavery. The Bushmen, like the Indian, were a hunter race that obstinately refused to adapt themselves to new conditions, and the result was that when they met a stronger people in the Kaffir, of South Africa, they were hunted off the face of the earth. The same thing, or something like the same thing, happened in America. At the time that the white people of New England and of the Southern states were offering a bounty for every Indian scalp they could obtain, they were sending ships across the ocean to get Negro slaves to furnish the necessary labour for opening up the country and tilling the farm. At the time that the Indians were fighting the white man in the Ohio valley they relentlessly killed the white men they captured, and, it is said, sometimes ate them, but spared the lives of the Negro prisoners, in order to sell them to the French settlers in Canada and the Mississippi valley.*

The fact is that, so far as the Indian refused to become a slave of the white man, he deprived himself of the only method that existed at that time for getting possession of the white man's learning and the white man's civilisation. To me it seems that the patience of the Negro, which enabled him to endure the hardships of slavery, and the natural human sympathy of the Negro, which taught him, finally, to love the white man and to gain his affection in return, was wiser, if you can speak of it in such terms, than the courage and independence of the Indian which prevented him from doing the same.

In the long run it is not those qualities which make a race picturesque and interesting, but rather those qualities which make that race useful, that fit it to survive and profit from contact with a civilisation higher than its own. So far as I have been able to learn, the white man, as yet, has never been able to

* It adds something to our notion of the condition of life in the early days in this country when slavery was first established, if we recall that many of the Indians of the United States were cannibals when the white man first met them. "For the purpose of terrifying their Indian enemies, the French commanders used to threaten to turn them over to the friendly Indians to be eaten, and they did not hesitate to carry out their threats when they wished to please their anthropophagous allies."—"Indiana: A Redemption from Slavery," J. P. Dunn, Jr., pp. 23, 24.

make the Indian of value, in any large way, in the great task of civilisation. While the Negro, in this country, at least, has steadily increased in numbers, the Indian has steadily decreased, until at the present time there are nearly ten million Negroes and less than three hundred thousand Indians in the United States. Not only has the Indian decreased in numbers, but he has been an annual tax upon the Government for food and clothing to the extent of something like $10,000,000 a year, to say nothing of the large amount spent in policing him. It has been estimated that the entire amount expended by the people of the United States is something more than a billion dollars.*

The Negro, on the contrary, for two hundred and fifty years, was brought to this country at an enormous expense, and during that time, judging, at any rate, by the prices which were paid for him, the value of

*The expenditure of the United States for these wards of the nation, in the fiscal year ending June 30, 1902, aggregated $10,049,584.86. From July 4, 1776, to June 30, 1890, the civil expenditures of the Government on account of the Indians aggregated a little more than $250,000,000.

The Indian wars of the United States have been more than forty in number. It is estimated that they have cost the lives of some 19,000 white men, women, and children, and of more than 30,000 Indians. The military expenditures have exceeded the civil expenditures doubtless more than four to one. It is impossible to get at thoroughly trustworty statistics, but it is estimated that something like two-thirds of the total expense of the army of the United States from 1789 to 1890, save during periods of foreign and civil wars, is directly or indirectly chargeable to the Indian account. Upon this basis, the total is more than $800,000,000. Add thereto the civil list, and we have more than a billion dollars expended on account of the Indians within a century and a quarter of our national existence. . . . A comparison of the military and the civil expenditures as above stated would indicate that it was much cheaper to support the Indian than to fight him. . . . History of the United States, Avery. Appendix, p. 361.

his services was constantly increasing. I venture to predict that when the economic history of the Negro comes to be written it will be found that, both in this country and in Africa, the black man has proved himself superior as a labourer to any other people in the same stage of civilisation.

In seeking to draw here a comparison between the red man and my own race I do not believe it is necessary for me to say that I am not influenced in any way by racial prejudices against the Indian. I think that when the first Indians were brought to Hampton I was disposed to feel, as most of the students did at that time, that since Hampton was established for the benefit of the Negro, the Indian should not have been permitted to come in. But it did not take me long, after getting in personal contact with individual Indians, to outgrow that prejudice. During the time that I had these young men under my charge, living in intimate daily contact with them as I did, I learned to admire the Indian.

Perhaps all of us were more kindly disposed toward the Indians as we learned that they, like ourselves, felt that they had suffered wrongs and had been oppressed. In this respect the presence of the Indians at Hampton has been, I believe, a valuable experience to the mass of the Negro students of the school. It taught me, at any rate, that other races than the Negro had had a hard time in this country, and that was, and is, a valuable thing for the young men of my race to know and understand. Just so far as we, as a race, learn that our trials and our difficulties are not wholly exceptional and peculiar to ourselves; that, on the contrary, other peoples have passed through the same period of trials and have had to stand the same tests, we shall cease to feel discouraged and embittered. On the contrary, we shall learn to feel that in our struggles to rise we are carrying the common burden of humanity, and that only in helping others can we really help ourselves. It was from my contact with the Indian, as I remember, that I first learned the important lesson that if I permitted myself to hate a man because of his race I was doing a greater wrong to myself than I could possibly do to him.

What is true of the Negro in comparison with the Indian is equally true in his comparison with any other primitive race. The fact seems to be, as I have said elsewhere, that the Negro is the only race that has been able to look the white man in the face during any long period of years and not only live but multiply.

So much has been said about Negro labour in this country, and so much has been said about Negro labour in Africa, that I feel disposed to quote at some length here a statement of the late Professor N. S. Shaler, formerly Dean of the Lawrence Scientific School, of Harvard University. Professor Shaler was not only a scientific man of broad and deep culture, but he was also a

Southern man, and had abundant opportunity to get the facts.

Professor Shaler says:

The Negroes who came to North America had to undergo as complete a transition as ever fell to the lot of man, without the least chance to undergo an acclimatising process. They were brought from the hottest part of the earth to the region where the winter's cold is of almost arctic severity; from an exceedingly humid to a very dry air. They came to service under alien taskmasters, strange to them in speech and purpose. They had to betake themselves to unaccustomed food and to clothing such as they had never worn before. Rarely could one of the creatures find about him a familiar face or friend, parent or child, or any object that recalled his past life to him. It was an appalling change. Only those who know how the Negro cleaves to all the dear, familiar things of life, how fond he is of warmth and friendliness, can conceive the physical and mental shock that this introduction to new things meant to him. To people of our own race it would have meant death. But these wonderful folk appear to have withstood the trials of their deportation in a marvellous way. They showed no peculiar liability for disease. Their longevity or period of usefulness was not diminished, or their fecundity obviously impaired. So far as I have been able to learn, nostalgia was not a source of mortality, as it would have been with any Aryan population. The price they brought in the market, and the satisfaction of their purchasers with their qualities, show that they were from the first almost ideal labourers.

A little further on Professor Shaler compares the Indian as a labourer with the Negro, pointing out the superiority of the black over the red man in this respect. It should be remembered in this connection, however, that almost everywhere, in Africa, the Negro before coming to America had reached a higher stage of civilisation than the Indian. He already had possession of some of the fundamental industries, like agriculture and the smelting of ores, while the system of slavery existing everywhere in Africa had long accustomed large portions of the population to the habit of systematic labour.

The Indians who first met the white man on this continent do not seem to have held slaves until they first learned to do so from him. It is interesting to note also that Indian slavery, as practised by both the white man and the Indian, seems to have maintained itself among the French population in the Mississippi valley and in Canada for a considerable time after it had begun to die out in the English seaboard colonies. Speaking of the Indian, as compared with the Negro slave, Professor Shaler says:

> If we compare the Algonquin Indian, in appearance a sturdy fellow, with these Negroes, we see of what stuff the blacks are made. A touch of housework and of honest toil took the breath of the aborigines away, but these tropical exotics fell to their tasks and trials far better than the men of our own kind could have done. . . . Moreover, the production of good tobacco requires much care, which extends over about a year from the time the seed is planted. Some parts of the work demand a measure of judgment such as intelligent Negroes readily acquire. They are, indeed, better fitted for the task than white men, for they are commonly more interested in their tasks than whites of the labouring class. The result was that before the period of the Revolutionary War slavery was firmly established in the tobacco-planting colonies of Maryland, Virginia, and North Carolina; it was already the foundation of their only considerable industry. . . . This industry (cotton), even more than that of raising tobacco, called for abundant

labour, which could be absolutely commanded and severely tasked in the season of extreme heat. For this work the Negro proved to be the only fit man, for while the whites can do this work, they prefer other employment. Thus it came about that the power of slavery in this country became rooted in its soil. The facts show that, based on an ample foundation of experience, the judgment of the Southern people was to the effect that this creature of the tropics was a better labourer in their fields than the men of their own race.

Referring to what he calls "the failure of the white man to take a larger share in the agriculture of the South," Professor Shaler says of the Negro as a farm labourer:

Much has been said about the dislike of the white man for work in association with Negroes. The failure of the white to have a larger share in the agriculture of the South has been attributed to this cause. This seems to be clearly an error. The dislike to the association of races in labour is, in the slaveholding states, less than in the North. There can be no question that if the Southern folk could have made white labourers profitable they would have preferred to employ them, for the reason that they would have required less fixed capital for their operation. The fact was and is, that the Negro is there a better labouring man in the field than the white. Under the conditions he is more enduring, more contented, and more trustworthy than the men of our own race.*

I have written at some length of the relations of the Negro and the Indian in this country because these relations are interesting in themselves and because they show how thoroughly the Negro, by uniting himself with the indigenous population of the country, has knitted himself into the life and rooted himself in the soil of America. I think I am perfectly safe in

*"Translation of our Race." Popular Science Monthly, Vol. 56, pp. 513, 524.

saying that the Negro in America has a great deal more of the blood of the original American in him than any other race on this continent, other than the native Indian himself. In fact, if we confine ourselves to certain parts of the West Indies and South America, the Negro is the only man who can still be said to represent, by inheritance of blood, the original American.

I have taken some pains to find out, as near as I was able, from the imperfect statistics at hand, the actual number of people of African descent in the Western world. Including the ten million persons of Negro blood in the United States, I believe I am safe in saying that there are in North and South America and the West Indies no less than twenty-one million descendants of the original slaves who were brought from Africa during the period of two hundred and fifty years in which the slave-trade existed.

CHAPTER VIII

THE NEGRO'S LIFE IN SLAVERY

SOME years ago one of the frequent subjects of discussion among the white people and the coloured people was the question: Who was responsible for slavery in America? Some people said the English government was the guilty party, because England would not let the colonies abolish the slave-trade when they wanted to. Others said the New England colonies were just as deep in the mire as England or the Southern states, because for many years a very large share of the trade was carried on in New England ships.

As a matter of fact there were, as near as I have been able to learn, three parties who were directly responsible for the slavery of the Negro in the United States. First of all there was the Negro himself. It should not be forgotten that it was the African who, for the most part, carried on the slave-raids by means of which his fellow African was captured and brought down to the coast for sale. When, some months ago, the Liberian embassy visited the United States, Vice-President Dossen explained to me that one reason why Liberia had made no more progress during the eighty-six years of its existence was the fact that for many years the little state had been engaged in a life-and-death struggle with native slave-traders who had been accustomed for centuries to ship their slaves from Liberian ports and were unwilling to give up the practice. It was only after the slave-trade had entirely ceased, he said, that Liberia had begun to exercise an influence upon the masses of the native peoples within its jurisdiction.

The second party to slavery was the slave-trader who, at first, as a rule, was an Englishman or a Northern white man. During the Colonial period, for instance, Newport, Rhode Island, was the principal headquarters of the slave-trade in this country. At one time Rhode Island had one hundred and fifty vessels engaged in the traffic. Down to 1860 Northern capital was very largely invested in the slave-trade, and New York was the port from which most of the American slave-smugglers fitted out.

Finally there was the Southern white man who owned and worked the bulk of the slaves, and was responsible for what we now ordinarily understand as the slave-system. It would be just as much a mistake, however, to assume that the South was ever solidly in favour of slavery as it is to assume that the North was always solidly against it. Thousands of persons in the Southern states were opposed to slavery, and numbers of them, like James G. Birney, of Alabama, took their slaves North in order to free them, and afterward became leaders in the anti-slavery struggle.

Like every other human thing, there is more than one side to slavery and more than one way of looking at it. For instance, as defined in the slave-laws in what was known as the Slave Code, slavery was pretty much the same at all times all over the South. The regulations imposed upon master and upon slave were, in several particulars, different for the different states. On the whole, however, as a legal institution, slavery was the same everywhere.

On the other hand, actual conditions were not only different in every part of the country, but they were likely to be different on every separate plantation. Every plantation was, to a certain extent, a little kingdom by itself, and life there was what the people who were bound together in the plantation community made it. The law and the custom of the neighbourhood regulated, to a certain extent, the treatment which the master gave his slave. For instance, in the part of Virginia where I lived both white people and coloured people looked with contempt upon the man who had the reputation of not giving his slaves enough to eat. If a slave went to an adjoining plantation for something to eat, the reputation of his master was damned in that community. On the whole, however, each plantation was a little independent state, and one master was very little disposed to interfere with the affairs of another.

The account that one gets of slavery from the laws that were passed for the government of slaves show that institution up on its worst side No harsher judgment was ever passed on slavery, so far as I know, than that which will be found in the decision of a justice of the Supreme Court of North Carolina in summing up the law in a case in which the relations of master and slave were defined.

The case I refer to, which was tried in 1829, was one in which the master, who was the defendant, was indicted for beating his slave. The decision, which acquitted him, affirmed the master's right to inflict any kind of punishment upon his slave short of death. The grounds upon which this judgment was based were that in the whole history of slavery there had been no such prosecution of a master for punishing a slave, and, in the words of the decision, "against this general opinion in the community the court could not hold."

It was a mistake, the decision continued, to say that the relations of the master and slave were like that of a parent and child. The object of the parent in training his son was to render him fit to live the life of a free man, and, as a means to that end, he gave him moral and intellectual instruction. With the case of the slave it was different. There could be no sense in addressing moral considerations to a slave. Chief-Justice Ruffin, of North Carolina, summed up his opinion upon this point in these words:

> The end is the profit of the master, his security, and the public safety; the subject, one doomed in his own person and his posterity to live without knowledge and without the capacity to make anything his own, and to toil that another may reap the fruits. What moral consideration shall be addressed to such a being to convince him, what it is impossible but that the most stupid must feel and know can never be true — that he is thus to labour upon a principle of natural duty, or for the sake of his own personal happiness. Such services can only be expected from one who has no will of his own, who surrenders his will in implicit obedience to that of another. Such obedience is the consequence only of uncontrolled authority over the body. There is nothing else which can operate to produce the effect. The power of the master must be absolute to render the submission of the slave perfect.

In making this decision Justice Ruffin did not attempt to justify the rule he had laid down on moral grounds. "As a principle of right," he said, "every person in his retirement must repudiate it. But in the actual condition of things it must be so; there is no remedy. This discipline belongs to the state of slavery. It constitutes the curse of slavery both to the bond and free portion of our population."*

This decision brings out into plain view an idea that

* "Slavery in the State of North Carolina," John Spencer Bassett.

was always somewhere at the bottom of slavery — the idea, namely, that one man's evil is another man's good. The history of slavery, if it proves anything, proves that just the opposite is true, namely, that evil breeds evil, just as disease breeds disease, and that a wrong committed upon one portion of a community will, in the long run, surely react upon the other portion of that community.

There was a very great difference between the life of the slave on the small plantations in the uplands and upon the big plantations along the coasts. To illustrate, the plantation upon which I was born, in Franklin County, Va., had, as I remember, only six slaves. My master and his sons all worked together side by side with his slaves. In this way we all grew up together, very much like members of one big family. There was no overseer, and we got to know our master and he to know us. The big plantations along the coasts were usually carried on under the direction of an overseer. The master and his family were away for a large part of the year. Personal relation between them could hardly be said to exist.

John C. Calhoun, South Carolina's greatest statesman, was brought up on a plantation not very much different from the one upon which I was raised. One of his biographers relates how Patrick Calhoun, John C. Calhoun's father, returning from his legislative duties in Charleston, brought home on horseback behind him a young African freshly imported in some English or New England vessel. The children in the neighbourhood and, no doubt, some of the older people, had never before seen a black man. He was the first one brought into that part of the country. Patrick Calhoun gave him the name of Adam. Some time later he got for him a wife. One of the children of the black man, Adam, was named Swaney. He grew up on the plantation with John C. Calhoun, and was for many years his playmate. Swaney lived to a great age, and in after years used to be fond of talking about the early years that he and John Calhoun had spent together. They hunted and fished together, and worked together in the fields.

"We worked in the field," Swaney is reported to have said, "and many a time in the hot brilin' sun me and Marse John has ploughed together."

I have taken these facts from an account of Calhoun's early life by Colonel W. Pinkney Stark, who has given, besides, a very excellent account of the institution of slavery as it existed in the early days in that part of the country in which he lived. At that time and in that part of the country the planter worked his own plantation. The overseer did not come in until later, and Colonel Stark believes that "whatever was most harsh in the institution of slavery was due to the rise of this middleman." He says:

Not far from the Calhoun settlement lived a man who had ridden with Sumter in the old war for liberty. During a long and active life he managed the business of the plantation himself. Toward the close of his life he consented to try an overseer, but in every case some difficulty soon arose between the middleman and the Negroes, in which the old planter invariably took sides with the latter and rid himself of the proxy. On rainy days the Negro women spun raw cotton into yarn, which was woven by his own weaver into summer goods, to be cut by a seamstress, and made by the other women, assisted by her, into clothing for the "people." The sheep were shorn and the wool treated in the same fashion for winter clothing. The hides of cattle eaten on the place were tanned into leather and made into shoes by his own shoemaker. He had his own carpenters, wheelwrights, and blacksmiths, and besides cattle and sheep the old planter raised his own stock of horses and mules. He grew his own wheat for flour, besides raising other small grain, corn, and cotton. He distilled his own brandy from peaches and sweetened it with honey manufactured by his home bees. His Negroes were well fed and clothed, carefully attended to in sickness, virtually free in old age, and supported in comfort till their death. The moral law against adultery was sternly enforced, and no divorce allowed. His people were encouraged to enjoy themselves in all reasonable ways. They went to a Methodist church in the neighbourhood on Sunday, and had besides a preacher of their own, raised on the place. The young people were supplied with necessary fiddling and dancing. I was present when he died, and heard him say to his son that he would leave him a property honestly made and not burdened with a dollar indebtedness. His family and friends gathered about his bedside when the time had come for him to go. Having taken leave of his friends, he ordered his Negro labourers to be summoned from the field to take farewell of him. When they arrived he was speechless and motionless, but sensible of all that was occurring, as could be seen from his look of intelligence. One by one the Negroes entered the apartment, and filing by him in succession took each in turn the limp hand of their dying master, and affectionately pressing it for a moment, thanked him for his goodness, commended him to God, and bade him farewell.

The faithful discharge of the duties of the proprietor of a plantation in former times demanded administrative as well as moral qualities of a high order. There was never a better school for the education of statesmen than the administration of a Southern plantation under the former régime. A well-governed plantation was a well-ordered little independent state. Surrounded with such environments, Calhoun grew at this school.*

The conditions of the Negro slave were harder on some of the big plantations in the Far South than they were elsewhere. That region was peopled by an enterprising class of persons, of whom many came from Virginia, bringing their slaves with them. The soil was rich, the planters were making money fast, the country was rough and unsettled, and there was undoubtedly a disposition to treat the slaves as mere factors in the production of corn, cotton, and sugar.†

---

*American Historical Assn. Report, Vol. II., 1899, p. 74 et seq.

† That the Negroes were overtasked to the extent of being often permanently injured, was evident from the complaints made by the Southern agricultural journals against the bad policy of thus wasting human property. An Alabama tradesman told Olmsted that if the overseers make "plenty of cotton, the owners never ask how many niggers they kill"; and he gave the further information that a determined and perfectly relentless overseer could get almost any wages he demanded, for when it became known that such a man had so many bales to the hand, everybody would try to get him. . . .

Louisiana sugar-planters did not hesitate to avow openly that, on the whole, they found it the best economy to work off their stock of Negroes about once in seven years, and then buy an entire set of new hands.—"History of the United States," James Ford Rhodes, Vol. I., p. 308.

And yet there were plantations in this region where the relations between master and slave seem to have been as happy as one could ask or expect under the circumstances. On some of the large estates in Alabama and Mississippi which were far removed from the influence of the city, and sometimes in the midst of a wilderness, master and slaves frequently lived together under conditions that were genuinely patriarchal. But on such plantations there was, as a rule, no overseer.

As an example of the large plantations on which the relations between master and slave were normal and happy I might mention those of the former President of the Confederacy, Jefferson Davis, and his brother, Joseph Davis, in Warren County, Mississippi.

The history of the Davis family and of the way in which their plantations, the "Hurricane" and "Brierfield," came into existence is typical. The ancestors of the President of the Confederacy came originally from Wales. They settled first in Georgia, emigrated thence to Kentucky, and finally settled in the rich lands of Mississippi. In 1818 Joseph Davis, who was at that time a lawyer in Vicksburg, attracted by the rich bottom-lands along the Mississippi, took his father's slaves and went down the river, thirty-six miles below Vicksburg, to the place which is now called "Davis's Bend."

There he began clearing the land and preparing it for cultivation.

At that time there were no steamboats on the Mississippi River, and the country was so wild that people travelled through the lonely forests mostly on horseback. In the course of a few years Mr. Davis, with the aid of his slaves, succeeded in building up a plantation of about five thousand acres, and became, before his death, a very wealthy man. One day he went down to Natchez and purchased in the market there a young Negro who afterward became known as Ben Montgomery. This young man had been sold South from North Carolina, and because, perhaps, he had heard, as most of the slaves had, of the hard treatment that was to be expected on the big, lonesome plantations, had made up his mind to remain in the city. The first thing he did, therefore, when Mr. Davis brought him home, was to run away. Mr. Davis succeeded in getting hold of him again, brought him back to the plantation, and then, as Isaiah, Benjamin Montgomery's son, has told me, Mr. Davis "came to an understanding" with his young slave.

Just what that understanding was no one seems now to know exactly, but in any case, as a result of it, Benjamin Montgomery received a pretty fair education, sufficient, at any rate, to enable him in after years, when he came to have entire charge, as he soon did, of Mr. Davis's plantation, to survey the line of the levee which was erected to protect the plantation from the waters of the Mississippi, to draw out plans, and to compute the size of buildings, a number of which were erected at different times under his direction.

Mrs. Jefferson Davis, in her memoir of her husband, referring to Benjamin Montgomery and to the manner in which Joseph Davis conducted his plantation, says:

> A maxim of Joseph E. Davis was: "The less people are governed, the more submissive they will be to control." This idea he carried out with his family and with his slaves. He instituted trial by jury of their peers, and taught them the legal form of holding it. His only share in the jurisdiction was the pardoning power. When his slave could do better for himself than by daily labour he was at liberty to do so, giving either in money or other equivalent the worth of ordinary field service. One of his slaves kept a variety shop, and on many occasions the family bought of him at his own prices. He shipped, and indeed sometimes purchased, the fruit crops of the Davis families, and also of other people in "The Bend," and in one instance credited one of us with $2,000 on his account. The bills were presented by him with promptitude and paid, as were those of others on an independent footing, without delay. He many times borrowed from his master, but was equally as exact in his dealings with his creditors. His sons, Thornton and Isaiah, first learned to work, and then were carefully taught by their father to read, write, and cipher, and now Ben Montgomery's sons are both responsible men of property; one is in business in Vicksburg, and the other is a thriving farmer in the West.

Some years after the settlement on the bottom-lands at Davis's Bend had been made, Mr. Jefferson Davis joined his brother and lived for several years upon an adjoining plantation. The two brothers had much the same ideas about the management of their slaves. Both of them took personal supervision of their estates, and Jefferson Davis, like his brother, had a coloured man to whom he refers as his "friend and servant, James Pemberton," who, until he died, seems to have had practically the whole charge of the Brierfield plantation in the same way that Benjamin Montgomery had charge of the Hurricane. After the war both of these plantations were sold for the sum of $300,000 to Benjamin Montgomery and his sons, who conducted them for a number of years until, as a result of floods and the low price of cotton, they were compelled to give them up.

Thornton Montgomery afterward moved to North Dakota, where for a number of years he owned and conducted a large wheat farm of 640 acres near Fargo. His brother Isaiah afterward founded the Negro town of Mound Bayou, Miss., of which I shall have more to say hereafter.

As illustrating the kindly relations and good will which continued to exist between the ex-President of the Confederacy, Jefferson Davis, and his former slaves, both during the years that they lived together on the plantation and afterward, Mrs. Davis has printed several letters written to her by them after Mr. Davis's death. The following letter was written by Thornton Montgomery, who is at present associated with his brother, Isaiah, in business at Mound Bayou.

CHRISTINE, NORTH DAKOTA, December 7, 1889.

MISS VARINA: I have watched with deep interest and solicitude the illness of Mr. Davis at Brierfield, his trip down on the steamer *Leathers*, and your meeting and returning with him to the residence of Mr. Payne, in New Orleans; and I had hoped with good nursing and superior medical skill, together with his great will-power to sustain him, he will recover. But, alas! for human endeavour, an over-ruling Providence has willed it otherwise. I appreciate your great loss, and my heart goes out to you in this hour of your deepest affliction.

Would that I could help you bear the burden that is yours today. Since I am powerless to do so, I beg that you accept my tenderest sympathy and condolence.

Your very obedient servant,

THORNTON.

To Mrs. Jefferson Davis, Beauvoir, Mississippi.*

From all that I have been able to learn, the early slaves, and by these I mean the first generation which were brought to America fresh from Africa, seem to have remained more or less alien in customs and sympathy to their white masters. This was more particularly the case on the large plantations along the Carolina coast, where the slaves came very little in contact with their masters, and remained to a very large degree and for a considerable time merely an African colony on American soil.

But the later generations, those who knew Africa only by tradition, were different. Each succeeding

*"Jefferson Davis, Ex-President of the Confederate States," A memoir by his wife, Vol. II., p. 934.

generation of the Creole Negroes — to use the expression in its original meaning — managed to pick up more and more, as it had the opportunity, the language, the ideas, the habits, the crafts, and the religious conceptions of the white man, until the life of the black man was wholly absorbed into that of the plantation upon which he lived.

The Negro in exile from his native land neither pined away nor grew bitter. On the contrary, as soon as he was able to adjust himself to the conditions of his new life, his naturally cheerful and affectionate disposition began to assert itself. Gradually the natural human sympathies of the African began to take root in the soil of the New World and, growing up spontaneously, twine about the life of the white man by whose side the black man now found himself. The slave soon learned to love the children of his master, and they loved him in return. The quaint humour of the Negro helped to turn many a hard corner. It helped to excuse his mistakes and, by turning a reproof into a jest, to soften the resentment of his master for his faults.

Quaint and homely tales that were told around the fireside made the Negro cabin a place of romantic interest to the master's children. The simple, natural joy of the Negro in little things converted every change in the dull routine of his life into an event. Hog-killing time was an annual festival, and the corn shucking was a joyous event which the whites and blacks, in their respective ways, took part in and enjoyed. These corn-shucking bees, or whatever they may be called, took place during the last of November or the first half of December. They were a sort of a prelude to the festivities of the Christmas season. Usually they were held upon one of the larger and wealthier plantations.

After all the corn had been gathered, thousands of bushels, sometimes, it would be piled up in the shape of a mound, often to the height of fifty or sixty feet. Invitations would be sent around by the master himself to the neighbouring planters, inviting their slaves on a certain night to attend. In response to these invitations as many as one or two hundred men, women, and children would come together.

When all were assembled around the pile of corn, some one individual, who had already gained a reputation as a leader in singing, would climb on top of the mound and begin at once, in clear, loud tones, a solo — a song of the corn-shucking season — a kind of singing which I am sorry to say has very largely passed from memory and practice. After leading off in this way, in clear, distinct tones, the chorus at the base of the mound would join in, some hundred voices strong. The words, which were largely improvised, were very simple and suited to the occasion, and more often than not they had the flavour of the camp-meeting rather than any more secular proceeding. Such singing I have never heard on any other occasion. There was something wild and weird about that music, such as I suspect will never again be heard in America.

One of these songs, as I remember, ran about as follows:

I.

Massa's niggers am slick and fat,
Oh! Oh! Oh!
Shine just like a new beaver hat,
Oh! Oh! Oh!

REFRAIN:

Turn out here and shuck dis corn,
Oh! Oh! Oh!
Biggest pile o' corn seen since I was born,
Oh! Oh! Oh!

II.

Jones's niggers am lean an' po';
Oh! Oh! Oh!
Don't know whether dey get 'nough to eat or no,
Oh! Oh! Oh!

REFRAIN:

Turn out here and shuck dis corn,
Oh! Oh! Oh!
Biggest pile o' corn seen since I was born,
Oh! Oh! Oh!

Little by little the slave songs, the quaint stories, sayings, and anecdotes of the slave's life began to give their quality to the life of the plantation. Half the homely charm of Southern life was made by the presence of a Negro. The homes that had no Negro servants were dreary by contrast, and that was not due to the fact that, ordinarily, the man who had slaves was rich and the man who had no slaves was poor.

The four great crops of the South — tobacco, rice, sugar, and cotton — were all raised by slave labour. In the early days it was thought that no labour except that of the Negro was suited to cultivate these great staples of Southern industry, and that opinion prevails pretty widely still. But it was not merely his quality as a labourer that made the Negro seem so necessary to the white man in the South; it was also these other qualities to which I have referred — his cheerfulness and sympathy, his humour and his fidelity. No one can honestly say that there was anything in the nature of the institution of slavery that would develop these qualities in a people who did not possess them. On the contrary, what we know about slavery elsewhere leads us to believe that the system would have developed qualities quite different, so that I think I am justified in saying that most of the things that made slavery tolerable, both to the white man and to the black man, were due to the native qualities of the African.

Southern writers, looking back and seeking to reproduce the genial warmth and gracious charm of that old ante-bellum Southern life, have not failed to do full justice to the part that the Negro played in it. The late Joel Chandler Harris, for instance, has given us in the character of "Uncle Remus" the type of the Negro story-teller who delights and instructs the young children of the "big house" with his quaint animal stories that have been handed down to the Negro by his African ancestors. The "Br'er Rabbit" stories of Uncle Remus are now a lasting element in the literature, not only of the South, but of America, and they are recognised as the peculiar contribution of the American Negro slave to the folk-lore stories of the world.

In my own state of Virginia, Mr. Thomas Nelson Page has given us, in "Uncle Billy" and "Uncle Sam," two typical characters worthy of study by those who wish to understand the human side of the Negro slave on the aristocratic plantations of that state. In Mr. Page's story, "Meh Lady," Uncle Billy was guide, philosopher and friend to his mistress and her daughter in the trying times of war and in their days of poverty. He hid their silver, refused to give information to the Union soldiers, prayed the last prayer with his dying mistress, comforted her lonely daughter, and at last gave her away in marriage. At the close of the wedding, the old man sits in front of his cabin door and thinks again of the old days. The musings of Uncle Billy Mr. Page tells in the following quaint dialect:

An' dat night when de preacher was gone wid he wife, and Hannah done drapt off to sleep, I wuz settin' in de do' wid meh pipe, an' I heah 'em setting dyah on de front steps, dee voices soun'in' low like bees, an' moon sort o' meltin' over de yard, an' I sort o' got to studyin', an' hit 'pear like de plantation 'live once mo', an' de ain' no mo' scufflin', an' de ole times done come back ag'in, an' I heah meh kerridge-horses stompin' in de stall, an' de place all cleared up again, an' fence all roun' de pahsture, an' I smell de wet clover blossoms right good, and Marse Phil and Meh Lady done come back, an' running all roun' me, climbing up on meh knees, calling me Unc Billy, an' pestering me to go fishing while somehow Meh Lady and de Cun'l, setting dyah on de steps wid de voices hummin' low like water runnin' in the dark.

In the story of "Marse Chan" Mr. Page lets Uncle Sam, the slave bodyguard, tell in the following language what happened to his young master during the Civil War on the field of battle:

Marse Chan he calls me, an he sez, "Sam, we 'se goin to win in dis battle, an den we 'll go home an' git married; an' I 'm goin' home wid a star on my collar." An' den he sez, "Ef I'm wounded, kyah me, yo' hear?" An' I sez, "Yes, Marse Chan." Well, jes' den dey blowed boots an' saddles an' we mounted — an' dey said, "Charge 'em," an' my King ef ever yo' see bullets fly, dey did dat day. . . . We wen' down de slope, I 'long wid de res' an' up de hill right to de cannons, an' de fire wuz so strong dyah our lines sort o' broke an' stop; an' de cun'l was kilt, an' I b'lieve dey wuz jes' 'bout to break all to pieces wen Marse Chan rid up an' cotch holt de flag and hollers, "Follow me." . . . Yo' ain' never heah thunder. Fust thing I knowed de Roan roll head over heels an' flung me up 'gainst de bank like yo' chuck a nubbin over g'inst de foot o' de corn pile.

An' dat what kep me from being kilt I 'spects. When I look 'roun' de Roan was lying dyah stone dead. 'Twan' mo'n a minit, de sorrel come gallupin' back wid his mane flying and de rein hangin' down on one side to his knee. I jumped up an' run over de bank an' dyah, wid a whole lot ob dead mens and some not dead yit, on de one side o' de guns wid de flag still in he han' an' a bullet right thru' he body, lay Marse Chan. I tu'n 'im over an' call 'im, "Marse Chan," but twan' no use. He wuz done gone home. I pick him up in my arms wid de flag still in he han' and toted 'im back jes' like I did dat day when he wuz a baby an' ole master gin 'im to me in my arms, an' say he could trus' me, an' tell me to tek keer on 'im long as he lived. I kyah'd 'im way off de battle-fiel' out de way o' de balls an' I laid 'im down under a big tree till I could git somebody to ketch de sorrel for me. He was kotched arter a while an' I hed some money, so I got some pine plank an' made a coffin dat evenin' an' wrap Marse Chan's body up in de flag an' put 'im in de coffin, but I did n't nail de top on strong, 'cause I knowed de old missus wan' to see 'im; an' I got a' ambulance an' set out fo' home dat night. We reached dyah de nex' evenin' arter travellin' all dat night an' all nex' day.

In the Palace of Fine Arts in St. Louis during the Exposition of 1904, there was a picture which made a deep impression on every Southern white man and black man who saw it, who knew enough of the old life to understand what it meant. Rev. A. B. Curry, of Memphis, Tenn., referring to this picture in a sermon in his home city on November 27, 1904, said:

When I was in the Palace of Fine Arts in St. Louis this summer, I saw a picture before which I stood and wept. In the distance was a battle scene; the dust of trampling men and horses, the smoke of cannon and rifles filled the air; broken carriages and dead and dying men strewed the ground. In the foreground was the figure of a stalwart Negro man, bearing in his strong arms the form of a fair-haired Anglo-Saxon youth. It was the devoted body-servant of a young Southerner, bearing the dead body of his young master from the field of carnage, not to pause or rest till he had delivered it to those whose love for it only surpassed his own; and underneath the picture were these words: "Faithful Unto Death"; and there are men before me who have seen the spirit of that picture on more than one field of battle.

The slaves in Virginia and the border states were, as a rule, far superior, or at least they considered themselves so, to the slaves of the lower South. Even in freedom this feeling of superiority remains. Furthermore, the mansion house-servants, of whom Mr. Page writes, having had an opportunity to share to a large extent the daily life of their masters, were very proud of their superior position and advantages, and had little contact with the field-hands. It is perhaps not generally understood that in slavery days lines were drawn among the slaves just as they were among the white people. The servants owned by a rich and aristocratic family considered that the servants of "a poor white man," one who was not able to own more than half a dozen slaves, were not in the same social class with themselves. And yet the life of these more despised slaves had its vicissitudes, its obscure heroisms, and its tragedies just like the rest of the world. In fact, it was from the plantation hands, as a rule, that the most precious records of slave-life came — the plantation hymns. The field-hands sung these songs and they expressed their lives.

I have frequently met and talked with old men of my race who have grown up in slavery. It is difficult for these old men to express all that they feel. Occasionally, however, they will utter some quaint humorous turn of expression in which there is a serious thought underneath.

One old farmer, who owns a thousand acres of land not far from Tuskegee, said: "We 's jes' so ign't out heah, we don' see no diff'rence 'twe'n freedom an' slav'ry, 'cept den we 's workin' fer someone else, and now we 's workin' fer oursel's."

Some time ago an old coloured man who has lived for a number of years near the Tuskegee Institute, in talking about his experience since freedom, remarked that the greatest difference he had found between slavery and freedom was that in the days of slavery his master had to think for him, but since he had been free he had to think and plan for himself.

At another time out in Kansas I met an old coloured woman who had left her home in Tennessee, directly after the war, and settled with a large number of other coloured people in what is called "Tennessee Town," now a suburb of Topeka, Kansas. In talking with her about her experiences in freedom and in slavery, I asked her if she did not sometimes feel as if she would like to go back to the old days and live as she had lived on the plantation.

"Sometimes," she replied, "I feel as I 'd like to go back and see my old massa and missus"— she hesitated a moment and then added, "but they sold my baby down South."

Aside from the slave-songs very little has come down to us from slavery days that shows how slavery looked to the masses of the people.

There are a considerable number of slave narratives, written by fugitive slaves with the assistance of abolitionist friends, but as these were composed for the most part under the excitement of the anti-slavery agitation they show things, as a rule, somewhat out of proportion. There is one of these stories, however, that gives a picture of the changing fortunes and vicissitudes of slave-life which makes it especially interesting. I refer to the story of Charity Bower, who was born in 1779 near Edenton, North Carolina, and lived to a considerable age after she obtained her freedom. She described her master as very kind to his slaves. He used to whip them, sometimes, with a hickory switch, she said, but never let his overseer do so. Continuing, she said:

My mother nursed all his children. She was reckoned a very good servant, and our mistress made it a point to give one of my mother's children to each one of her own. I fell to the lot of Elizabeth, the second daughter. Oh, my mistress was a kind woman. She was all the same as a mother to poor Charity. If Charity wanted to learn to spin, she let her learn; if Charity wanted to learn to knit, she let her learn; if Charity wanted to learn to weave, she let her learn. I had a wedding when I was married, for mistress did n't like to have her people take up with one another without any minister to marry them. . . . My husband was a nice, good man, and mistress knew we set stores by one another. Her children promised they never would separate me from my husband and children. Indeed, they used to tell me they would never sell me at all, and I am sure they meant what they said. But my young master got into trouble. He used to come home and sit leaning his head on his hands by the hour together, without speaking to anybody. I see something was the matter, and begged him to tell me what made him look so worried. He told me he owed seventeen hundred dollars that he could not pay, and he was afraid he should have to go to prison. I begged him to sell me and my children, rather than to go to jail. I see the tears come into his eyes. "I don't know, Charity," he said; "I 'll see what can be done. One thing you may feel easy about: I will never separate you from your husband and children, let what will come."

Two or three days after he come to me, and says he: "Charity, how should you like to be sold to Mr. Kinmore?" I told him I would rather be sold to him than to anybody else, because my husband belonged to him. Mr. Kinmore agreed to buy us, and so I and my children went there to live.

Shortly after this her new master died and her new mistress was not so kind to her as he had been. Thereupon she set to work to buy the freedom of her children.

"Sixteen children I 've had, first and last," she said, "and twelve I 've nursed for my mistress. From the time my first baby was born, I always set my heart upon buying freedom for some of my children. I thought it was more consequence to them than to me, for I was old and used to being a slave."

In order to save up money enough for this purpose she set up a little oyster board just outside her cabin which adjoined the open road. When anyone came along who wanted a few oysters and crackers she would leave her washing and wait upon them. In this way she saved up $200, but for some reason or other she never succeeded in getting her mistress's consent to buy one of the children. It was not always easy for a master to emancipate his slave in those days, even if he wanted to do so. On the contrary, as she says, "One after another — one after another — she sold 'em from me."

It was to a "thin, peaked-looking man who used to come and buy of me," she says, that she finally owed her freedom. "Sometimes," she continued, "he would say, 'Aunt Charity, you must fix me up a nice little mess, for I am poorly to-day.' I always made something good for him; and if he did n't happen to have any change I always trusted him."

It was this man, a Negro "speculator," who, according to her story, finally purchased her with her five children and, giving her the youngest child, set her free.

"Well," she ended, "after that I concluded I 'd come to the free states. Here I am takin' in washing; my daughter is smart at her needle; and we get a very comfortable living."

There was much in slavery besides its hardship

and its cruelties; much that was tender, human and beautiful. The heroic efforts that many of the slaves made to buy their own and their children's freedom deserve to be honoured equally with the devotion that they frequently showed in the service of their masters. And after all, considering the qualities which the Negro slave developed under trying conditions, it does not seem to me there is any real reason why any one who wishes him well should despair of the future of the Negro, either in this country or elsewhere.

CHAPTER IX

SLAVE INSURRECTIONS AND THE NEGRO "PERIL"

SOMETHING like twenty-five insurrections of the slaves took place in the United States, according to Professor Albert Bushnell Hart, previous to the American Revolution. This is taking no account of the outbreaks that took place before that time in Louisiana, nor of those that took place in the other Spanish, French, and English colonies in the West Indies.*

After the English invasion of Jamaica in 1655, for instance, the Negro slaves who had fought with their Spanish masters against the English, betook themselves to the mountains and maintained a number of little insurgent governments for nearly a hundred years until, in 1738, these independent governments were formally constituted and their right of existence recognised. They continued until 1796, when their attempt to build roads and improve the condition of their villages opened the way for attacks by the English and resulted in their downfall. It is said, however, that even to this day some of the wild descendants

* "Slavery and Anti-Slavery," p. 51.

of those maroons are still living in the mountainous passes of Jamaica.

The insurrection of the slaves which finally resulted in the establishment, in 1804, of the little Black Republic of Haiti was a part of the revolutionary movement that began in France in 1789. Much has been said and written about the frightful cruelties which characterised the revolution in this island, but any one who will compare what took place in Haiti and Santo Domingo with the events which took place during this period in France will not find, I believe, much to say, considering all of the circumstances, in disparagement of these revolting slaves and their heroic leader, Toussaint L'Overture.

The most important, because the most far-reaching in their effects, of these efforts of Negro slaves to gain their freedom by force, were the attempted insurrection of Denmark Vesey in 1822 and the outbreak under Nat Turner in 1831. These two events, following closely upon the bloody revolution in Haiti and the disturbances in other parts of the West Indies, made a profound impression upon the people of the Southern States.

But even before the memorable insurrection of Nat Turner, two Negroes, Gabriel and Jack Bowler, were the leaders, in 1800, of an attempted revolt in Virginia. These two slaves got together and organised something like a thousand Negroes in

Henrico County, and with this force marched on the city of Richmond. A swollen stream, impassable owing to a recent storm, forced them to halt. They disbanded, expecting to renew the attempt the following night, but the plot was discovered and the citizens of Richmond were aroused before the attack could be made. A reward was offered for Gabriel and Jack Bowler. They were caught and executed.

Twenty-two years later, in Charleston, S. C., an extensive conspiracy was organised by a free Negro, Denmark Vesey. Vesey was known among his people as a deep student of the Bible and exerted a marked influence over them, particularly through their religious meetings which, then as now, were of the nature of popular assemblies for the discussion of all questions relating to the welfare of the race. Vesey's plot failed of its purpose, and he was caught, duly tried and, with thirty-four others, put to death.

When a boy in Virginia I recall the stories that were told around the cabins by the older slave men and women of the "Prophet" Nat Turner, as he was called, and of the dreadful incidents that took place during the insurrection of 1831. Nat Turner was a slave preacher in Southampton County, Virginia. During his boyhood days, as I have heard, his mother, who was known to be a very religious woman, taught him that, like Moses, he was to be the deliverer of his race. She took great pains to give him the advantage of what lore and learning she possessed, and taught him verses and parts of chapters from the Bible, particularly from the Prophets of the Old Testament. He was nursed in the quaint and primitive theology of the plantation hymns, which helped to stimulate the belief in his mission to free his people.

He grew up to be a silent, dreamy kind of man, going, whenever he could, to the caves of the mountains to brood over the condition of the slaves.

It appears to have been Turner's plan to collect a large number of slaves and take refuge in the Dismal Swamp, in the extreme southeastern section of Virginia. On August 21, 1831, with the belief that he was executing the will of God, Nat Turner started forth with six companions who were soon joined by others, making a force of sixty men. Their plan was to exterminate, as far as they were able, the white race about them. In a short time sixty white people on different plantations had been killed. The local militia and United States troops were called out. The insurgents resisted, but the resistance proved useless, and after more than a hundred of them had been killed the uprising was crushed. Forty-three Negroes in all were put on trial, of whom twenty-one were acquitted, twelve were convicted and sold out of the state, while twenty others, including Nat Turner and one woman, were convicted and hanged.

When the John Brown raid took place at Harper's Ferry in 1859, five coloured men were a part of his little band. Of the five men, three were free-born Negroes and two were fugitive slaves. Two of them, Dangerfield Newby and Lewis Leary, were killed during the fighting; John A. Copeland and Shields Green were captured, tried, and executed; Osborne Anderson was the only one to escape from the scene of the disaster.

Newby was tall, well-built, and about thirty years of age, with a pleasing face. Leary came originally from North Carolina and was a member of the colony of Southern coloured people at Oberlin, Ohio. He was twenty-four years of age and quite well educated.

Copeland, who was related to Leary, was twenty-two years of age and came from Oberlin. His letters, written from the jail to relatives, show him to have been a young man of intelligence and courage. In a letter to his brother, written shortly before his execution, were these words, which can be read with profit to-day after a lapse of nearly fifty years:

> My jailer, Captain John Avis, is a gentleman who has a heart in his bosom as brave as any other. He met us at Harper's Ferry and fought us as a brave man would do. And since we have been in his power he has protected us from insult and abuse which cowards would have heaped upon us. He has done as a brave man and gentleman would do. Also one of his aids,

Mr. John Sheats, has been very kind to us and has done all he could to serve us. And now, Henry, if fortune should ever throw either of them in your way, and you can confer the least favour on them, do it for my sake.

On the morning of his execution Copeland wrote a long letter to his family in Oberlin from which the following extract is taken:

Let me tell you that it is not the mere fact of hanging to meet death, if I should express regret, but that such an unjust institution should exist as the one which demands my life, and not my life only, but the lives of those to whom my life bears but the relative value of zero to the infinite.

Shields Green was a fugitive slave from South Carolina, twenty-four years of age, with no knowledge of letters, but he is said to have possessed considerable natural ability and a courage which showed that, if better trained, he might have become a man of some importance. He had come to Chambersburg, Pa., the meeting-place of those who were to aid Brown, with Frederick Douglass. Douglass tells how, when he turned to leave the Chambersburg quarry, where his interview with John Brown was had, that, on telling Green he could return with him to Rochester, N. Y., the Negro turned and looked at the bowed figure of John Brown, then asked, "Is he going to stay?"

"Yes," was the answer.

Green looked again at Brown, then at Douglass, and slowly said: "Well, I guess I goes wid de ole man."

When the fight had begun at Harper's Ferry some of the men soon saw that resistance was useless and decided to try to make their escape. Green came under fire while on his way to the arsenal. One of the men told Green he had better go with them. He turned and looked toward the engine-house, before the door of which stood its few defenders and asked: "You think der 's no chance?"

"Not one," was the reply.

"And de ole captain can't get away?"

"No," said the men.

"Well," he replied, slowly, with a long, lingering look, "I guess I 'll go back to de ole man."

In prison Green was constantly sending expressions of consolation and of devotion to Brown and, on the morning of John Brown's execution, Green sent him word that he was glad he came, and that he waited willingly for his own death.

Anderson, born free in Pennsylvania, was twenty-four years of age. He was well-educated and by trade a printer. He was a man of natural ability, simple in manner and address. He wrote a very interesting pamphlet of the raid after his escape entitled, "A Voice from Harper's Ferry." He served during the latter part of the Civil War in one of the Negro regiments, and died in Washington in 1871.

The great slave insurrection which, during the whole period of slavery, was frequently expected and always feared, never actually took place; but the fear of such a general outbreak always haunted the South and helped to harden the hearts of the Southern people against the Negro race. This fear was responsible, for instance, for the passage of laws which made it difficult, if not impossible, in many of the Southern states, for a master to emancipate his slaves; made it a crime for him to teach his slaves to read and write; and imposed such limitations and burdens on the free Negroes as reduced that unfortunate class to a condition often counted worse than that of slavery.

In the relations which existed between the white man and the black man in slavery, just as in the relations which exist to-day between the races in the South, there was much that was strange and contradictory, much that was and is hard to understand. For instance, it seems to me that in Virginia, at any rate, the relations between master and slave were usually kindly. The master frequently trusted his slave, usually cared for and protected him, and had for him, in many instances, a feeling of genuine affection. And yet the slaveholder was never able to shake off his sense of danger of an uprising of the slaves. "The night-bell is never heard to toll in the city of Richmond," said John Randolph of Roanoke, referring to this fear, "but the anxious mother presses her infant more closely to her bosom."

As a result of his experience in slavery the Southern white man seems to have learned to make a pretty complete distinction between the individual Negro, whom he knows and protects, and the Negro as a race, whom he denounces in the political campaign and sometimes flaunts in the faces of strangers who do not understand the situation in the South. These two ways of looking upon and dealing with the Negro are well represented in the cases of ex-Governor Vardaman, of Mississippi, and Senator Tillman, of South Carolina, both of whom, ordinarily so violent in all their public utterances in regard to the Negro, are frequently spoken of by coloured men who know them as unusually kind in all their personal relations with the Negro. Mr. Vardaman and Mr. Tillman, it would seem, hate the Negro in the abstract, but they get along very well with the actual black man who is their neighbour.

It is sometimes said that the vague, impersonal sort of fear which the master felt for the Negro during slavery was due to his knowledge of the savage instincts of the black man which, unless proper precautions were taken, might at any moment break out and overwhelm the country. I am more inclined to the opinion, however, that the majority of the Negroes who were brought to this country, either because of their previous training in Africa or because of their natural disposition, were more submissive, more disposed to attach themselves and remain faithful to their masters, than any other race or class of people would have been under similar circumstances.

I am disposed to believe that the real reason why the white man feared the black man was because he felt the injustice of the condition of slavery, and realised that it was but human nature that, when the slave began to understand his position, he should seek to become free.

When I hear of a certain type of public man of the present day, either in the press or on the political platform, talking about the danger in which the white race is placed by reason of the presence of the Negro in this country I cannot but feel that these men, in their efforts to stir up prejudice against the Negro, are moved by a bad conscience. If they really believe there is danger from the Negro it must be because they do not intend to give him justice. Injustice always breeds fear.

When I hear people talking about the savage instincts of the Negro and about the danger with which they are threatened in consequence, I wish these people could know and talk, as I have, with some of the men and women who have gone as missionaries to Africa and have spent years of their life alone in the midst of the wildest and most uncivilised peoples of that continent, with never so much as a thought of fear. There are scores of cases in all the Southern States where a few white people live surrounded by coloured people without fear of insurrection or murder, because they have convinced the coloured people that they want to do the fair thing by them, that they are anxious to help them, and to see them make progress. I know personally of a case where for ten years a half-dozen white women have lived in a community surrounded by thousands of coloured people and with no white man near to protect them, but they have never had the least fear of violence because they went there to help the coloured people.

In looking into the history of these insurrections and conspiracies I have been impressed with the fact that, so far as concerns the leaders of them, none of these outbreaks seems to have been inspired by revenge or to have been due to the ill-treatment which the slaves had received.

Denmark Vesey was not a slave. In 1822 he drew a fifteen-hundred-dollar prize in a lottery and bought his freedom for $600. His real reason for organising the conspiracy of which he was the author seems to be revealed in the explanations he made to some of his fellow-conspirators in inducing them to join him.

"He said," according to the confession of one of these men, "he did not go with Creighton to Africa because he had not a will; he wanted to stay and see what he could do for his fellow-creatures."

To another witness he stated that "he was satisfied with his own condition, being free, but, as all his children were slaves, he wished to see what could be done for them."

Denmark Vesey was a man of some education. He had travelled all over the world with his master, who was a ship captain. In his talks with the slaves he not only quoted the Bible, citing the passage about the deliverance of the children of Israel, but he read the speeches in Congress, particularly one speech of a certain Mr. King who, he said, was "the black man's friend," adding that "he, Mr. King, had declared he would continue to speak, write, and publish pamphlets against slavery the longest day he lived, until the Southern States consented to emancipate their slaves, for that slavery was a great disgrace to the country."

Nat Turner was a very different type of man. He was a dreamer, as I have said, and a fanatic. So deeply was he himself imbued with the belief that he was inspired, that his presence impressed with a sense of awe, not merely the Negro slaves, but many of the white people who came in contact with him after his arrest and before his execution.

He is described as a man of ordinary stature, having "the true Negro face, every feature of which is strongly marked."

Mr. Gray, the gentleman who took his confession, says of him:

> It has been said that he was ignorant and cowardly, and that his object was to murder and rob for the purpose of obtaining money to make his escape. It is notorious that he was never known to have a dollar in his life, to swear an oath, or drink a drop of spirits. As to his ignorance, he certainly never had the advantages of education; but he can read and write, and for natural intelligence and quickness of apprehension is surpassed by few men I ever have seen. As to his being a coward, his reason, as given, for not resisting Mr. Phipps, shows the decision of his character. When he saw Mr. Phipps present his gun, he said he knew it was impossible for him to escape, as the woods were full of men; he therefore thought it was better for him to surrender, and trust to fortune for his escape.
>
> He is a complete fanatic, or plays his part admirably. On other subjects he possesses an uncommon share of intelligence, with a mind capable of attaining anything, but warped and perverted by the influence of early impressions. I shall not attempt to describe the effect of his narrative, as told and commented on by himself, in the condemned hole of the prison: the calm, deliberate composure with which he spoke of his late deeds and intentions; the expression of his fiend-like face when excited by enthusiasm; still bearing the stains of the blood of helpless innocence about him, clothed with rags, and covered with chains, yet daring to raise his manacled hands to Heaven, with a spirit soaring above the attributes of man. I looked on him, and the blood curdled in my veins.

The history of these conspiracies proves that the very contact of the slave with his master tended to breed a desire for freedom. Every slave who became educated sufficiently to read the Bible or to read the ordinary school books came into contact with the sentiments and traditions of a people that was proud of its independence, and the slave learned from his master the desire to be free. Frederick Douglass got his first notions of freedom from reading the great orations of William Pitt, Lord Chatham, Fox, and Sheridan in a book called "The Columbian Orator," which he picked up by chance.

Once this notion of freedom got into the mind of a slave with a vigorous intellect it never left him. In Frederick Douglass's "Narrative," published in 1845, he tells us that when he was a slave in Maryland on the shores of Chesapeake Bay he often watched the ships as they sailed by, and as they passed he would express himself in this way:

> You are loosed from your moorings, and are free, I am fast in my chains and am a slave! You move merrily before the gentle gale, and I sadly before the bloody whip! You are freedom's swift-winged angels that fly round the world, I am confined in bands of irons! O that I were free! O that I were one of your gallant decks, and under your protecting wing!

It is as true to-day as it was before the war that, while the personal relations of the white man and the black man in the South are frequently all that could be desired, the natural development of these good relations is hindered and held back by the impersonal fear which the white man seems to have of the Negro race as a whole. The success of the Negro as well as that of the white man is, for that reason, hindered by the efforts to force upon the South a system which does not fit the desires or the needs of either race. Ever since the war, for instance, the normal political development of the South has been stunted by the fear, or the ghost of the fear, that the Negro would some time or other again secure the upper hand in the South as he was supposed to have done directly after the war. As a matter of fact, the Negro was never in control in the South. The people who were in control were representatives of the Republican party in the North who came South and used their influence with the Negro and with the Government at Washington to control the course of events. Just such a condition never will and never can arise again. Even if it were possible, the Negro does not desire it any more than the white man. What he desires most is the good will of his white neighbours and the opportunity for the peaceful development of those fundamental interests which are the same for both races.

The Negro gained just as little from the temporary power which he held during the Reconstruction time as he did from the successful and unsuccessful insurrections by which he sought to gain his freedom before the war. He has no desire to try that experiment again.

Scarcely a month or a week has passed since the Negro became free that some newspaper has not expressed a fear or made a prediction that there was going to be an uprising or insurrection of the

Negroes at some time in some part of the country. That uprising has never taken place. The nearest to anything like an uprising of the Negroes in the South since emancipation took place at the end of the seventies, when, as a result of real or fancied oppression in some of the Southern states, delegates from fourteen states and territories met in Nashville, Tenn., May 7, 1879, and advised the coloured people of the South to "emigrate to those states and territories where they can enjoy all the rights which are guaranteed by the laws and Constitution of the United States." As a result of this advice 40,000 emigrants, within the period of a few months, poured into Kansas, largely from the "Black Belt" of Mississippi and Louisiana. This movement created such embarrassment among the planters in the region from which the emigration took place, and such distress among the immigrants themselves, because of their helplessness when they reached their destination, that the movement became an object of national concern, and it required the most energetic efforts upon the part of Frederick Douglass and other leaders of the race to prevent the movement assuming larger and more dangerous proportions.

The chances for another such movement, or for an uprising of any kind, grow less every year, just in proportion as the Negro himself gains in property and in intelligence; in proportion as he enters into the business of the community in which he lives, and becomes a permanent and definite factor in its industrial life. The only possible chance for such an uprising at the present time would be in a community where the Negro has little or no interest at stake, and such communities are now few in the Southern states.

I can best illustrate what I have in mind by referring to a specific instance which I came across during a trip of observation through Mississippi in the fall of 1908. During that visit I spent a day in Marshall County where, although the Negro population outnumbers the white more than two to one, there has not been, with one exception, an outbreak of any character between the races since the Civil War. I inquired of the coloured and the white people there how it was that peace and harmony prevailed in their community. I received practically the same answer from both races, which was in substance this: In that community the coloured people are large owners of farm land; they are successful farmers; they own in the principal town of the county, Holly Springs, valuable business blocks; they are not only engaged in farming, but they are engaged in business, selling groceries, dry-goods, buying and selling cotton. Besides the coloured people of Mississippi own several important schools and colleges in Holly Springs. A racial outbreak would cost the Negroes of the county quite as much as the white people, and this fact has helped to bring about racial peace. What is true in that community is equally true in others where the Negro is making real progress.

In these places the people of both races have discovered that their material and moral interests are so interlaced that if one race suffers the other must suffer too.

One Negro in Marshall County, Mr. E. H. McKissack, is the Treasurer of the State Odd Fellows organisation, which handles practically $200,000 each year. This money, which is distributed among the different banks in Holly Springs, is a visible evidence of the way in which the material interests of the races are bound together. I was told during my visit that, whenever the least danger of racial conflict arose in Marshall County, the leading coloured men and the leading white men were in the habit of taking counsel together, in order to form plans that would result in the maintenance of peace and friendly relations. On one occasion, for instance, when the son of a poor white woman was murdered by a coloured man, the coloured people were the first to get together and hold a mass meeting, in which a considerable sum of money was collected and presented to the mother of the murdered boy.

In recent years we have had several outbreaks of mobs, sometimes in the North, sometimes in the

South, but I have noticed this difference between a mob in the North and a mob in the South: A mob in the South is more short-lived than the one in the North, and with few exceptions, does not seek to visit its punishment upon the innocent as well as upon the guilty. There is a reason for this. In the South every Negro, no matter how worthless he may be as an individual, knows one white man in the town whose friendship and protection he can always count upon; perhaps he has gained the friendship of this white man by reason of the fact that some member of the white man's family owned him or some of his relatives, or it may be that he has lived upon this white man's plantation, or that some member of his family works for him, or that he has performed some act of kindness for this white man which has brought them into sympathetic relations with each other. It is generally true, as I have said before, that in the South every white man, no matter how bitter he may seem to be toward the Negro as a race, knows some one Negro in whom he has complete confidence, whom he will trust with all that he has. It is the individual touch which holds the two races together in the South, and it is this individual touch between the races which is lacking, in a large degree, in the North.

In bringing to a close what I have written on the subject of Negro insurrections I am tempted to say a word on the subject of Negro courage. While certain people have fallen into the habit of denouncing the Negro because he is unduly ambitious, and because he refuses to remain, as they say, "in the place for which God made him," there are others who claim that the Negro is too submissive. These latter insist that, if he had the courage to stand up and denounce his detractors in the same harsh and bitter terms that these persons use toward him, in a short time he would win the respect of the world, and the only obstacle to his progress would be removed.

It is interesting, sometimes amusing, and sometimes even pathetic, to note the conception of "bravery" and "courage" which some coloured men, who put their faith in this solution of the Negro problem, occasionally apply to other members of their race. For a long time after freedom came, and the same is not infrequently true at the present time, any black man who was willing, either in print or in public speech, to curse and abuse the white man, easily gained for himself a reputation for great courage. He might spend but thirty minutes or an hour once a year in that kind of "vindication" of his race, but he got the reputation of being an exceedingly brave man. Another man, who worked patiently and persistently for years in a Negro school, depriving himself of many of the comforts and necessities of life, in order to perform a service which would uplift his race, gained no reputation for courage. On the contrary, he was likely to be denounced as a coward by these "heroes," because he chose to do his work without cursing, without abuse, and without complaint.

There is an element of white people which has gained a reputation for courage by abusing the Negro in the same way that certain of the Negroes have gained a reputation by abusing the white man. No account is taken by these people of the kind of courage shown by the white man in the South who, in an unostentatious way, is helping to lift the Negro to a higher plane of usefulness. It requires no real courage for a man to stand up before a sympathetic audience and denounce wrongs that had been committed by people thousands of miles away. Neither does it require any real courage for five hundred armed men to march out and kill one helpless individual.

The encouraging thing about the relations of the races in the United States is that an increasing number of white men and black men are learning that the highest courage is that of the man or the woman who is helping some one else to be more useful or more happy; that, in the last analysis, it is not the courage that hurts some one and destroys something, but the courage that helps some one and builds something up which the world needs most.

CHAPTER X

THE FREE NEGRO IN SLAVERY DAYS

SOME time in the fall of 1828, Benjamin Lundy, the Quaker abolitionist, met by accident, in a Boston boarding house, a young man by the name of William Lloyd Garrison, who was then publishing a total abstinence newspaper, the *National Philanthropist.* The next year, after returning from a visit to a colony of emancipated slaves which he had succeeded in settling in the island of Haiti, Lundy announced in his paper that William Lloyd Garrison had joined him at Baltimore, Maryland, and would henceforth be associated with him in the publication at that city of *The Genius of Universal Emancipation,* the first abolition newspaper in the United States.

This meeting of Benjamin Lundy and William Lloyd Garrison and their subsequent association in Baltimore marks the point in time when the agitation for the emancipation of the Negro was transferred from the Southern to the Northern States, and slavery became for the first time a National issue. After the Southampton uprising in 1831, the abolition societies, which up to that time had existed in different parts of the South, almost wholly disappeared. With the exception of a few individuals like Cassius M. Clay who, as late as 1845, published an anti-slavery weekly, the *True American*, at Lexington, Kentucky, there was no public opposition to slavery in any of the Southern States.

Opposition to slavery, though silenced in the South, never wholly ceased there, and the evidence of its existence was the Free Negro. In spite of the efforts that were made to limit and check emancipation of the slaves, the number of free Negroes continued to increase in the Southern as well as the Northern States, and the existence of this class of persons was the silent protest of the Southern slaveholder against the system which he publicly defended and upheld.

Under the conditions of slavery, the position of the free Negro was a very uncomfortable one. He was, in a certain sense, an anomaly, since he did not belong to either class. He was distrusted by the white people, and looked down upon by the slaves. In spite of this fact, individual slaveholders — sometimes by providing in their wills for the emancipation and transportation of their slaves to a free state or to Liberia, sometimes by permitting individual slaves to buy their own freedom — were constantly adding to the number of "free persons of colour." Among the most illustrious of those who freed their slaves were George Washington, John Randolph, and Chief-Justice Roger B. Taney, author of the famous Dred Scott decision.

When a master liberated his slaves by will, it was frequently with the explanation, expressed or understood, that he believed slavery was morally wrong. When he allowed them to buy their own freedom, it was a practical recognition that the system was economically a mistake, since the slave who could purchase his own freedom was one whom it did not pay to hold as a slave. This fact was clearly recognised by a planter in Mississippi who declared that he had found it paid to allow the slaves to buy their freedom. In order to encourage them to do this he devised a method by which they might purchase their freedom in instalments. After they had saved a certain amount of money, by extra labour, he permitted them to buy one day's freedom a week. With this much capital invested in themselves they were then able to purchase, in a much shorter time, a second, a third, and a fourth day's freedom, until they were entirely free.

A somewhat similar method was sometimes adopted by certain ambitious freedmen for purchasing the freedom of their families. In such a case the father would purchase, for instance, a son or a daughter. The children would then join with their father in purchasing the other members of the family. It was in this way, I have been informed by Mr.

Monroe Work, who is at present a teacher at Tuskegee, that his grandfather purchased his wife and ten of his children, including Mr. Work's father. The grandfather, Henry Work, after securing his own freedom, went first to Cincinnati, and then to Decatur, Michigan, where he owned a farm, and on this farm he and his children earned the money to purchase one by one the other members of the family. How much it cost the family to free itself in this way Mr. Work says he was unable to learn. He knows, however, that his father sold at one time for $1,400. When Henry Work died there were still three of his children in slavery whom he had not been able to redeem. Ex-President Gibson, of the Negro State of Liberia, told me that his father purchased himself and most of the other members of the family in installments and transported them to Liberia. Two sons, who did not care to go back to Africa, were left in slavery in this country, but with the understanding that after a certain time they were to become free.

In this and other ways, in spite of the fact that there were at this time something like 30,000 fugitives in Canada and 20,000 colonists in Africa and elsewhere, the number of free Negroes in the United States increased from 59,466 in 1790 to 434,495 in 1860. This was about 10 per cent. of the whole Negro population at that time. Of these free Negroes considerably more than half — 262,000 — were in the Southern States. In the South, the three states of

Maryland, Virginia, and North Carolina contained by far the largest number of the "free citizens of colour," as they were sometimes called. At the census of 1860, the slave population of Maryland was something like 87,000 and the number of free Negroes was 83,942. From 1830 to 1860 the slave population of Maryland decreased nearly 16,000 while the population of free Negroes increased something over 31,000.

In estimating the number of slaves who were, in one way or another, given their freedom by their masters, some account should be taken of those who were, for one reason or another, re-enslaved. A free Negro might be sold into slavery to pay taxes or to pay fines, and in Maryland free Negroes might be sold into perpetual slavery for the crime of entering the state. In 1829 the practice of selling any free Negro, who could not account for himself, in order to pay the jail fines, had become such a scandal as to attract public attention.

There were other means by which a considerable number of free Negroes were re-enslaved. The practice of kidnapping, in spite of severe laws against it in all the Southern states, was carried on to a very great extent. In his book on the domestic slave-trade, Professor Collins, of Claremont College, Hickory, N. C., estimates that the number of free Negroes kidnapped and sold into slavery "must have ranged from a few hundred to two or three thousand,"

and he adds, "it appears quite certain that as many were kidnapped as escaped from bondage, if not more."*

A disposition to free slaves for personal considerations of one kind or another began at a very early period. In York and Henrico counties, Virginia, as far back as the middle of the seventeenth century, we find records of the emancipation of Negro slaves. For example, Thomas Whitehead, of York, emancipated his slave John, and bequeathed to him, among other things, two cows and the use of a house and as much ground as he could cultivate. He further showed his confidence in the discretion and the integrity of this Negro slave by appointing him guardian of Mary Rogers, a ward of Mr. Whitehead. He also made him trustee of her property, but the court refused to allow him to fill either one or the other of these positions.† Another instance recorded about this time was that of John Carter, of Lancaster, Virginia, who was one of the largest slaveholders in the colony. He gave freedom to two of his Negro slaves who were married to each other. To each he gave a cow and a calf and three barrels of Indian corn. He also instructed his heirs to allow them the use of convenient firewood, timber, and as much land as they could cultivate. He provided that the

* "The Domestic Slave-Trade of the Southern States," Winfield H. Collins M. A., p. 94.

† "Economic History of Virginia in the Seventeenth Century," Bruce, Vol. II., p. 123.

two daughters of this couple should receive their liberty when they reached their eighteenth year, and, as a provision for them when they reached that age, he gave each a yearling with its increase, which was to be permitted to run with the cattle of his wife after his death.*

In the interval between 1635 and 1700, although the Negro slaves were few in number, and most of the labour was performed by white servants, there were a number of persons of African blood in the colony of Virginia who raised themselves to positions of some importance. Several of them were able to write at a time when there were very few schools and education was a decided luxury. Several had obtained patents to land. For instance, in 1654, one hundred acres of land in Northampton County were granted to Richard Johnson, a Negro, and in the description of this tract reference was made to the contiguous estates of John Johnston and Anthony Johnson, both Negroes. There are in the records of Northampton County, also, evidences that a suit was begun by Anthony Johnson for the purpose of recovering his Negro servant.

During the early years of slavery, the free Negroes seem to have had about the same rights under the law that other free persons had, except, as I have already stated, they were not allowed to hold persons of white blood as bond-servants. It appears that,

*"Economic History of Virginia in the Seventeenth Century," Bruce, Vol. II., p. 124.

until after the Revolution, Negro freemen were allowed to vote in every state, except Georgia and South Carolina. Between 1792 and 1834 the four bordering states, Delaware, Maryland, Virginia, and Kentucky, denied suffrage to the Negro. In North Carolina, Negroes who paid a public tax took part in the election until 1835, when a new constitution excluded them from the suffrage. New Jersey took away the suffrage of the Negro in 1807, Connecticut in 1814, and Pennsylvania in 1838. New York, in 1821, required from them an unusually high property qualification.*

These changes were all evidences of the steady growth in the United States, both North and South, of a caste system which excluded the Negro from the ordinary privileges of citizenship exclusively upon the ground of his colour. In 1803 Ohio demanded a bond of five hundred dollars for Negroes who came into the state. A Negro, even though a free man, could not at that time testify in a case in which a white man was a party, and Negroes were not admitted to the public schools. Similar provisions were made by Illinois, Indiana, and Iowa when they became states. Illinois prohibited the entrance of Negroes to the state at any time. In 1833 Judge Dagget, of Connecticut, twenty-four years before the Dred Scott decision, held that a free Negro was a person and not a citizen. This was in the trial of the

* "Slavery and Abolition," Hart, pp. 53, 83.

case against Prudence Crandall, the young Quakeress who had established a school for Negroes in Canterbury, Connecticut, contrary to a law which provided that no school could be established for coloured people who were not inhabitants of Connecticut.

The effect of the agitation for abolition seems to have made the condition of the free Negroes steadily worse, particularly in the Southern states. In some of these states, they were forbidden to sell drugs, in others they might not sell wheat and tobacco, and in still others to peddle market produce or own a boat was against the law. In several states it was against the law for a free Negro to cross the state line; in others, a slave who was emancipated was compelled to immediately leave the state.

Notwithstanding the hardships and difficulties under which the free Negro population laboured, both in the North and in the South, those who have had occasion to study the local history of the Southern States have found that the number of Negroes who had succeeded in making some impression upon their community, either by their native qualities or by their success in business, was more considerable than is usually imagined. Solomon Humphreys, for instance, after purchasing his freedom, became a well-known business man in Georgia. Benjamin Lundy found at San Antonio a Negro who, after purchasing his own freedom and that of his wife and family, had become the owner of several houses and lots.*

The number of free Negroes in North Carolina was considerable because, in spite of the rigorous laws against the free coloured people, conditions were more lenient than those of any other Southern state. The result was that many free Negroes crossed into North Carolina and settled, undisturbed, in the northern or southern counties. Speaking of this class of people, Professor John Spencer Bassett says:

> They were well-diggers, shoemakers, blacksmiths, fiddlers, hucksters, peddlers, and so forth. Besides, they were easily called in to help the whites on occasions of need. There were a very few who accumulated money and some of these became slave-owners. Although it was against the law for them to come into the state, their arrival was tolerated both because the law was recognised as severe and because their services were wanted in the community. Many of them had Indian blood in their veins, and when such was the case they were a little distant toward the slaves. . . . I have been speaking of free Negroes who lived in the country districts. In towns they fared better and accumulated wealth.†

Professor Bassett gives an account of several free Negroes, of whom he had been able to obtain records, who were citizens of Newbern, Craven County, North Carolina. One of the men to whom he refers was John C. Stanley, the son of an African-born slave woman, who was liberated by the General

---

* *Cf.* Hart's "Slavery and Anti-slavery," p. 90.

† Johns Hopkins University Studies: "Slavery in the State of North Carolina," by John Spencer Bassett, p. 43.

Assembly under the petition of Mrs. Lydia Stewart, his mistress. Because he got his start in the barber business, he was generally known as "Barber Jack." He became the owner of several plantations on which he employed sixty-four slaves, of which he was the owner, and as many more bound free Negroes. He had three sons, John, Alexander, and Charles. John became an expert book-keeper, and was employed in that capacity by a prominent firm. John C. Stanley amassed a fortune, or what was supposed to be a fortune in those days, of something like $40,000. Speaking of some of the other successful Negroes of whom he was able to obtain the records, Professor Bassett says:

> Many of the free Negroes were in circumstances of independent thrift, and from many parts of the state I have had evidence that some Negroes were slaveholders. In Newbern especially there were a number of such thrifty coloured men. Notable among these was John Good. He was a son of his master, and for a long time a slave. When the master died, his two surviving children, who were daughters, had but little property besides this boy, John, who was a barber. John took up the task of supporting them. He boarded them in good houses and otherwise provided for them well. His faithfulness won him many friends among the best citizens, and when both of his mistresses were married these friends united to persuade the owners to liberate him as a reward for his services. . . . There were other thrifty and notable free Negroes in the same place, as, for example, John Y. Green, a carpenter and contractor; Richard Hazel, a blacksmith of means; Albert and Freeman Morris, described as "two nice young men," and thoroughly respected, tailors by trade; and Scipio, slave of Dr. Hughes, who was a blacksmith and owner of a livery stable. Another was Fellow Bragg, a tailor who was

thoroughly conscientious and so good a workman that prominent people were known to move their custom to the shops at which he was employed in order that he might work on it. Most of these men moved to Cincinnati sooner or later. What became of them I do not know. The conditions here recorded for Newbern were not unusual for North Carolina towns in general. Everywhere there were usually a number of prosperous free Negroes. Most of them were mulattoes, not a few of them were set free by their fathers and thus they fell easily into the life around them.*

Among the descendants of the free coloured people of Newbern, North Carolina, with whom I am personally acquainted is the Hon. John P. Green, who was for twelve years a justice of the peace in Cleveland, Ohio, four years a member of the Ohio House of Representatives, two years a member of the State Senate, and for nine years at the head of the Postage-stamp Distribution Bureau of Washington, filling in the intervals of his public service with practice at the Cleveland bar. His father was a master tailor in Newbern, and a member of a family of free coloured people whose traditions go back something more than one hundred years.

Charles W. Chesnutt, author of "The Conjure Woman" and other popular stories of Southern life, was descended from free coloured people in Fayetteville, North Carolina. Mr. Chesnutt informs me that a coloured man by the name of Matthew Leary is still remembered in Fayetteville who, before the war, was the owner of considerable land, a number of

* Johns Hopkins University Studies: "Slavery in the State of North Carolina," by John Spencer Bassett, p. 45.

slaves, a brick store in the business part of the town, and a handsome residence in a good neighbourhood. His sons gained some prominence in North Carolina during the Reconstruction era. Matthew Leary, Jr., went into politics and afterward became a clerk in one of the Government offices in Washington. A younger brother, Hon. John S. Leary, was the first coloured man in North Carolina to be admitted to the bar, of which he remained a respected member until he died at Charlotte, N. C. He was, I understand, at one time a member of the North Carolina Legislature.

Another of the successful free coloured people of North Carolina was James D. Sampson, who began life as a house carpenter and became in the course of time a man of considerable wealth and some local distinction. I have been informed that one time the Legislature passed a bill granting his family special privileges which were not permitted to other free people of colour. His children, John, Benjamin, and Joseph, were all educated in the North. Benjamin graduated from Oberlin College and afterward became a teacher at Wilberforce, Ohio. John P. Sampson published at Cincinnati, during the war, the *Coloured Citizen*. After the war he was commissioned by General Howard to look after the coloured schools established by the Freedmen's Bureau in the Third District of North Carolina. He was elected treasurer and assessor of Wilmington, and was candidate for Congress, but was defeated because of the fact, it is said, that his father had been the owner of slaves before the war. While it was true that James D. Sampson owned a number of slaves, it is said that many, if not all, of them were held in trust in order to secure them practical freedom. Recently, George M. Sampson, a grandson of James D. Sampson, visited Tuskegee. He is now a teacher in the State Normal School at Tallahassee, Florida.

There is no reason to believe that the coloured people of North Carolina made more progress in a material way than they did in some of the other states in the South. For instance, in the city of Charleston, South Carolina, there was a colony of "free persons of colour" who were proud of the fact that they sprang from a generation of free ancestors going back to before the Revolutionary War. In the list of taxpayers in the city of Charleston for 1860 the names of three hundred and sixty "persons of colour," whose property was assessed in that year, are given. They owned real estate which was valued for taxation at $724,570. Of these three hundred and sixty taxpayers, one hundred and thirty owned slaves, aggregating three hundred and ninety in number. The largest number of slaves held by a coloured person was fourteen. In this list of "persons of colour" thirteen are classed as Indians, but it is quite certain that these so-called Indians were largely mixed with Negro blood. Like so many other communities, there were Indians in Charleston who had been but partially absorbed by coloured people with whom they had been associated.

In 1860 the population of Charleston was 48,409, of whom 26,969 were white, 17,655 slaves, and 3,785 were "free persons of colour." It would appear from the figures given that these free coloured people probably owned, including slaves, a million dollars' worth of property. Among the slaves held by coloured people of Charleston were a number who were actually free men, and only nominally slaves. For instance, Richard Holloway, who was a prominent man among the free coloured people in Charleston, owned Charles Benford, who was his friend, and with him one of the leaders in the Methodist Church, at that time. The circumstances were these: Charles Benford had arranged with his white master to purchase his freedom, but at that time the laws were such that it was difficult for a master to free his slaves, particularly if the slave purchased his own freedom. In order to get around this law Charles Benford asked his friend, Richard Holloway, to purchase him, Benford himself furnishing the money for the purchase.

There were a number of other slaves held in trust by the free coloured people of Charleston. The wealthiest family in Charleston, among the free coloured people, were the Westons. They had among the various members of the family taxable property to the amount of $80,000. They also owned thirty-six slaves, nine of whom they held as trustees. It is said that the number of slaves held by St. Philip's Church, which was the aristocratic church of the city, amounted to something over one hundred. These consisted for the most part of slaves who had actually bought their freedom and whom the church held in trust.

Of the free coloured people of Louisiana, of whom there were a very considerable number before the war, many were slaveholders and large owners of land. There were a number of settlements of Creole Negroes, as they were called, in various parts of Louisiana. When Frederick Law Olmsted visited that state in 1853, he visited one of these settlements in the neighbourhood of Natchitoches. The information which he obtained in regard to these people was to the effect that they were "honest and industrious and paid their debts quite as promptly as the white planters, and were, as far as anyone could judge, good citizens in all respects!" One of them, he learned, had lately spent $40,000 in a law suit, and it is believed that they were increasing in wealth. Several of these coloured planters were worth four or five hundred thousand dollars. The little town of Washington, near Opelousas, in St. Landry Parish, was formerly called Negroville from the number of free Negroes living in that village. A number of them, according to Olmsted, were wealthy and thriving. They owned some of the best cotton and sugar plantations.

"An intelligent man whom I met at Washington," he said, "who had been travelling most of the time for two years in the plantation districts, told me that the free Negroes in the state in general, so far as he had observed, were equal in all respects to the white Creoles. Much the larger part of them were poor, thriftless, unambitious, and lived wretchedly, but there were many opulent, intelligent, and educated. The best house and most tasteful grounds that he had visited in the state had belonged to a nearly full-blooded Negro — a very dark man. He and his family were well educated and, though French in their habitual tongue, they spoke English with a liberal tongue and one much more eloquent than most of the liberally educated whites. They had a private tutor in their family, and owned, he thought, a hundred and fifty slaves.

It is near here, in the adjoining parish of St. Martin, that my friend Paul Chretien lived. His father was a free coloured man who made his money in the neighbourhood of Calcasieu, but afterward returned to St. Martin and built himself a beautiful home there in which his son, whose name I have mentioned, is now living.

A considerable portion of the Negro population of Mobile, Alabama, at the present day are the descendants of these Creole Negroes whose freedom was guaranteed to them by the France treaty which transferred Louisiana to the United States in 1803. There is an island in Mobile Bay, about twenty miles below the city, Mon Louis Island, which is owned by the descendants of two families. The lower end of the island was settled by the veterans of the Revolutionary War, who lived to a great age; the upper part of the island was settled by a man known as Captain Jack Collins, but his real name was Maximilian Collins, who settled on this island in 1808. He left a large tract of land to his descendants with the injunction that they should sell none of it; it has remained in their hands up to the present time, and there has grown up there, as a result, a little patriarchal colony made up of the descendants of the free Negro, Captain Jack, and the descendants of his slaves. The oldest living descendant of this patriarch is the widow of the late Belthair Durette, who had seventy-two grandchildren, fifty-two great-grandchildren, ninety-seven of whom are living in this community of Mon Louis.

I have mentioned here several cases which indicate that, even in the South and before the Civil War, the Negro had made some progress along material lines. It is impossible to tell, of course, how much property these people possessed. But the aggregate value of the property of the 262,000 Negroes in the South in 1860 has been estimated at something like twenty-five millions of dollars. I should judge, from what I have been able to learn, that that was a low estimate.

The question might very well be asked, considering the success that individuals were able to make before the war, why it was that the great mass of the Negro people who were free did not do better? In reply to that I might say that there were the same reasons and others why the Negro should not get on or succeed that there were why the class known as the "poor whites" in the South did not succeed. If the conditions of slavery operated to keep the poor white man in a low stage of civilisation, they certainly operated to keep the free Negro in a still lower stage.

Not only did the free people of colour have to meet all the difficulties to which I have referred, but it was against the law for them to meet together in any large number in order to cooperate to improve their condition. The great benefits of cooperation which go so far to extend to the mass of individuals the benefits which are obtained by a few were denied them.

In spite of this fact, in Charleston, Baltimore, Washington, New York, and in other places where there were large numbers of free Negroes, little societies for mutual helpfulness were established. For instance, in 1790 there was formed in Charleston what was known as the "Brown Fellowship Society." This society was started at the suggestion of the director of St. Philip's, of which a number of free Negroes were members. Besides cultivating a spirit of fellowship among its members, it sought to provide school privileges for their children and to provide relief and extend aid to worthy persons of their colour. One of the first things they did was to purchase a burial lot for their dead. This organisation befriended helpless orphans; one of these orphans was the well-known Bishop Daniel A. Payne, the founder of Wilberforce University. This organisation still maintains its existence, and celebrated a few years ago its centennial. The records have all been preserved, and one of the most interesting of these is one which commemorates, in a formal way, the expulsion of one of its members on suspicion of having assisted in kidnapping and selling into slavery a free coloured man. The success of this first organisation led to the establishment of other similar organisations. "The Humane and Friendly Society" was established in 1802; "The Friendly Union," in 1813; and later still, "The Friendly Moralist," and the "Brotherly Association," and the "Unity and Friendship." Each of these had its own burial plot and system of mutual benefit.

After the attempted conspiracy of Denmark Vesey, in 1822, all these organisations came under suspicion, and there was a time when they were kept up under the greatest difficulties, but they never ceased to exist. There were similar organisations, as I have said, in several of the larger cities of the South.

Frederick Douglass, while living in Baltimore, attended one of these societies, known as the "East Baltimore Mental Improvement Society." This society was formed by a number of free coloured young men who, like Frederick Douglass, were engaged, as ship caulkers. In this organisation he frequently took prominent part, although, being a slave, he would naturally have been excluded. He has said that the society of the young men he met there aided him considerably in completing the education that he had already begun in secret. As Baltimore probably had more free coloured people at the time than any other city, with the exception of Washington, it was natural that there should be a large number of these societies of a literary and mutual-benefit and benevolent character. Baltimore, in fact, seems to have been the home of the Negro mutual benefit societies, many of which now in existence date back to 1820.

The New York African Society, for mutual relief, which has been in existence for over a hundred years in New York City, held its first meeting in a coloured school-house in Rose Street in 1808, nearly twenty years before the final emancipation of the slaves in New York State. Although it has not increased its membership in recent years, this society has become, I understand, comparatively wealthy as a result of its earlier investments. The first property owned by this society was on Baxter Street not far from the spot that afterward became notorious under the name of Five Points. It was purchased in 1820 for $1,800, and when it was sold later the funds were used to purchase a five-story flat at No. 43 West Sixty-sixth Street and another building at No. 27 Greenwich Avenue, both of which the society still owns.

In Maryland these beneficial organisations were especially exempt from the general prohibition against public meetings of free coloured people In other places in the Southern States there was no such exemption and, although the law was usually got around in some way or other, not infrequently members of these organisations were arrested, fined, and sometimes sent to prison. Frederick Law Olmsted records one such instance in Washington, D. C., in the first chapter of his journals of "In the Seaboard Slave States."

He says:

> The coloured population voluntarily sustain several churches, schools, and mutual assistance and improvement societies, and there are evidently persons among them of no inconsiderable cultivation of mind. Among the police reports of the city newspapers, there was lately (April, 1855) an account of the apprehension of twenty-four "genteel coloured men" (so they were described), who had been found by a watchman assembling privately in the evening, and been lodged in the watch-house. The object of their meeting appears to have been purely benevolent, and, when they were examined before a magistrate in the morning, no evidence was offered, nor does there seem to have been any suspicion, that they had any criminal purpose. On

searching their persons there were found a Bible, a vclume of Seneca's "Morals"; "Life in Earnest;" the printed constitution of a society, the object of which was said to be "to relieve the sick, and bury the dead"; and a subscription paper "to purchase the freedom of Eliza Howard," a young woman, whom her owner was willing to sell at $650. I can think of nothing that would speak higher for the character of a body of poor men, servants and labourers, than to find, by chance, in their pockets, just such things as these.*

Nothing contributed more to keep the free Negroes from making the great advancement that they did during the period of slavery than the fact that they were not allowed to organise and unite their efforts for their own improvement in any large way. On the other hand, nothing has more prevented and held back the progress of the coloured people since slavery than the fact that they have had to learn how to unite their efforts in order to improve their condition.

---

* "Seaboard Slave States," by Frederick Law Olmsted, pp. 14, 15.

CHAPTER XI

FUGITIVE SLAVES

IN THE latter part of the year 1852 was organised or rather re-organised, in the rooms of the Anti-slavery Society, at 107 North Fifth Street, Philadelphia, what was known as the "Vigilance Committee." The chairman of this committee was a coloured man, Robert Purvis. He was descended from a free coloured woman of Charleston, whose mother was said to have been a Moor. His father, Robert Purvis, was an Englishman. He was brought to Pennsylvania by his parents in 1819; was a member of the Anti-slavery Convention in 1833, and was one of the signers of its declaration of sentiments. When the fiftieth anniversary of the Anti-slavery Society was held in Philadelphia, December 4, 1883, he was one of the three original signers who were present. The other two were John G. Whittier, the poet, and Elizur Wright, the anti-slavery editor. The Secretary of the Philadelphia Vigilance Committee was William Still.

This Vigilance Committee, which was the successor of an earlier organisation of the same name that dates at least as far back as 1838, soon became the principal directing body for all the numerous lines of the Underground Railroad which centred in Philadelphia at that time. As secretary of this organisation, William Still kept a record of all the fugitive slaves who passed through the hands of this committee from the time of its organisation until the breaking out of the Civil War. During the period of the Civil War he kept this record hidden, but in 1872 it was published in the form of a book called "The Underground Railroad."

This book is one of the most remarkable records in existence, concerning the history of slavery. It is made up in large part of the letters that were written by the different agents of the Underground Railroad to the secretary of the Vigilance Committee, and of letters written by fugitive slaves, sometimes while they were en route to Canada, and sometimes after they had reached their destination. They tell, in words of the fugitives themselves, of the difficulties, sufferings, fears of runaway slaves, and of all the various devices which they used to escape from bondage to freedom.

Of his own motives for keeping this record, Mr. Still says:

Thousands of escapes, harrowing separations, dreadful longings, dark gropings after lost parents, brothers, sisters, and identities, seemed ever to be pressing on my mind. While I knew the danger of keeping strict records, and while I did not then dream that in my day slavery would be blotted out, or that the time would come when I could publish these records, it used to afford me great satisfaction to take them down, fresh from the lips of fugitives on the way to freedom, and to preserve them as they had given them.*

Sometimes these fugitives reached free soil packed in boxes, shipped as merchandise by rail or by steamship, from some of the nearby Southern ports. This was the case of Henry Box Brown, who was shipped from Richmond, Va., by James A. Smith, a shoe dealer, to William H. Johnson, Arch Street, Philadelphia. He was twenty-six hours on the road from Richmond to Philadelphia. Though the box was marked "This side up," in the course of his journey, Mr. Brown was compelled to ride many miles standing on his head. When the box arrived at the anti-slavery office, there was the greatest apprehension lest, in the course of the journey, the fugitive had perished and the society would find itself with a corpse upon its hands. Mr. Still described, in the following words, the scene when this box was opened in the presence of a number of prominent members of the Anti-slavery Society:

All was quiet. The door had been safely locked. The proceedings commenced. Mr. J. Miller McKim, Secretary of the Pennsylvania Anti-slavery Society, rapped quietly on the lid of the box and called out, "All right!" Instantly came the answer from within, "All right, sir!"

The witnesses will never forget that moment. Saw and hatchet quickly had the five hickory hoops cut and the lid off, and the marvellous resurrection of Brown ensued. Rising up in his box,

* Quoted in Siebert's "The Underground Railroad," pp. 7, 8.

he reached out his hand, saying, "How do you do, gentlemen?" The little assemblage hardly knew what to think or do at the moment. He was about as wet as if he had come up out of the Delaware. Very soon he remarked that, before leaving Richmond, he had selected for his arrival-hymn (if he lived) the psalm beginning with these words: "I waited patiently for the Lord, and He heard my prayer." And most touchingly did he sing the psalm, much to his own relief, as well as to the delight of his small audience. He was then christened Henry Box Brown, and soon afterward was sent to the hospitable residence of James Mott and E. M. Davis, on Ninth Street, where, it is needless to say, he met a cordial reception from Mrs. Lucretia Mott and her household.*

Other attempts were made after that time to ship fugitive slaves out of the South as express packages. In 1857, a young woman was shipped from Baltimore to Philadelphia in a box of freight. After reaching Philadelphia, this box with its living freight, after having been turned upside down several times, was left standing nearly all of one night at the freight shed, and it was not secured by the persons to whom it was consigned until ten o'clock the next day. When the box was opened the young woman inside was unconscious and could not speak for some time. She recovered, however, and eventually escaped to Canada.

Samuel A. Smith, who shipped Henry Box Brown from Richmond to Philadelphia, attempted, shortly after this successful venture, to send two other slaves by express to the anti-slavery office. The deceit, however, was discovered and

*"The Underground Railroad," William Still, pp. 83, 84.

Smith was arrested, convicted, and sentenced to eight years in prison, and served out his time in the penitentiary.

Frequently fugitives were secreted upon steamships and sailing vessels. There was usually a coloured steward on these vessels who was willing to run the risk of assisting a fugitive to escape. Men dressed themselves as women, and women dressed themselves as men in order to escape from slavery. Sometimes fugitives travelled hundreds of miles in skiffs in order to reach free soil.

William Still, the author of the book on "The Underground Railroad," had a singular experience. One summer day in 1850, as he was engaged in mailing the weekly issue of the *Pennsylvania Freeman*, two coloured men entered the office. One of these was a stranger, a man who had purchased his freedom and gone to Philadelphia in the hope of finding his relatives.

"I am from Alabama," he said, speaking slowly and deliberately. "I have come in search of my people. My little brother and I were kidnapped about forty years ago, and I thought by coming to Philadelphia and having notices published and read old people would remember about it, and I could find my mother and people."

"Where were you kidnapped from?" asked Mr. Still.

"I don't know," was the reply.

"Don't you know the name of the place?"

"No."

"Don't you know the name of any town, river, neighbourhood or state?"

"No."

"What was your name?"

"Peter."

"What was your brother's name?"

"Levin."

"What were the names of your father and mother?"

"Levin and Sidney."

By the time the dialogue had reached this point William Still was so fully convinced that the stranger was one of his long-lost brothers that he scarcely knew what to do.

"I allowed a full hour to pass," he says, in relating the circumstance, "meanwhile plying him with questions before intimating to my brother the discovery I had made. Then seating myself by his side, I said, 'I think I can tell you about all your kinsfolk — mother, father, and all,' and then I went on to say, 'You are an own brother of mine.'"

Such proved to be the case. It seems that Peter Still had been stolen from his parents when they were living on a farm in New Jersey, in an obscure little settlement of Free Negroes and fugitive slaves called "Springtown," in Cumberland County.*

* Springtown is one of the several little Negro communities still existing in New Jersey.

The father of William Still and his brother, Peter, had purchased his own freedom from his master, about 1800. The mother was a fugitive slave. Peter had been carried from his mother when he was six years old and taken to Alabama. After he had grown to be a young man he made up his mind to save money by performing extra labour, to buy his freedom. Fearing that his master would be unwilling to sell him his freedom, he secured the friendly offices of a Jew named Friedman who made the purchase and set him free.

After reaching Philadelphia and finding his brother William, as has been described, Peter Still made several attempts to secure the freedom of his wife and children, whom he left in slavery in Alabama. It was in an attempt to secure the freedom of Peter Still's wife and children that Seth Concklin, the Shaker Abolitionist, lost his life. Seth Concklin was one of the few white men who, in their efforts to rescue the slaves, penetrated the slave country. He succeeded in bringing the fugitives by boat down the Tennessee and up the Mississippi and the Wabash rivers, as far as Vincennes, when he and they were captured and taken back. Concklin was killed in an attempt to escape.*

* Among the other Northern white men who went into the South to abduct slaves were the Reverend Calvin Fairbank, the Reverend Charles T. Torrey, and Dr. Alexander M. Ross, of Canada. Mr. Fairbank carried off from the neighbourhood of Covington, Ky., the Stanton family, father, mother, and six children, by packing them in a load of straw. The Reverend Charles T. Torrey went to Mary-

One of the most singular and interesting figures among the people who were engaged in the work of the "Underground Railroad" was Harriet Tubman. She escaped from slavery some time about 1849, when she was between twenty and twenty-five years of age. It was the fear that she and her brothers were to be "sold South" that finally led her to make the attempt to escape. She started, with her brothers, from her home in Maryland, guided, as she said, only by the North Star. But after the fugitives had made some distance, the brothers, who feared that they would not succeed, turned back and Harriet went on alone. After making her own escape, she went back repeatedly to different parts of the South and aided in the escape of other fugitives. Many of the slaves who had escaped to Canada, and who had learned to have complete faith in "Moses," as they called her, employed her to secure the freedom of their friends. The fugitives in Canada believed that she had a charmed life. As a matter of fact, Harriet Tubman succeeded, in the course of nineteen different trips into the South, in bringing more than three hundred slaves from the South into the

land and from there sent some four hundred slaves over different routes to Canada. Dr. Alexander M. Ross made extensive tours through various slave states for the purpose of spreading information about Canada and the routes by which that country could be reached. He made trips into Maryland, Kentucky, Virginia, and Tennessee. He went to New Orleans, and from that point set out upon a journey, in the course of which he visited Vicksburg, Selma, and Columbus, Mississippi, Augusta, Georgia, and Charleston, South Carolina. — "The Underground Railroad," Siebert, p. 28.

Northern states and Canada, and in no case was a fugitive under her care ever captured. During the Civil War, she was employed in the secret service of the Federal Army, and, in the last year of the war, carried papers which admitted her through the lines of the Union Army in any part of the country, wherever she cared to go. She was still living, in 1908, in retirement at Auburn, New York.

The most distinguished fugitive who escaped from slavery was Frederick Douglass, who secured a "sailor's protection," which certified that he was a free American sailor. Armed with this on Monday, September 3, 1838, he boarded the train at Baltimore and rode directly to New York City. From there he went into New Bedford, where he found refuge in the home of a coloured man by the name of Nathan Johnson. After Frederick Douglass went to live in Rochester, New York, his home there became one of the principal stations of the "Underground Railroad," which ran from New York City through Albany to the Great Lakes and Canada.

He has told, in his autobiography, the manner in which fugitives were brought to his home, concealed there, and then hurried on to the little town of Charlotte, seven miles from Rochester, and there placed on board a little lake steamer en route for Canada.

"On one occasion," he said, "I had eleven

fugitives at the same time under my roof. And it was necessary for them to remain with me until I could collect sufficient money to get them on to Canada.

"But," he added, "it is due to the truth to state that we seldom called in vain upon a Whig or a Democrat for help. Men were better than their theology and truer to humanity than to their politics or their offices."

He refers here to the fact that at one time, when a master was in the office of a United States Commissioner, getting the papers necessary for the arrest of three young men who had escaped from slavery in Maryland, the law-partner of the commissioner, a distinguished Democrat, sought him out, told him what was going on in his office, and urged him by all means to get these young men out of the way of pursuit.

In Syracuse, New York, there was another station of the "Underground Railroad," conducted by another fugitive slave. This was the Rev. J. W. Loguen, afterward a bishop of the A. M. E. Zion Church. "Jarm" Loguen, as he was called, was born a slave in Kentucky. His mother came of free parents in Ohio, but was kidnapped and sold in Kentucky when she was a child. She seems to have been a woman of great sense and character, and after her son grew up he inherited from her, apparently, a determination to be free.

He and another young man made their escape on horseback. They reached the Ohio River, crossed the ice, and finally, after a long series of adventures, during which they spent some time with the Indians, and passed several weeks in a settlement of fugitive slaves in Indiana, crossed the river at Detroit into Canada. They remained for some time on British soil, but Loguen finally returned to the United States and settled in Northern New York.

Although he had no education when he left Kentucky, young Loguen was industrious, thrifty, and succeeded in making money. He used the first money he accumulated to secure for himself an education at the Oneida Institute, Whitesboro, New York, a school started for coloured children by the noted Abolitionist, Beriah Green. Afterward, he went to Syracuse to live and interested himself, as a minister and anti-slavery leader, in the welfare of the coloured people of that city. It was while he was there that the famous "Jerry Rescue" took place, in which some of the citizens stormed the United States Commissioner's Office and forcibly carried off a fugitive named Jerry, who had been arrested under the recently enacted Fugitive Slave Law. At this time, Syracuse was the home of Samuel J. May and Gerrit Smith, and this first case under the Fugitive Slave Law was at once a defiance and a test of the abolitionist temper of the people of that city.

Though thousands of fugitive slaves succeeded in making their escape by routes that led from the South through Pennsylvania and New York, and also through New England, by far the larger number of the fugitives passed through the State of Ohio. In all the little coloured settlements in Ohio, Indiana, and Illinois, and in the larger cities like Cincinnati, there were men who were known to be fugitive slaves. Some of these men were slowly paying for their freedom from their earnings in the free states. In his life of Salmon P. Chase, Prof. Albert Bushnell Hart, of Harvard University, refers to a theological student who was known to have provided for his education "from the instalments thus paid by a man for his own flesh, and to have charged the poor Negro twelve per cent. on deferred payment." As further illustration of the number and variety of these cases, he mentions a Negro child in a charitable school who excused her absence with the explanation, "I am staying at home to help buy father."

After the passage of the Fugitive Slave Law, September 26, 1850, large numbers of these fugitive slaves living in Ohio became frightened for fear that they were to be sent back into slavery and fled into Canada. At that time, J. C. Brown, a free man who had paid $1,800 for his freedom, organised a colonisation society for the purpose of inducing coloured people to leave the State of Ohio and settle in Canada.

"At this time," says Mr. Brown, "Cincinnati was full of women, without husbands, and their children. These were sent by planters from Louisiana, Mississippi, and some from Tennessee, who had got fortunes and had found that white women could live in those states, and in consequence, they had sent their slave wives and children to Cincinnati and set them free."

These people were now, of course, in a state of terror and their former masters were of course anxious to get them upon free soil where there would be no doubt of their security. It was at this time that a number of refugees in different parts of Canada, sprang up. Under Mr. Brown's direction, four hundred and sixty people were settled in the township of Biddulph, near Little York. These were joined afterward by fifteen families from Boston, Mass. They purchased twelve hundred and twenty acres which were divided into tracts of from twenty-five to fifty acres to a family.

One of the most romantic of the fugitive slave stories is that of William and Ellen Craft. William Craft was a slave on a plantation near Macon, Georgia. He had learned the trade of cabinet-maker and had become so proficient in that craft that, in addition to his daily work for his master, he had been able to earn a considerable sum of money for himself by work performed in his leisure moments. William Craft was a black man, but on this same plantation there was another slave, a young woman, who was almost white. They became acquainted with each other and after a time they were married. They had not lived together very long before the fear that they might at some time be sold and thus parted from one another, made them think about the possibilities of escape from slavery. After studying over the matter for some time, William Craft hit upon a plan.

There were always white people in the slavery times who were willing for the sake of a little money to carry on a secret traffic with the slaves. From one of these white men he secured a suit of men's clothing that would fit his wife. He had the suit made in the latest fashion in order to make the disguise as complete as possible. He secured shoes, hat, neckties, all the other pieces of wearing apparel necessary to complete the wardrobe of a wealthy young planter. In this disguise, Ellen Craft, having secured a permit from her mistress for a visit of a few days to a neighbouring plantation, took the train at Macon for Savannah. The husband, William, having secured a similar permit for himself, boarded the same train and, passing himself off as the Negro servant of his wife, they made the journey out of slavery into freedom together.

At Savannah they took the boat for Charleston.

From Charleston they went to Wilmington, North Carolina, and from there took the train to Philadelphia. They had a great many curious and exciting adventures on the way. The young "planter" who, in order to more fully disguise herself, had tied a bandage around her head, as if she had a toothache, seemed to arouse the interest and sympathy of a number of people, who gave her advice how to keep her Negro servant from running away from her when she reached free soil. Both at Savannah, when they were boarding the boat, and at Wilmington, when they were taking the train to the North, they found it was the rule to require passengers to register their names. As neither of them could read and write, Ellen Craft had put her right hand in a poultice and supported it with a sling about her neck, pretending that she was suffering from rheumatism. Even then, it was with the greatest difficulty that she was able to persuade the agents of the steamship and railway companies to sign her name for her. At length, however, they reached Philadelphia in safety and for several days found refuge in the home of philanthropic Quakers in that city. From there, they went to Boston, where William Craft secured employment at his trade as cabinet-maker.

They had left their home in Macon in 1848. Two years later the Fugitive Slave Law was passed and a determined effort was made by many Southern slave-holders to get possession of their runaway slaves, who were living in freedom in many parts of the North. It was not long before such an effort was made to get possession of the two fugitives from Macon. For some months they lived in daily apprehension of being seized and carried away. Finally, upon learning that a warrant had been issued for their arrest, some of their anti-slavery friends smuggled them aboard one of the ships leaving Boston for England. Arriving in Liverpool they went directly to friends in London. Shortly after their arrival there they went to live in the town of Hammersmith, not far from London, which was their home for a number of years. William Craft secured employment in the African trade, and took several ship-loads of merchandise out to Africa where he was able to dispose of them with special advantage because he was of the same colour and race as the people with whom he sought to trade.

After emancipation and the Civil War had made it possible for them to return to the country of their birth, William and Ellen Craft came back to Boston and lived for several years in Cambridge, Massachusetts, where their children were educated. While they were in England several children were born to them, one of them, William, is still living there. Another has since become the wife of Dr. W. D. Crum, who was collector of customs at

Charleston, South Carolina, under President Roosevelt. A grandson of William and Ellen Craft, Henry K. Craft, who was graduated from Harvard University in 1908, is, at the time this is written, in charge of the electrical plant and the teaching of Electrical Engineering at Tuskegee Institute. William and Ellen Craft finally returned to Georgia and passed their last days in a comfortable home not far from Savannah.

Directly and indirectly, the fugitive slaves probably did more to bring about the abolition of slavery than any other one agency. The Northern people learned from the lips of these fugitives — from the strange, romantic, pathetic, and tragic stories they told — that the slaves, no matter how ignorant or how different in colour or condition they might seem, were very much the same kind of human beings as themselves. They learned from the sufferings of these fugitives, from the desperate efforts which they made to escape, that no matter what might be said to the contrary the slaves wanted to be free.

At the same time, the fugitive slaves learned in the United States, in their very efforts to be free, something about the nature of freedom that they could not have learned in Africa. Slavery, however hard or cruel it might be, appeared to the native African, as it did to the Greek and Roman, to be the natural condition of the majority of men. It was only after the African slaves learned the language of their masters and possessed themselves to some extent of their masters' ideas that they began to conceive that the natural condition of man was not slavery but freedom.

When the fugitive slaves came in contact with the anti-slavery people of the North they made the acquaintance for the first time of a people who hated slavery in a way and with an intensity which few of them had ever felt or known. They learned from these anti-slavery people to believe in freedom for its own sake, not only for themselves but for every one. They were transformed in this way from fugitive slaves to abolitionists. They became, as a result, the most determined of anti-slavery people, and many of them devoted their lives most unselfishly to securing the freedom of other members of their race.

In 1860 it was estimated that the number of Negroes that journeyed annually from Canada to the slave states to rescue their fellows from bondage was about five hundred. These persons carried the Underground Railroad and the Underground Telegraph into nearly every Southern state. *

* "The Underground Railroad," Siebert, p. 28.

CHAPTER XII

NEGRO SETTLEMENTS IN OHIO AND THE NORTHWEST TERRITORY

A FEW miles west of Xenia, Ohio, is a quiet little community of which one occasionally sees the name in the newspapers, but in regard to which very little is known by the outside world, even among its immediate neighbours. This is the Negro town of Wilberforce, which is, however, not a town in the ordinary sense of the word, but rather a suburb of Xenia, from which it is distant an hour's walk and with which it is connected only by stage.

What distinguishes Wilberforce from other communities in the North is the fact that it is the home of what is, so far as I know, the first permanent Negro institution of learning established for Negroes and by Negroes in the United States. A few years ago, I visited this community in order to take part in the semi-centennial celebration of the founding of the University there. During my visit I was especially impressed with the quiet charm of the surroundings, the comfort and simplicity of the homes I visited, and the general air of culture and refinement which pervaded the whole community. I doubt if there is any Negro community in the United States in which, in proportion to the population, there is so large a number of beautiful and well-conducted homes. Besides that, there was an air of permanence and stability about this community which one does not meet elsewhere, even in the quiet and orderly suburbs that one frequently finds in the neighbourhood of a good Negro school. Here, at any rate, it seemed to me, a certain number of coloured people had found themselves, had made a permanent settlement on the soil and were at home.

The history of Wilberforce goes back to a time before the War. In its origin, this is representative of a number of other Negro communities that were established in different parts of Ohio during that period. Most of these communities have disappeared and been forgotten, but there are many coloured people in all parts of the Northern states who trace their history back to one or another of these little Negro settlements that were started partly by fugitive slaves and partly by free coloured people, who left the South in order to find a home in the free soil of the Northwest Territory.

The thing that gives a peculiar and interesting character to many of these ante-bellum Negro settlements is that they were made by Southern slave-holders who desired to free their slaves and were not able to do so under the restrictions that were imposed upon emancipation in the Southern States. Many of the coloured people in these settlements were the natural children of their master. For example, John M. Langston, the first coloured man to represent Virginia in the Congress of the United States, was freed by the terms of his father's will, in 1834. In his autobiography, he has given a vivid description of the manner in which he, in company with the other slaves who had been freed at his father's death, made a long journey across the mountains from Louisa County, Virginia, to Chillicothe, Ohio. Before his election to Congress from Virginia, Mr. Langston graduated in 1849 from Oberlin University, had been admitted to the bar of Ohio in 1854, and elected clerk of several Ohio townships. He was the first coloured man in Ohio, it is said, to be elected to any sort of office by popular vote.

When John Randolph, of Roanoke, Virginia, died, he gave freedom to all his slaves and provided that they should be transported to some other part of the country, "where not less than two thousand and not more than four thousand acres of land should be purchased for them." The Randolph Freedmen went to Ohio with the purpose of settling in Mercer County, but they were not allowed to enter upon the land which had been purchased for them, because the German settlers in that part of the country did not want them there. The community was soon after scattered, but descendants of the Randolph slaves are still living in the neighbourhood of Piqua and Troy, in Miami County, Ohio. The most noted of them, as I have learned, is Goodrich Giles, whose father was a member of the original immigrants. Mr. Giles now owns four hundred and twenty-five acres of land just out of Piqua. He is said to be worth something over $50,000. Two years ago, a sort of family reunion of the descendants of the Randolph slaves was held in Ohio, and, as a result of the gathering, an organisation was formed among a few of the descendants for the purpose of investigating their claims to the land in Mercer County which was purchased for them under the terms of John Randolph's will, but of which they never secured possession.

The little community at Wilberforce grew out of a similar effort of a number of Southern planters to secure a foothold in a free state for their former slaves. In 1856 there was already a considerable number of the free Negroes settled at what was then known as Tawawa Springs. In that year it was decided to establish at this place a school for these coloured immigrants and refugees. At the time of the breaking out of the War this school had nearly one hundred pupils. Many of them were the coloured children of the white planters who had been sent North to be educated. With the breaking out of the Civil War, however, the support this school received from its Southern patrons ceased. The institution soon fell into decay and, in March, 1863, it was sold for a debt of ten thousand dollars to the African Methodist Episcopal Church. This was the origin of Wilberforce.

Of the little colony of Negro refugees who settled in this neighbourhood before 1861, there still remain a few families. The memories of others are preserved in the names of some of their descendants who occupy farms in the neighbourhood. But the community has continued to grow. A few farmers, attracted by the advantages of the University, have purchased farms in the neighbourhood; a few former students, who have made a success elsewhere, have gone back there to make their home. The rest of the community is made up of the officers of the school and their families, together with some four hundred students.

One thing that has given character to this little town, and made it attractive as a residence for Negroes, is the number of distinguished men of the Negro race who have lived and worked there. Among others whose memories are still preserved there is Bishop Daniel A. Payne, who was, more than any one else, responsible for the existence of the colony. He lived there for many years until he died in 1892. Bishop Benjamin W. Arnett, who was a real force in Ohio affairs during his connection with Wilberforce, lived in this community for thirty-five years. It is said that he was the first coloured man in the United States to represent a constituency where the majority were white, and the first to be foreman of a jury where all the other members were white. As member from Green County to the Ohio Legislature in 1886 and 1887, he was largely responsible for the repeal of the remnant of what were known as the "Black Laws."

Much was said during the anti-slavery agitation of the efforts of the Southern Church to justify African slavery. There was, in fact, a very serious attempt to find justification in the Bible for slavery, but any one who will study the history of Christianity in the South and its influence upon slavery cannot fail to see that, in spite of all that was said by individual preachers and in spite of all that was done by church organisations, there was always a large number of white slave-holders in the South who felt deep down in their hearts that slavery was wrong. In his will, written in 1819, John Randolph says: "I give my slaves their freedom, to which my conscience tells me they are justly entitled. It has long been a matter of deepest regret to me that the circumstances under which I inherited them and the obstacles thrown in the way by the laws of the land have prevented me in emancipating them in my lifetime, which it is my full intention to do in case I can accomplish it."

These words pretty well express the deepest sentiment of a great many people who held slaves before the Civil War, but owing to the obstacles thrown in the way of emancipation, did not go so far as John Randolph and actually free their slaves. I have often thought that the peculiar interest which former slave-holders have manifested in their former slaves was due to this feeling that they had a special responsibility toward these people whom they had held at one time under conditions which their consciences could not entirely justify.

As a matter of fact, the whole character of the anti-slavery campaign in Ohio differed from the anti-slavery movements in New York and in New England from the fact that so large a number of the people who were engaged in the movement in Ohio were either themselves men who had moved into a free territory in order to free their slaves, or they were the descendants of people who had been slave-holders.

Benjamin Lundy, the man who first interested William Lloyd Garrison in the subject of abolition, was a Southerner who had emigrated from Virginia to Ohio, and started his first paper, *The Genius of Universal Emancipation*, at Mount Pleasant,

Ohio, a little Quaker settlement. James G. Birney, who, while he lived at Huntsville, Alabama, was a member of the American Colonisation Society, finally freed his slaves and moved with them to Cincinnati, where he became the leader in the anti-slavery movement of Ohio. Dr. John Rankin, the famous pastor of Ripley, Ohio, whose house, standing on a hill, and visible from the Kentucky shores, was descended from the Southern abolitionists of East Tennessee. Among the fugitives who took refuge in Dr. Rankin's house was the original of Eliza Harris, the character in "Uncle Tom's Cabin," who crossed the Ohio River on the drifting ice with her child, and was sheltered for several days at this house on the hill.

Another Southerner who became a prominent abolitionist was the famous Levi Coffin, the Quaker, representative of a large number of Quakers who left North Carolina at various times before the Civil War because they had grown to feel that slavery was wrong. Levi Coffin was the man who bore the title of President of the Underground Railroad, and in his reminiscences he has told stories of hundreds of fugitives, whom he aided to escape from bondage. It is said that he aided no less than two thousand fugitives to make their way through Ohio to Canada. Quakers coming from North Carolina settled in an early day near Steubenville, and in a little town called Smithfield there still live descendants of the Negro colonists from North Carolina settled there by Quaker masters.

Not only in Ohio, but in Indiana and in Michigan there were scattered settlements of free Negroes, many of whom had been sent thither by the Quakers of North Carolina. In Hamilton County, Indiana, a family named Roberts settled on about a thousand acres of land in Jackson Township. These were joined, afterward, by other families, until there was a considerable settlement there, which finally gained the name of Robert's Settlement. There was another settlement very much like this, in Randolph, and still another in Wayne County.

A recent investigator says:

> It is not generally known that in the North there are thousands of acres of land to which no individual white man has ever held title; the only title under the Government of the United States has been in the name of Negroes. But this is a fact and a large part of these lands exist in Indiana. In Jackson Township, Hamilton County, the Roberts family entered 960 acres of land between 1835 and 1838, and during the lifetime of its original holders, added several hundred acres more to it, all of which was unimproved. In 1907, about 700 acres of the original 960 acres were owned by Negroes and 627 acres besides, making a total of 1,327, the larger part of which is now under cultivation. In Randolph County 2,000 were entered between 1822 and 1845 by a dozen different Negro immigrants, chiefly from North Carolina. In Grant County was what is known as the Weaver Settlement. In Vigo County, before 1840, the holdings of Negroes amounted to 4,000, in this settlement, one man, Dixon Stewart, having acquired more than 600 acres.*

* *Southern Workman*, March, 1908; "Rural Communities in Indiana," Richard R. Wright, Jr., pp. 165, 166.

The interesting thing about these settlements scattered throughout the Northwest Territory is, as I have suggested, that they represented to a very large extent the efforts of the Southern people to bring about the emancipation of their own slaves. This is particularly true in the case of the Quakers. Early in the eighteenth century the Quakers began to consider the question of sinfulness of holding other members of the human race in the condition of servitude. As early as 1688, a small body of German Quakers of Germantown, Pennsylvania, presented a protest to the Yearly Meeting against the "buying, selling, and holding of men in slavery," and in 1696, the Yearly Meeting, although not yet prepared to take action, sent out the advice that "the members should discourage the introduction of slaves and be careful of the moral and intellectual training of such as they held in servitude." From 1746 to 1767 the Quaker, John Woolman, of New Jersey, travelled through the Middle and Southern states teaching that "the practice of continuing slavery is not right." And that "liberty is the natural light of all men equally." *

The minutes of the various Yearly Meetings of the Quaker societies show a steady progress in respect to the sentiment in regard to slave-holding, and in 1776 the Eastern Quarterly Meeting of the

---

* "Rise and Fall of the Slave Power in America," Henry Wilson, vol. i, pp. 8–10.

North Carolina Yearly Meeting advised Friends to manumit their slaves. Friends were prohibited from importing, buying, or selling slaves, and in 1780 they were prohibited by the Yearly Meeting from hiring them. In 1818, it is recorded regarding slaves that "none held them."

But under the laws as they then existed, it was not without considerable difficulty that Friends, who desired to emancipate their slaves, were permitted to do so. In order to evade this law it became the custom of Friends to confer upon their slaves practical emancipation, allowing them to hire themselves out and use for themselves the money they earned, although their masters still exercised a nominal control over them. In 1817, a case came before the court in which William Dickinson conveyed a slave to the trustees of the Quaker Society of Contentnea to be held in a kind of guardianship until he could be manumitted under the laws of the state. When this case came before the Supreme Court of North Carolina, Chief Justice Taylor declared that this practice of the Quakers was emancipation in everything but name, and therefore contrary to the law. A few years later another case occurred in which Collier Hill left his slaves to four trustees, one of whom was "Richard Graves of the Methodist Church," with the injunction to keep the slaves for such purposes as "they, the trustees, could judge most for the glory of God, and the good of the said slaves." The court held that, as it did not appear that "any personal benefit to the legatees," was intended, the will "was held to constitute them trustees for the purpose of emancipation and that such a purpose was illegal."

It was the difficulties which Southern slave-holders who wanted to ameliorate the condition of their slaves encountered when they undertook to assist their servants to freedom that led the Quakers and so many other Southern people, to found the settlements I have referred to in Ohio and elsewhere in the Northwest Territory.

In the early years of the Colonisation Movement the Quakers, with other Southern abolitionists, had supported the Colonisation Society, believing that that was one method of solving the problem. But, as experience proved that that was a wholly inadequate remedy, and as many of the coloured people did not desire to leave the country in which they had been born and bred, people who desired to free their slaves were more and more induced to send them to the Northwest Territory.

In 1835, the Pennsylvania Young Men's Society, a Quaker organisation, interested themselves in promoting the emigration of free coloured people to Africa. They looked at the matter in a very practical way and sent out twenty-six Negro colonists, all of whom were proficient in the trades.

The emigrants were blacksmiths, carpenters, potters, brickmakers, shoemakers, and tailors. Altogether one hundred and twenty-six emigrants were sent out in this way, and these established themselves at Port Cresson, on the coast of what is now Liberia. These Negro colonists were, however, to such an extent under the influence of the Quaker doctrine that, when they were attacked by the native chiefs, the head of the colony refused to resort to arms. The result was that eighteen of the colonists were killed, the houses were all destroyed and those who were not killed were obliged to flee for their lives.*

Some time in the early part of the last century a number of Quakers, who were dissatisfied with conditions in the Southern states, moved from North Carolina to Cass County, Michigan. They brought with them a number of their former slaves. And these made the nucleus for a settlement of free Negroes which was constantly recruited by fugitives from the other side of the Ohio River. In 1847, this Quaker settlement had become so notorious as a refuge for fugitive slaves that a determined effort was made on the part of some of the slave-holders to recapture their runaways. A number of slave-holders, or their representatives, mounted and well-armed, crossed the Ohio River in that year and, riding across the intervening states, made

* "Liberia," Sir Harry Johnston, Vol. I, p. 155.

a bold and determined effort to regain possession of their property. The effort to recapture the fugitives was successfully resisted by the Quakers, coloured people, and the other residents of the community, and the only result was to advertise Cass County, Michigan, as a place where Negroes might live with a reasonable freedom from capture by their former masters. After the raid a still larger number of fugitives poured into the county, the majority of them settling in Calvin Township.

In 1847, the same year in which the Negro communities in Cass County were raided, a large slave holder by the name of Saunders, who lived in Cabell County, Virginia — now part of West Virginia — died, and when his will was opened it was found that he had not only freed all his slaves but had made a generous provision for the purchase of a tract of land in some free State to be divided among these people. The Saunders ex-slaves, forty-one in number, started northward in 1849 and, after a long journey, attended by many hardships, they finally reached Calvin Township, Cass County, Michigan, a few days before Christmas.

Sometime in the latter part of 1902, or the early part of 1903, I visited Cass County and had an opportunity to study, at first hand, the success which the descendants of these Saunders ex-slaves and the other fugitives had made in that county. At this time, I found that Calvin Township contained a population of 759 Negroes and 512 whites. In addition to these a large Negro population had overflowed into the adjoining county of Porter, and to some extent all but two of the towns in the county. Among the men I met there at that time was a farmer by the name of Samuel Hawkes, who, I was informed, on good authority, was worth something like $50,000. Another farmer whose name I recall was William Allen. He was born in Logan County, Ohio, but his parents were among that numerous class of free coloured people who moved from North Carolina to the free soil, in order to preserve their freedom. When I visited his farm, I found he had fifty head of cattle, ten horses, three hundred sheep, and twenty-five hogs. He had paid taxes during the previous year to the amount of $191.00, on property in the two townships of Porter and Calvin. He had been a justice of the peace for eighteen years, but resigned that office, because, as he said, "it took too much time away from the farm."

One of the supervisors of Calvin Township was a farmer by the name of Cornelius Lawson. Of the eight schools in Calvin, four of them were taught by coloured teachers. As we drove through the township, I discovered, posted up beside the road, a notice of the annual school meeting. It was signed by C. F. Northrup, director. Mr. Northrup, as I was informed, is a Negro.

Among other things which attracted my attention during my visit was the existence in Calvin of the Grand Army Post, named after Matthew Artis, who was one of the large number of coloured soldiers who enlisted from this township during the War. The commander of the Post at the time of my visit was Bishop Curtis, who was a member of the 54th Massachusetts Regiment, took part in the attack on Fort Wagner and, it is said, was shot with a fragment of the same shell which killed his commander, Robert Gould Shaw.

At the present time, Negroes hold the offices of supervisor, clerk, road commissioner, and school director in the township of Calvin. There are two highway commissioners, two justices of the peace, two constables, two members of the Board of Review, who are Negroes. None of these men, I may add, are professional politicians, and none of them were elected because of their colour. In fact, as near as I could learn, there is no question of colour, but merely of fitness for the duties of offices in the politics of Cass County.

In a recent study of this township, under the title of "Negro Governments in the North," Richard R. Wright, Jr., says:

The Negroes, who make up the township, are, as a rule, landowners. There are one hundred and sixty-three Negroes on the tax books; they own 8,853.73 acres of land, assessed at $224,062, and with a market value possibly of $400,000. Some of these were included among the land-owners mentioned having property in other townships and counties also; and some own city property. The wealthiest of them owns about 800 acres in all, several pieces of city property, and has personal property amounting to more than $18,000. Several families are reported to be worth from $50,000 to $100,000 and one to be worth more than $150,000.

I have stated the facts in regard to this Negro colony in Cass County at some length because they illustrate what has gone on in a number of other similar colonies in Ohio and neighbouring states. They show, at any rate, the efforts of those Southern people, who sought to give to their slaves the advantage of freedom, were not entirely in vain.

The history of these efforts of Southern white people and the Southern Negroes to lessen, to some extent, the evils of slavery by emigration to the free soil of the Northwest Territory, seems to me one of the most important chapters in the Story of the Negro. It should not be forgotten in this connection that Abraham Lincoln was himself born in the South and that many, if not most of the leaders of the abolition movement in Ohio and Indiana, were in full sympathy with that portion of the Southern people who wanted to do away with slavery. They represented the heart and conscience of thousands of others whose voices were drowned in the factional political strife which grew up as a result of the anti-slavery agitation.

I feel a peculiar interest in the work of those men because I believe that the men in the South, who quietly, earnestly, and unostentatiously are seeking to better conditions in the South to-day, are, in a certain sense, the direct descendants of those Southern anti-slavery people of Ohio and the Middle West. At any rate, they are following in the traditions and working in the spirit of these earlier men.

CHAPTER XIII

THE NEGRO PREACHER AND THE NEGRO CHURCH

ONE of the interesting documents relating to the early history of the Negro in the United States is a paper, written in the quaint, old-fashioned style of a hundred years ago, and entitled: "Narrative of the Proceedings of the Coloured People During the Awful Calamity in Philadelphia, in the Year 1793; and a Refutation of Some of the Censures Thrown Upon Them in Some Publications."

In the year 1792 and 1793, Philadelphia was stricken with a sort of plague. Hundreds of people died and hundreds more left the city, frequently leaving the dead unburied in the houses. It was believed at this time that Negroes were exempt from this epidemic and a call was made upon them to act as nurses and to assist in burying the dead. After the epidemic was over the terror-stricken inhabitants returned again to the city and the charge was made that the coloured people, who had acted as nurses, had demanded exorbitant prices for their services. The narrative to which I have referred is an answer to that charge. In this account of the epidemic, the authors tell how they were induced to take up this work, not because of any reward for themselves, but in answer to an appeal to the coloured people to come forward and assist "the distressed, perishing, and neglected sick."

The narrative goes on to describe the distress which the plague brought on the city; it relates in detail a number of instances of the heroism of Negro nurses during the period when the city was in a condition of panic fear; and concludes with a full account of the way in which the monies, which came into their hands, were expended. From this report it appears that one hundred and seventy-seven pounds, of the four hundred and eleven expended, was contributed from their own pockets, not counting, as the report adds, "the cost of hearses, and maintenance of our families for seventy days, and the support of five hired men during the respective times of their being employed; which expenses, together with sundry gifts we occasionally made to poor families, might reasonably and properly be introduced to show our actual situation in regard to profit."

This narrative of the plague in Philadelphia and of the services of the coloured people to the citizens during this trying period is the more interesting because one of the authors of this account, Richard Allen, was the founder and first Bishop of the African Methodist Church and the other, Absalom Jones, established the First African Church of St. Thomas, which is sometimes called the first Negro church in

America, although it is probable that there were several churches in some of the Southern states which were earlier in origin.

Both Allen and Jones, who were the leaders of the coloured people of Philadelphia at that time, had been slaves and both had purchased their freedom. Richard Allen was born February 14, 1760, a slave to Benjamin Chew, of Philadelphia. He was afterward sold with his father and mother, and his three brothers and sisters, to a man by the name of Stokeley, in Delaware. Of his master Richard Allen says, in his autobiography, "He was more like a father to his slaves than anything else."

After he purchased his freedom, Allen became an itinerant preacher, working, meanwhile, as a common labourer at whatever he could get to do. During the Revolution he was employed as a teamster hauling salt. He had his regular places of stopping along the road, where he would preach to whoever were willing to come together to listen to him. In 1784, he attended the General Conference, at Baltimore, Maryland, which was the first General Conference of the Methodist Church in America, and in 1786 he came to Philadelphia, Pennsylvania. About this time, because of the influx from the country, the coloured population of Philadelphia was increasing rapidly and the white congregation of St. George's Church, where they attended, determined to force them into the galleries. Allen had already made a move in the direction of a separate church, so that the coloured people were already prepared, to some extent, for secession. The crisis was reached one Sunday morning when the attempt was made to move Jones and Allen from their accustomed places in the body of the church into the gallery, whereupon they and their followers rebelled and walked out. On April 17, 1787, the coloured portion of this congregation formed, under the leadership of Allen and Jones, what was known as the Free African Society. The preamble of the articles of association, upon which this society was founded, is interesting as showing the thoughts which were stirring in the minds of the leaders of the coloured people at that time. The preamble is as follows:

> Whereas, Absalom Jones and Richard Allen, two men of the African Race who, for their religious life and conversation, have obtained a good report among men, these persons from a love of the people of their own complexion whom they beheld with sorrow, because of their irreligious and uncivilised state, often communed together upon this painful and important subject in order to form some kind of religious body; but there being too few to be found under the like concern, and those who were, differed in their religious sentiments; with these circumstances they laboured for some time, till it was proposed after a serious communication of sentiments that a society should be formed without regard to religious tenets, provided the persons live an orderly and sober life, in order to support one another in sickness, and for the benefit of their widows and fatherless children.

The Free African Society prepared the way for the African Methodist Episcopal Church, which may be said to have come into existence four years later, in 1790, when Allen and a few followers withdrew from the Free African Society and started an Independent Methodist Church. Allen's congregation worshipped at first in a blacksmith shop on Sixth, near Lombard Street. The other members of the society then became members of the Episcopal Church under the leadership of Jones and, in 1794, built St. Thomas Church, at the corner of Fifth and Philadelphia streets.

The little society maintained by Allen in the blacksmith shop grew rapidly in membership. Some time in 1794, also, Bethel Church was erected by Allen and his followers. About this same time the coloured people withdrew from the white congregations in Baltimore and New York, and in 1816 a conference was held at the Bethel Church in Philadelphia, which resulted in the establishment of the African Methodist Episcopal Church, with Richard Allen as first Bishop.

Six years after Allen withdrew from the Free African Society in Philadelphia, coloured members of the Methodist Episcopal Church in New York decided to hold separate meetings, in which they "might have an opportunity to exercise their spiritual gifts among themselves, and thereby be more useful to one another." They erected a church, which was dedicated in 1800, and to which they gave the name, African Methodist

Episcopal Zion. This congregation formed the nucleus of what is now known as the "Zion" Methodist connection. From 1801 to 1820 this organisation was under the pastoral supervision of the Methodist Episcopal Church, but during that time it had its own preachers. In 1820 this arrangement was terminated and a union of coloured Methodist congregations in New York, New Haven, Long Island, and Philadelphia was formed. These churches together became the African Methodist Episcopal Zion Connection.

Directly after the War the two coloured branches of the Methodist Church invaded the Southern states. At that time, there were 207,742 coloured members of the Methodist Church, South. Within a few years, much the larger proportion of the coloured members of the Southern Methodist Church joined either one or the other of the African Methodist connections so that in 1866 the Methodist Church, South, had only 78,742 coloured members. In that year, the Church authorised these coloured members, with their preachers, to organise separate congregations, and in 1870 two Bishops were appointed to organise the coloured conferences into a separate and independent church. This new connection took the name of the Coloured Methodist Episcopal Church.

In 1908, representatives of the three coloured Methodist connections met in the First Council of the

United Board of Bishops. This council met in Washington, D. C. Its purpose was to bring the three more important organisations among the coloured Methodists into closer working relations with each other, in the hope that eventually a compact organisation might be formed which would unite in one body more than 13,000 churches and over 1,500,000 communicants.

The Negro seems, from the beginning, to have been very closely associated with the Methodist Church in the United States. When the Reverend Thomas Coke was ordained by John Wesley as Superintendent or Bishop of the American Society in 1784, he was accompanied on most of his travels throughout the United States by Harry Hosier, a coloured minister who was at the same time the Bishop's servant and an evangelist of the Church. Harry Hosier, who was the first American Negro preacher of the Methodist Church in the United States, was one of the notable characters of his day. He could not read or write, but he was pronounced by Dr. Benjamin Rush the greatest orator in America. He travelled extensively through the New England and Southern states and shared the pulpits of the white ministers whom he accompanied. But he seems to have excelled them all in popularity as a preacher.

It is said that on one occasion, in Wilmington, Delaware, where Methodism early became popular, a number of citizens, who did not ordinarily attend the Methodist Church, came together to hear Bishop Asbury. The church was so crowded that they were not able to get in, so they stood outside and listened, as they supposed, to the Bishop, but in reality they heard Harry Hosier. They were greatly impressed, and before leaving, one of them was heard to remark that "if all Methodist preachers could preach like the Bishop, more of us would like to hear him." Some one replied that "that was not the Bishop, but his servant." This served to raise the Bishop still higher in their estimation, for they concluded, if the servant was so eloquent what must the master be.* Harry Hosier remained popular as a preacher to the last. Francis Asbury, Associate-bishop, stated that the best way to get a large congregation was to announce that Harry was going to preach. He died in Philadelphia in 1810.

From the first the Methodist Church was strongly anti-slavery although the sentiment against slavery was always stronger in the North than in the South. The struggle which led to the separation of the Southern and Northern churches, in 1844, was brought about because of the censure voted against Bishop Andrew for having married in Georgia a woman who owned slaves. But even after the separation, the Southern organisation maintained, at least formally,

* Stevens's "History of the M. E. Church," pp. 174, 175. Quoted in Williams's "History of the Negro Race in America," p. 467, vol. ii.

its protest against slavery. The first edition of its discipline, in 1846, declared:

> That we are as much as ever convinced of the great evil of slavery. Therefore, no slave-holder shall be eligible to any official position in our Church hereafter, where the laws of the state in which he lives will admit of emancipation and permit the liberated slaves to enjoy freedom. When any travelling preacher becomes an owner of a slave or slaves, by any means, he shall forfeit his ministerial character in our Church, unless he executes, if it be practicable, a legal emancipation of such slaves, conformable to the laws of the state in which he lives.*

Methodism had started in England among the poor and the outcast; it was natural, therefore, that when its missionaries came to America they should seek to bring into the Church the outcast and neglected people, and especially the slaves. In some parts of the South the Methodist meeting-houses were referred to by the more aristocratic denominations as "the Negro churches." This was due to the fact that the Methodists often began their work in a community with an appeal to the slaves.

Methodism began in the early part of the nineteenth century in Wilmington, North Carolina, in this way. A Methodist preacher by the name of William Meredith began his work among the slaves. Through the penny collections which he took from the black people and the scanty contributions of the poor whites, he purchased a lot and completed a building. Bishop Francis Asbury visited the church

*"Slavery in the State of North Carolina." Johns Hopkins University Studies, John Spencer Bassett, p. 55.

in 1807, and John Charles, a coloured preacher, delivered a sermon in the same church at sunrise the same day.*

The Methodist Church in Fayetteville, North Carolina, was started earlier than that at Wilmington, but in much the same way. The story of the founding of that church is told in some detail in Bassett's History of Slavery in North Carolina. The author says:

> Late in the eighteenth century, Fayetteville had but one church organisation, the Presbyterian, and that had no building. One day there arrived in town Henry Evans, a full-blooded free Negro from Virginia, who was moving to Charleston, South Carolina, where he proposed to follow the trade of shoemaking. He was, perhaps, free-born; he was a Methodist and a licensed local preacher. In Fayetteville, he observed that the coloured people "were wholly given to profanity and lewdness, never hearing preaching of any denomination." He felt it his duty to stop and work among them. He worked at his trade during the week and preached on Sunday. The whites became alarmed and the Town Council ordered him to stop preaching. He then met his flock in the "sand hills," desolate places out of the jurisdiction of the Town Council. Fearing violence, he made his meetings secret and changed the place of meeting from Sunday to Sunday. He was particular to violate no law, and to all the whites he showed the respect which their sense of cast superiority demanded. Public opinion began to change, especially when it was noticed that slaves who had come under his influence were more docile for it. Some prominent whites, most of whom were women, became interested in his cause. They attended his meetings and through their influence opinion was reversed. Then a rude frame building was erected within the town limits and a number of seats were reserved

* "Early Methodism in Wilmington," Dr. A. M. Chreitzberg, in the annual publication of the Historical Society of the North Carolina Conference, 1897, quoted in "Slavery in North Carolina," p. 57.

for the whites, some of whom became regular attendants at his services. The preacher's reputation spread. The white portion of the congregation increased till the Negroes were crowded out of their seats. Then the boards were knocked from the sides of the house and sheds were built on either hand and in these the blacks were seated. By this time the congregation, which had been unconnectional at first, had been taken into the regular Methodist connection and a regular white preacher had been sent to it. But the heroic founder was not displaced. A room was built for him in the rear of the pulpit, and there he lived till his death in 1810. . . . His last speech to his people is noteworthy. Directly after the morning sermon for the whites it was customary to have a sermon for the blacks. On the Sunday before Evans's death, as the latter meeting was being held, the door of his little shed room opened and he tottered forward. Leaning on the altar rail he said: "I have come to say my last word to you. It is this: None but Christ. Three times I have had my life in jeopardy for preaching the gospel to you. Three times I have broken the ice on the edge of the water and swam across the Cape Fear to preach the gospel to you, and if in my last hour I could trust to that, or anything but Christ crucified, for my salvation, all should be lost and my soul perish forever." Of these words Bishop Capers justly says that they were worthy of St. Paul.*

During the Colonial times the Baptists, to which denomination at the present time the majority of the Negroes in the United States belong, were a persecuted people, not only in New England but in Virginia. At that time this sect drew its followers very largely from the poorer people who did not own slaves, and it was therefore natural that its members should be opposed to slavery. The Baptist Church, however, did not, as did the Methodists, make an effort to draw the Negroes into the churches, but

* "Slavery in the State of North Carolina," pp. 57–59.

took care to bring under religious influence the slaves of their own members, and paid particular attention to the relations of the master and slave. In 1778, it was decided that a marriage between slaves ought to be respected, even though it was against the law of the land. In 1783 the Sandy Creek Association of North Carolina declared that a master should give his servants the liberty to attend family prayers in his house, that he should exhort them to attend, but not use force. Among the older coloured bishops and ministers, in both the Methodist and Baptist churches, there are a number who attribute their religious life to the influence and teachings which they received through this personal contact with their masters and masters' families.

John Jasper, the famous pastor of the Sixth Mount Zion Baptist Church, Richmond, Virginia, always spoke with the greatest reverence of his former master. The Reverend John Jasper was known as a preacher for sixty years in and about Richmond, twenty-five of which he was a slave. He became a national figure as a result of his efforts to prove by the Bible, that "the sun," as he put it, "do move." Recently, William E. Hatcher, a Southern white man, who knew Jasper for many years, admired him for his sincerity and valued him for the influence that he exercised over his people, has written the story of John Jasper's life. One of the interesting incidents related in this book is that of Jasper's conversion. At the time this took place he was a slave of Mr. Samuel Hargrove, and was employed as a tobacco stemmer in a tobacco factory in Richmond. One day he fell to shouting, while he was at work, and nearly started a revival in the tobacco factory. His master, hearing the uproar, called him into the office. Jasper explained what had come over him and that he really did not mean to make any noise. His own account of what then happened, which Mr. Hatcher has given in his own words, is as follows:

Mars' Sam was settin' wid his eyes a little down to de flo' an' wid a pritty quiv'r in his voice he say very slo': "John, I b'lieve dat way myself. I luv de Saviour dat you have jes' foun', now as you did." Den Mars' Sam did er thing dat nearly made me drop to de flo'. He git out of his chair, an' walk over to me an' giv' me his han', and he say: "John, I wish you mighty well. Your Saviour is mine, an' we are bruthers in de Lord." When he say dat, I turn 'round an' put my arm agin de wall, an' held my mouf to keep from shoutin'. Mars' Sam well know de good he du me.

Art'r awhile he say: "John, did you tell eny of 'em in thar 'bout your conversion?" And I say: 'Yes, Mars' Sam, I tell 'em fore I kno'd it, an' I feel like tellin' everybody in de worl' about it." Den he say: "John, you may tell it. Go back in dar an' go upstars an' tell 'em all 'bout it, an' den downstars an' tell de hogshed men an' de drivers an' eberybody what de Lord has dun for you."

By dis time Mars' Sam's face was rainin' tears, an' he say: "John, you needn' work no mo' to-day. I giv' you holiday. Art'r you git thru tellin' it here at de factory, go up to de house an' tell your folks; go 'round to your neighbours an' tell dem; go enywhere, you wan' to an' tell de good news. It'll do you good, do dem good, an' help to hon'r your Lord an' Saviour."

John Jasper always contended that his master made a preacher of him. "Oft'n as I preach," he said in one of his sermons, "I feel that I'm doin' what my ol' marster tol' me to do. If he was here now, I think he would fil' up dem kin' black eyes of his, an' say: 'Dat's right, John; still tellin' it; fly like de angel, an' wherever you go carry de Gospel to de people.'"*

John Jasper was born in 1812, and did not secure his freedom until 1864. He preached, as slave and freeman, for something over sixty years. When he died, in 1899, the Richmond *Dispatch* said of him:

> He was a national character, and he and his philosophy were known from one end of the land to the other. Some people have the impression that John Jasper was famous simply because he flew in the face of the scientists and declared that the sun moved. In one sense, that is true, but it is also true that his fame was due, in great measure, to a strong personality, to a deep, earnest conviction, as well as to a devout Christian character. Some preachers might have made this assertion about the sun's motion without having attracted any special attention. The people would have laughed over it, and the incident would have passed by as a summer breeze. But John Jasper made an impression upon his generation, because he was sincerely and deeply in earnest in all that he said. No man could talk with him in private, or listen to him from the pulpit, without being thoroughly convinced of that fact. His implicit trust in the Bible and everything in it, was beautiful and impressive. He had no other lamp by which his feet were guided. He had no other science, no other philosophy. He took the Bible in its literal significance; he accepted it as the inspired word of God; he trusted it with all his heart and soul and mind;

* "John Jasper," by W. E. Hatcher, pp. 26–29.

he believed nothing that was in conflict with the teachings of the Bible — scientists and philosophers and theologians to the contrary notwithstanding.

John Jasper was a survival of the ante-bellum days. He was representative of the "old-time" Negro preacher, of the men who were the natural leaders of the slaves on the plantation. He lived in a period, however, when, in many respects, the ante-bellum preacher was on the decline. In the early days, before the severe restrictions were put upon the education of the slaves, many of these men were educated and some of them preached in the white churches.

Among the most noted of the early Negro preachers was George Lisle, who began preaching to the slaves at Savannah, Georgia, during the War of the Revolution. After the evacuation of the country by the British in 1782 and 1783 he went with his master to Jamaica. The existence of the Baptist Church among the Negroes in Jamaica is due to this man. Before his departure for Jamaica he baptised a slave of Mr. Jonathan Bryan, by the name of Andrew.

Andrew Bryan became in after years a great preacher. At the present time there are two churches in Savannah, one of them the Bryan Baptist in the Yamacraw District and the other the First African, both of which claim descent from the little congregation of slaves which Andrew Bryan drew around him in the years after his baptism and previous to 1788, when he was solemnly ordained to the ministry and his congregation formally constituted a church.

The story of the struggle of this little congregation to maintain its existence against the prejudice that existed at that time is interesting because it shows the quality of some of these early slave preachers. In his volume, "The Gospel Among the Slaves," the Reverend W. T. Harrison, of the Methodist Church, South, says of the origin of the First Baptist Church in Savannah:

> Their evening assemblies were broken up and those found present were punished with stripes. Andrew Bryan and Samson, his brother, converted about a year after him, were twice imprisoned, and they with about fifty others were whipped. When publicly whipped, and bleeding under his wounds, Andrew declared that he rejoiced not only to be whipped, but would freely suffer death for the cause of Jesus Christ; and that while he had life and opportunity he would continue to preach Christ. He was faithful to his vow, and by patient continuance in well-doing he put to silence and shame his adversaries, and influential advocates and patrons were raised up for him. Liberty was given Andrew by the civil authority to continue his religious meetings under certain regulations. His master gave him the use of his barn at Brampton, three miles from Savannah, where he preached for two years with little interruption.

Toward the close of the year 1792, the Church which Andrew Bryan had founded began to build a place of worship. The city gave the lot for the purpose and the building, which still stands on the old site, though it is not the original structure erected in 1972, has become one of the historic landmarks of the city.

Among the other famous ante-bellum Negro preachers was a man known as Jack of Virginia, of whom Dr. William S. White, of the Southern Presbyterian Church, has written a biography. "Uncle Jack," as he was popularly known, was an African preacher of Nottoway County, Virginia. He had been captured from his parents in Africa and brought over in one of the last cargoes of slaves admitted to Virginia. He was sold to a remote and obscure plantation in Nottoway County which, at that time, was in the backwoods where there was almost no opportunity for religious life and instruction. In some way or other, however, he came under the influence of the Reverend Dr. John Blair Smith, President of Hampden-Sydney College, and of Dr. William Hill, and Dr. Archibald Alexander, of Princeton, both of whom were at that time young theological students. He learned to read from his master's children and became, as Professor Ballagh says in his work on Slavery in Virginia, "so full of the spirit and knowledge of the Bible that he was recognised among the whites as a powerful expounder of Christian doctrine, was licensed to preach by the Baptist Church, and preached from plantation to plantation within a radius of thirty miles, as he was invited by overseers or masters."

His freedom was purchased by a subscription of white people, and he was given a home and a patch of land for his support. It is said that he exercised such remarkable control over the members of his flock that masters, instead of punishing their slaves, often referred them to the discipline of their pastor, of which they stood in greater dread. Professor Ballagh says that the most refined and aristocratic people paid tribute to him, and he was instrumental in the conversion of many whites. He preached for forty years among blacks and whites alike, but voluntarily gave up his preaching in obedience to the law of 1832, which was passed as a result of the Nat Turner Insurrection. Dr. William S. White, his biographer, speaking of Jack of Virginia's relations with the white people in his neighbourhood, says:

> He was invited into their houses, sat with their families, took part in their social worship, sometimes leading the prayer at the family altar. Many of the most intelligent people attended upon his ministry and listened to his sermons with great delight. Indeed, previous to the year 1825, he was considered by the best judges to be the best preacher in that county. His opinions were respected, his advice followed, and yet he never betrayed the least symptoms of arrogance or self-conceit. His dwelling was a rude log cabin, his apparel of the plainest and coarsest materials. This was because he wished to be fully identified with his class. He refused gifts of better clothing, saying, "These clothes are a great deal better than are generally worn by people of my colour, and, besides, if I wear them, I find I shall be obliged to think about them even at meeting."*

Another noted Negro preacher was Ralph Freeman, who was a slave in Anson County, North

* "The African preacher," quoted by Ballagh in "Slavery in Virginia," pp. 110–112.

Carolina, in the neighbourhood of the Rock River. He was ordained a regular minister and travelled about, preaching at various places in his own and adjoining counties. It is said that the Rev. Joseph Magee, a white Baptist minister, became much attached to Ralph. They used to travel and preach together and it was agreed between them that the survivor should preach the funeral of the one who died first.

It so happened that the Rev. Joseph Magee died first and the task of preaching his funeral sermon fell to Ralph. In the meantime, however, his friend had moved to the West, and the coloured preacher was sent for all the way from North Carolina to come and fulfil the promise he had made in earlier years. Ralph Freeman continued to preach for a number of years. At last his lips were closed also, much to his sorrow, by the law which forbade Negroes to preach to white congregations.

Although Negro Baptists did not succeed in organising an independent National Church until after the War, coloured Baptists were the first among the Negroes to set up separate churches for themselves. In 1836, coloured Baptists in the North began to draw together. The Providence Baptist Association was organised in that year in Ohio. Two years later the Wood River Baptist Association was organised in Illinois. These local or district organisations, as they were afterward called, grew rapidly after the Civil War. About 1876 the New England states formed an organisation which aimed to be national in its character. In 1880 the Negro Baptists of the Southern states met at Montgomery, Alabama, to form a Foreign Mission Convention. Six years later the Southern states formed the American National Convention, and in 1894, at Montgomery, Alabama, measures were taken to bring together into one organisation all the coloured Baptist organisations in the United States, seeking to be national in character. By 1897 this national Baptist organisation had been completed.

According to statistics furnished by the eighty-nine state organisations and six hundred district associations there were, in 1908, 18,307 organised Negro Baptist churches, and 17,088 ordained preachers in the United States. According to these same statistics the total membership of these churches is 2,330,535. The total expenditures of the coloured Baptist Church for church, Sunday-school and educational work in 1907 is reported to have been $2,525,025.66.

The two great independent Negro denominations, the Methodist and the Baptist, were the first to break away from the older church organisations of the white people. These two organisations contain by far the larger number of the Negroes of the

United States. Perhaps this is the reason that they were the first to seek to establish independent Negro churches. In all the other religious denominations, with the exception of the Roman Catholics, Negroes have separate churches, which stand in a relation of greater or less dependence upon the denominations to which they belong.

The Catholics were the first to send missionaries to Africa. Therefore the Catholic Church is the First Christian Church into which Negroes were received as members. As far back as 1490, two years before the discovery of America, Catholic missionaries visited the mouth of the Kongo River. For several centuries after this a Negro Catholic kingdom existed in that part of Africa. It was eventually overthrown, as a result of wars with neighbouring peoples. Saint Benedict, the Moor, who died in Palermo, Sicily, in 1589, and was afterward canonised by the Catholic Church, was the son of a Negro slave woman. Some of the first Negroes to reach America were Catholics. They came over with the early Spanish discoverers.

Negro Catholics have never been numerous in the United States, except in Maryland, which was a Catholic colony, and in Louisiana. In 1829, a number of Catholic refugees came to Baltimore from Santo Domingo, and at this time there was founded, in connection with the Oblate Sisters of Providence Convent, the St. Francis Academy for Girls. The

Sisters of Providence, who founded the convent and seminary, were coloured women who first came to Baltimore with the Santo Domingo refugees. A few years later, in 1842, an order known as the Sisters of the Holy Family was founded among the free coloured women of New Orleans. The sisters of this order now have charge of three asylums, one of which is the Lafon Boys' Asylum, donated by Mr. Thomy Lafon, the Negro philanthropist, in 1893. The same order carries on schools at Baton Rouge, Mandeville, Madisonville and Lafayette, Louisiana; at Galveston and Houston, Texas; and Pine Bluff, Arkansas. The same Sisterhood has a government school at Stann Creek, British Honduras.

Outside the Catholic Church the first religious denomination in the United States to receive Negroes was the Protestant Episcopal Church. In 1624, only five years after slavery was introduced into Virginia, a Negro child named William was baptised and from that time the names of Negroes can be found upon the register of most of the older churches in Virginia. The first eminent coloured minister in the Episcopal Church in the United States was Alexander Crummell, who was born in New York City in 1818, but his father was a native of the Gold Coast, Africa. After his graduation at Cambridge University, England, Mr. Crummel went to Africa as a missionary. He was for a time a professor in the

Liberian College, in Liberia. Later he returned to the United States and was, for twenty-two years, rector of the St. Luke's Church, Washington, D. C. He is the author of several books upon Africa, and upon the Negro in the United States. In 1897 he established the American Negro Academy, which was designed to bring learned men of the Negro race together and to publish the results of their investigations, particularly upon subjects of interest to the Negro race.

Something like one hundred and fifty Negroes have been ordained as ministers in the Episcopal Church since Alexander Crummell entered that ministry in 1839. In 1874, James Theodore Holly was consecrated Bishop of Haiti and eleven years later Samuel David Ferguson was made Missionary Bishop of Cape Palmas, and adjacent regions in West Africa. There are several Negro archdeacons of the Episcopal Church in the Southern states. One of them is James S. Russell, who was a student at Hampton Institute, at the time I was there, and is now principal of the flourishing Episcopal school for Negroes at Lawrenceville, Virginia.

For some reason or other, probably because its teachings did not address themselves to the comprehension of the slaves, or did not appeal to their emotions, the Presbyterian Church was never as popular among the coloured people as the Methodist and Baptist churches were. Notwithstanding this fact, there were numerous coloured people who were members of the Presbyterian Church in the Southern states before the War. Among them was one free Negro by the name of John Chavis, who became famous. He was a full-blooded Negro and was born in Granville County, North Carolina, about 1763. He early in life attracted the attention of the white people and was sent to Princeton College as an experiment, to see if a Negro could take a collegiate education. The experiment succeeded and Chavis became so thoroughly educated that he afterward became a minister and preached with considerable success until 1831, when he was silenced by the law forbidding Negroes to preach.

After that he set himself up as a school-teacher, teaching in Granville, Wake and Chatham counties in North Carolina. Among his patrons were the best people in the neighbourhood. Willie P. Mangum, afterward United States Senator, and Priestley Mangum, his brother, Archibald and John Henderson, sons of Chief-Justice Henderson, Charles Manly, afterward Governor of the state, Dr. James L. Wortham, of Oxford, North Carolina, and many other men who did not become prominent, were his pupils. Reverend James H. Horner, who is said to have been one of the best teachers in North Carolina, said of John Chavis: "My father not only went to school to him, but boarded in his family. The school was the best at that time to be found in the state."

In his study of Slavery in the State of North Carolina, John Spencer Bassett says:

> From a source of the greatest respectability I learned that this Negro was received as an equal socially and asked to table by the most respectable of the neighbourhood. Such was the position of the best specimen of the Negro race in North Carolina in the days before race prejudices were aroused.*

After the Civil War large numbers, as many as seventy per cent., it is said, of the coloured members of the Presbyterian Church went into the African Methodist and into the Baptist churches. Others joined the Northern Presbyterian church, which had begun to establish schools and missions in the South among the Negroes directly after the War. In 1902, the Presbyterian Church, North, had eleven Presbyteries in the Southern states with two hundred and nine ministers, only seven of whom were white.

In spite of the large secession from the Presbyterian Church, South, a considerable number of coloured people still clung to the Southern branch of that Church. In the latter part of the Nineties, however, these coloured churches, at their own request, were set apart from the white churches and organised under the title of the Afro-American Presbyterian Church.

---

* "Slavery in the State of North Carolina," Johns Hopkins University Studies, p. 75.

The Congregational Church, through the medium of the American Missionary Association, began, directly after the War, to raise large sums of money and establish schools for the Freedmen. A number of these schools, like the one at Hampton, have now become independent of the organisation which started them. But a large number of schools are still being supported in different parts of the South by funds of the American Board. Around these schools there has usually grown up a coloured Congregational church. At first, these churches were located, for the most part, in the cities, but in recent years as the schools in the country districts have increased, the number of churches outside the city has multiplied. In 1902, the number of coloured Congregational churches was 230; the number of ministers and missionaries, 139, and the number of church members, 12,155.*

In 1890, the United States Census Bureau undertook a complete census of the religious denominations. Since that time no complete and systematic study of all the denominations has been made. The following table, however, prepared by Dr. H. K. Carroll, who had charge of the preparation of the church statistics of the Eleventh Census, although it does not agree entirely with the statistics furnished by the religious societies, probably shows

* "The Negro Church, a Social Study," p. 151.

pretty accurately the growth and relative percentage of strength of the different denominations:

Denomination	*Ministers*	*Churches*	*Communicants*
Regular Baptist	13,751	19,030	1,864,877
Church of God (Baptist)	71	93	8,500
Christian	88	34	956
Union American Methodist Episcopal	138	255	18,500
African Methodist Episcopal . .	6,170	6,920	858,323
African American Methodist Protestant	200	125	4,000
African Methodist Episcopal Zion .	3,986	3,280	583,106
Congregational Methodist . . .	5	5	319
Zion Union Apostolic (Methodist) .	30	32	2,346
Coloured Methodist Episcopal .	2,727	2,758	224,700
Evangelical Missionary (Methodist)	92	47	5,014
Cumberland Presbyterian . .	80	150	13,020
Total	27,338	32,729	3,583,661
Coloured members in Methodist Episcopal Churches	2,161	3,611	299,985
Coloured members in other bodies (est'd)	900	1,400	150,000
Grand total . . .	30,399	37,740	4,033,646
Grand total in 1890 . .		23,770	2,674,177
Gains in eighteen years .		13,970	1,359,469

These figures show that nearly half of the Negro population of the United States are members of one or the other of the great religious denominations. This means that, among the Negro population, the church plays a much more important part than it does among the white population, since considerably more than two-thirds of the white population are not enrolled in any church organisation. The influence of the Negro Church is particularly strong in the Southern states. In fact there is hardly a community or a plantation in the South so remote, or so obscure, that it does not possess some sort of place where the coloured people meet and worship.

These churches are not always what they should be. The coloured preacher is often ignorant and sometimes even immoral, but in spite of this fact the Church remains the centre for all those influences that are making for the welfare and the upbuilding of the communities in which they are situated. All these churches are connected more or less directly with the larger denominational organisations and thus serve, to some extent, to connect the people in them with the life and progress of the outside world.

I shall have something to say in a subsequent chapter in regard to the social work of the Negro Church. I wish to emphasise at this point, however, that the Negro Church represents the masses of the Negro people. It was the first institution to develop out of the life of the Negro masses and it still retains the strongest hold upon them. As the Negro Church grows stronger materially and spiritually so do the masses of the Negro people advance. There is no better indication of the progress of the masses of the people than the growth and development of these great Negro organisations.

CHAPTER XIV

THE NEGRO ABOLITIONISTS

A GOOD many stories have been told about John Randolph of Roanoke, and his peculiar opinions in regard to slavery. One of these concerns his reply to a man who asked him who, in his opinion, was the greatest orator he had ever heard. John Randolph was a great orator himself, and he had known Patrick Henry, but, in reply to this question, he said: "The greatest orator I ever heard was a woman. She was a slave. She was a mother, and her rostrum was the auction block." With that he arose and imitated the thrilling tones with which this slave woman had appealed to the sympathy and to the justice of the bystanders, concluding with an indignant denunciation of them and of the traffic in which they were engaged.

"There," said Mr. Randolph, in conclusion, "was eloquence. I have heard no man speak like that."

This story will serve to illustrate what was, from the beginning, the strongest force in the abolition of slavery in the South. I mean the appeal which the slaves made, themselves, not merely in words but in actions, to the sympathy of their masters. It was the faithful servants of the Southern masters who were the first Negro abolitionists.

This appeal which the Negro made for freedom merely through his humanity made its deepest impression, apparently, upon those people who had come to this country to obtain liberty for themselves. One of the very earliest of the anti-slavery men in the country was Anthony Benezet, the son of Huguenot parents who escaped from France on account of the revocation of the Edict of Nantes. He established and taught an evening school in Philadelphia for the instruction of Negroes and, as early as 1780, he made an effort to induce the Legislature of Pennsylvania to begin the work of emancipation. Anthony Benezet, after coming to America, joined the order of Friends, or Quakers as they were called. The people of this sect, who were more persecuted than any of the other English denominations that came to America to obtain religious freedom, were the first to give and to demand for the Negro emancipation.

Another thing that early aroused sympathy for the Negro slave was the sufferings of Americans who had been carried by the Barbary pirates into slavery in Africa. This was particularly true in Massachusetts and in New England, where a large proportion of the people were engaged in shipping, and consequently suffered more heavily from these piratical attacks. Among other Americans carried into African slavery was one of the first graduates of Harvard University, and in 1793, no less than one hundred and fifteen Americans were held in slavery in Algiers. The fact of the sufferings of the white slaves taken to Africa is frequently mentioned by the early abolitionists in Massachusetts as a reason for freeing the black slaves in America. One of the earliest books written in this country, which obtained any reputation abroad, was the story of the "Algerine Captive," which describes the hardships of these white slaves in Africa, and seeks to turn the sentiment aroused by this foreign white slavery against the black slavery at home.*

As a rule the Negro was not an anti-slavery agitator. In the South the free Negroes were frequently themselves slave-holders. Nevertheless, free Negroes were known to be in sympathy with the desire of the slaves to be free. That was one reason why they were regarded by slave-holders

* In an elaborate State paper John Jay, while Secretary for Foreign Affairs, in referring to the connection between white slavery in Africa and black slavery in America said: "If a war should take place between France and Algiers and in the course of it France should invite the American slaves there to run away from their masters, and actually receive and protect them in their camp, what would Congress, and indeed the world, think and say of France, if, on making peace with Algiers, she should give up those American slaves to their former Algerine masters? Is there any other difference between the two cases than this, namely, that the American slaves at Algiers are white people, whereas the African slaves at New York were black people?" Quoted in a lecture, "White Slavery in the Barbary States," before the Boston Mercantile Library Association, 1847. "The Works of Charles Sumner," vol. i, p. 449.

with so much distrust. In the North free Negroes were very largely engaged in the work of the Underground Railroad. In his history of that institution, Professor Wilbur H. Siebert has preserved the names of more than one hundred and forty coloured people, who maintained Underground Railroad stations in different parts of the United States. In Massachusetts there were Henry Box Brown and William Wells Brown, both of them fugitive slaves. Henry Box Brown was so named from the manner in which he escaped from slavery. William Wells Brown was born in Lexington, Kentucky, in 1816. He was taken as a boy to St. Louis, Missouri, and was employed by Elijah P. Lovejoy, the anti-slavery agitator, who was at that time editor of the St. Louis *Times*. It was here that be got his first education. After a year in Mr. Lovejoy's printing-office, young Brown was hired out to a captain of one of the river steamboats. In 1834 he escaped from the boat and came North. He obtained a position as a steward on one of the steamers on Lake Erie, where he was of great service to fugitive slaves, making their way to Canada. It was said that in a single year he gave free passage across the lake to sixty-five fugitives.

A little later, when he was living in Buffalo, he organised a "vigilance committee" to protect and aid fugitive slaves. During all this time he employed his evenings in study and, in 1843, he was engaged as a lecturer by the Anti-slavery Society, continuing in that position until 1849, when he went abroad.

Another agent of the Underground Railroad in Massachusetts was Charles Lenox Remond, who was born and brought up in Salem, Massachusetts, and as a consequence had the advantage of excellent school training. He became an anti-slavery lecturer in 1838, and went to England in 1846, as a delegate to the World's Anti-slavery Convention. In New York the principal agents of the Underground Railroad were Dr. James McCune Smith, David Ruggles, Bishop J. W. Loguen, the Rev. James W. C. Pennington, and Frederick Douglass. David Ruggles was one of the very early members of the Underground Railroad, and is said to have been connected with the work almost from the beginning. He edited for a number of years a quarterly magazine called the *Mirror of Liberty* and died in 1849.

Dr. James McCune Smith was born in New York, but received his medical education in Scotland. After his return to America he became an active writer for the newspapers and magazines and contributed a number of papers upon the history and progress of the Negro race. James W. C. Pennington was born a slave in 1809, on the plantation of Colonel Gordon, in Maryland, where he learned the trade of blacksmith. He joined the Presbyterian Church, studied in Germany, where he received the degree of Doctor of Divinity from the University of Heidelberg, and, upon his return to America, became the pastor of the Shiloh Church in New York City. He died in 1871.

In Pennsylvania, Robert Purvis, the only coloured man to sign the Declarations of the First American Anti-slavery Convention in Philadelphia in 1833, was the most prominent anti-slavery man of the coloured race. In 1850, he became chairman of the General Vigilance Committee, of which William Still was secretary.* During this time William Whipper, who afterward took a prominent part in the anti-slavery agitation, was a lumber merchant in the little town of Columbia, in the county of Lancaster, in the southeastern corner of Pennsylvania. At this time, this county was one of the principal avenues of escape for fugitive slaves and the coloured lumber merchants, Smith and Whipper,

* In an article published in *The Atlantic Monthly*, describing this first anti-slavery convention, John G. Whittier, the Quaker poet, mentions Robert Purvis and other coloured members of that convention. He says: "The president, after calling James McCrummell, one of the two or three coloured members of the convention, to the chair, made some eloquent remarks upon those editors who had ventured to advocate emancipation. At the close of his speech a young man rose to speak, whose appearance at once arrested my attention. I think I have never seen a finer face and figure, and his manner, words, and bearing were in keeping. 'Who is he?' I asked one of the Pennsylvania delegates. 'Robert Purvis, of this city, a coloured man,' was the answer. He began by uttering his heartfelt thanks to the delegates who had convened for the deliverance of his people. He spoke of Garrison in terms of warmest eulogy, as one who had stirred the heart of the nation, broken the tomb-like slumber of the church, and compelled it to listen to the story of the slave's wrongs. He closed by declaring that the friends of coloured Americans would not be forgotten. 'Their memories,' he said, 'will be cherished when pyramids and monuments have crumbled in dust. The flood of time is sweeping away the refuge of lies; is bearing on the advocates of our cause to a glorious immortality.'" *The Atlantic Monthly*, vol. xxxiii, pp. 168, 169.

were known to be active agents of the Underground Railroad. From 1847 to 1860, according to a letter written to William Still, the author of the Underground Railroad, Mr. Whipper expended as much as a thousand dollars a year in assisting fugitive slaves. After the passage of the Fugitive Slave Law in 1850, the coloured population at Columbia decreased from 943 to 487 by emigration and in 1861, when the War broke out, Mr. Whipper was preparing to go to Canada himself.

The number of coloured people engaged in the Underground Railroad was, as I have already said, much larger in Ohio than in any other of the Northern states. At Oberlin, Portsmouth, and Cincinnati, Ohio, and Detroit, Michigan, there were a number of Negroes who worked with the white abolitionists of these cities, in assisting fugitives on their way to Canada. In the neighborhood of Portsmouth, Ohio, slaves were assisted across the river by a barber of the town of Jackson, whose name was Poindexter. At Louisville, Kentucky, there was a coloured man by the name of Wash Spradley, who helped many slaves to escape into the free states across the river. Professor Siebert gives the names of more than one hundred coloured men who were known to be actively engaged in assisting in the escape of fugitive slaves in the State of Ohio. He says:

> George W. S. Lucas, a coloured man of Salem, Columbiana County, Ohio, made frequent trips with the closed carriage of

Phillip Evans between Barnesville, New Philadelphia, and Cadiz, and two stations, Ashtabula and Painesville, on the shore of Lake Erie. Occasionally Mr. Lucas conducted parties to Cleveland and Sandusky and Toledo, but in such cases he went on foot or by stage. His trips were sometimes a hundred miles or more in length. George L. Burroughes, a coloured man of Cairo, Illinois, became an agent for the Underground Road in 1857 while acting as porter of a sleeping-car running on the Illinois Central Railroad between Cairo and Chicago. At Albany, New York, Stephens, a Negro, was an agent for the Underground Road for a wide extent of territory. At Detroit there were several agents, among them George De Baptiste and George Dolarson.*

There were fewer stations of the Underground Railroad maintained in Illinois by coloured people than in most of the other Western states. Chicago, however, was the centre of anti-slavery sentiment and there early sprang up in that city a small colony of free Negroes who sometimes assisted fugitive slaves from Missouri to escape. Among the early coloured settlers of Chicago was John G. Jones, who for many years had a tailor shop on Dearborn Street near Madison and was, at the time of his death, in 1879, one of the wealthiest Negroes in Illinois. A few years ago, when Mrs. Jones was visiting her niece, who is the wife of Lloyd G. Wheeler, formerly Business Agent of Tuskegee Institute, I learned that her husband had been for many years a friend of John Brown and when, in the winter of 1858 and 1859, he made his sensational "rescue" of the Missouri slaves,

* "The Underground Railroad," Wilbur H. Siebert, p. 70.

Brown stopped at Mr. Jones's house on his way to Canada.

In addition to those I have already mentioned, there is evidence that there was a pretty well-organised body of coloured people engaged in the Underground Railroad extending the whole length of the Great Lakes from Detroit, Michigan, to Buffalo, New York. This organisation was known as the "Liberty League." John Brown was well acquainted with the members of this organisation and, when he held his famous "convention" at Chatham, Canada, shortly before the raid on Harper's Ferry, it was from the ranks of this organisation that he drew, in all probability, the largest number of his members. Among these were Dr., afterward Major, Martin R. Delany. Dr. Delany, who was chairman of the Chatham Convention, was not merely a physician but a traveller, soldier, lecturer, and editor. He was for a time editor of the anti-slavery paper published at Pittsburgh, Pennsylvania, called the *Mystery*. After the passage of the Fugitive Slave Law he decided to go to Canada. In association with Professor Campbell he was a member of the Niger Valley Exploring Expedition, and afterward lectured upon Africa in various parts of England. During the Civil War he served as a soldier and was a member of General Saxton's staff while the latter was in command at Port Royal, South Carolina. Dr.

Delany died January 24, 1885, at the age of seventy.

Among the early Negro abolitionists were Richard Allen and Absalom Jones, the founders of "The Free African Society," of Philadelphia. This society opened a communication with the Negroes in Boston, Newport, Rhode Island and other places and coöperated with the abolition societies in 1790, in studying the conditions of the free blacks. In 1799 and 1800, Absalom Jones led the Negroes of Philadelphia to draw up a petition to the Legislature, praying for the immediate abolition of slavery, and to send another petition to Congress against the Fugitive Slave Law, and in favour of prospective emancipation for all Negroes.

These two men, Richard Allen and Absalom Jones, were, a little later, supported in their efforts for abolition by James Forten, a sail-maker by trade; a man of education, and of considerable means. James Forten received his education in the school of the Quaker abolitionist, Anthony Benezet, and is described as "a gentleman by nature, easy in manner and easy in intercourse." In 1814, Mr. Forten, with the assistance of Jones and Allen, assisted in raising 2,500 coloured volunteers for the protection of the city of Philadelphia, which was then threatened by the English war-ships. A battalion was also formed for service in the field, but, before it reached the front, the war with Great Britain had come to an end.

In 1817, James Forten was chairman of the first convention of free Negroes held in Philadelphia. It is said that he drew up the first resolutions of protest against the work of the Colonisation Society, which declared "that we never will separate ourselves voluntarily from the slave population in this country. They are our brethren by the ties of blood, of suffering and of wrong, and we feel that there is more virtue in suffering privations with them than in gaining fancied advantages for a season." Mr. Forten was a firm friend and supporter of William Lloyd Garrison, who refers to him as "the greatly esteemed and venerated sailmaker of Philadelphia." In the early days of the anti-slavery agitation, when Garrison found so little support for his paper that he believed he would have to give it up, James Forten several times came to his rescue, at one time sending him fifty-four dollars for twenty-seven subscribers to the *Liberator*, and at another time assuming a considerable part of the indebtedness which that paper had incurred.

James Forten was born in 1766, in Philadelphia; he died in 1842. He was a friend of Whittier, the Quaker poet, among whose uncollected poems are some verses, written in 1833, but first published in the New York *Independent*, November, 1906, entitled, "To the Daughters of James Forten." Two grandchildren of James Forten are now living in Washington, D. C. One of these is the wife of Dr. Charles B. Purvis, son of Robert Purvis, and formerly surgeon-in-chief of the Freedman's hospital; the other is Mrs. Charlotte Forten Grimke, the wife of the well-known Presbyterian minister, Rev. Francis J. Grimke.

One of the interesting results of the anti-slavery agitation was the opening of Oberlin College to Negroes. This grew out of the anti-slavery discussions which took place among the students of Lane Seminary, at Cincinnati, Ohio. Out of one hundred or more students in attendance in 1833, more than half were Southerners. In 1834, there was a debate in the Chapel on the subject of slavery which lasted for eighteen consecutive nights. During that debate James Bradley, a former slave, who had purchased his freedom, was allowed to give his testimony. He made a speech lasting two hours, speaking in favour of the abolition of slavery and of the measures of the Colonisation Society. Bradley was born in Africa, but stolen from that country when he was a child. His master, who lived in Arkansas, died when he was eighteen years old. For some years afterward he acted as manager of the plantation for his mistress, and finally purchased his time by the year. After five years he paid $655 for his freedom and emigrated to free territory with $200 in his possession.

As a result of that debate, two Southern students became abolitionists, and afterward the students generally began to start Sunday and day schools for Negro children in Cincinnati. A report of the debate, which was written by one of these Southern students and published in pamphlet, says of Bradley: "He is now a beloved and respected member of this institution."

When in August, 1834, the trustees of the school voted that thenceforth there should be no discussion of slavery in any public room of the Seminary, fifty-one of the students left the school in a body. Just about this time, December, 1833, the Oberlin Collegiate Institution had been established, and the seceding students were invited to come there. The result was that Oberlin was open to students, "irrespective of colour." Since that time it is probable that nearly as many coloured students have been graduated from Oberlin as have been graduated from all other colleges in the North put together, outside of a few schools exclusively for Negroes. It is interesting to note that this result was brought about, to some extent, at least, by the eloquence of an untutored Negro orator.

Negro anti-slavery agitators, largely because of their lack of education, were almost always more influential as speakers than they were as writers.

Nevertheless, the Negro people were not wholly without anti-slavery writers during the period of the struggle for freedom. The first Negro paper published in the United States was an anti-slavery sheet called *Freedom's Journal*." This was published by John B. Russwurm, a graduate of Bowdoin College. The circumstances under which it was established were these: There was published in New York City a paper which was violent in its attacks upon coloured Americans. Some of the prominent coloured men, among them the Rev. Samuel Cornish, met at the home of Boston Crummell and determined to establish a paper through which they could answer these attacks. As a result of this conference the *Freedom's Journal* was launched. Among the contributors was David Walker, the author of "Walker's Appeal," a little pamphlet printed in 1829.* The "Appeal" was, so far as I am able to learn, the first attack upon slavery made by a Negro through the medium of the press. Another contributor to this paper was Stephen Smith, who, as a lumber merchant at Columbia, Pennsylvania, amassed a considerable fortune, with which he afterward endowed a home for aged and

* David Walker was born at Wilmington, North Carolina, in 1785, of a free mother by a slave father. He early went to Massachusetts to live and in 1827, having obtained a little education, he began business in Brattle Street, Boston. In 1829, he published his "Appeal," which was widely circulated, and stirred the South as no other anti-slave pamphlet up to that time had done. This pamphlet was the subject of a message of Governor Giles to the Legislature of Virginia in which he referred to the "Appeal" as a seditious pamphlet sent from Boston. "History of the Negro Race in America," Williams, vol. ii, appendix, p. 553.

infirm Negroes in Philadelphia, giving the institution $50,000 during his lifetime and $50,000 more at his death. This paper seems to have been favourable to the work of the Colonisation Society. Its first two numbers contain among other things an article entitled, "The Memoirs of Paul Cuffe," who some years before had taken a ship-load of free coloured people to Sierra Leone.

John Brown Russwurm was born in 1799, at Port Antonio, Jamaica. He was taken to Quebec by his father, who was a white man, and there put to school. Shortly after, his father came to Maine and married. After his father died, Mrs. Russwurm, who had become deeply interested in her stepson, gave him a college education. After leaving college, he was for a time the teacher of the coloured public school in Boston. In 1829, he went to Africa and became superintendent of the public schools of Liberia. At the same time he edited the *Liberia Herald*. In 1836, he was appointed Governor of Maryland, at Cape Palmas, and continued in that position until his death in 1851.

Another paper of some influence, known as the *Coloured American*, was started in 1837, by Philip A. Bell. The editor of this paper, which was published at 9 Spruce Street, New York City, was Charles B. Ray. Between the date of the publication of the *Coloured American* and Frederick Douglass's *North Star*, which was started ten years later, in

1847, several other papers were launched by coloured men. One of these was the *National Watchman*, edited by William G. Allen. He was assisted for a time by Henry Highland Garnet. Mr. Garnet had a remarkable career. He was born in slavery in Kent County, Maryland, December 23, 1815. His grandfather had been an African chief but was captured and sold to the slave-traders, and afterward became the property of Colonel William Spencer. His father escaped from slavery and sought protection with Thomas Garrett a Quaker and noted anti-slavery man. In 1825, he went to New York, where Henry Highland Garnet, his son, entered the African Free School on Mulberry Street. Among the students at the African Free School at this time were Charles L. Reason, afterward head of the coloured high school in Philadelphia, George T. Downing, at one time a noted caterer in Washington, D. C., and Ira Aldridge, the coloured actor.

Young Garnet subsequently attended the high school established for coloured people on Canal Street, and when this was closed he went to the famous school at Canaan, New Hampshire, and finally was graduated at the Oneida Institute at Whitesboro, New York. In 1850 he visited Great Britain, from there he went as a delegate to the Peace Conference, at Frankfort-on-the-Main; was a missionary for some time to Jamaica; chaplain of a coloured regiment during the War; president of Avery Institute at Pittsburgh, Pennsylvania; the first coloured man to hold religious services in Representatives' Chamber of Congress at Washington, D. C. He finally died as Minister Resident in Liberia, February 14, 1882.

After Frederick Douglass entered the anti-slavery field most of the efforts of the coloured people to secure their freedom centered about him. He was an orator of unusual gifts and devoted himself with such singleness of purpose to the task of securing freedom and recognition for his people that he soon became the recognised leader of the coloured people.

Among those who were associated with Frederick Douglass at this time were Samuel R. Ward, H. Ford Douglass, John M. Langston, William Howard Day, and Mifflin W. Gibbs. William C. Nell, the author of a book on "The Coloured Patriots of the Revolution," assisted him for some time in the publication of the *North Star*. Mr. Nell was a friend of Garrison and other anti-slavery men, and when he died in Boston, May 25, 1874, William Lloyd Garrison was one of the speakers at his funeral.

Contemporaneous with Frederick Douglass's paper, *The North Star*, which was published at Rochester, was the *Ram's Horn*, published by W. A. Hodges at 141 Fulton Street, New York City, and *The Alienated American*, published by William

Howard Day, at Cleveland, Ohio. A little later, in 1855, *The Mirror of the Times*, published by Mifflin W. Gibbs, was started at San Francisco, California.

The anti-slavery people to whom I have thus far referred were for the most part fugitive slaves or coloured men who were under the influence of the Northern abolitionists. But there were other Negroes in the Southern states who, by their lives and actions, exercised a very positive influence upon anti-slavery sentiment in the South. In a "History of the Anti-slavery Leaders of North Carolina," Professor John Spencer Bassett, of Trinity College, has given a sketch of one of these men, Lunsford Lane, whom he reckons among the four prominent abolitionists of North Carolina.

Lunsford Lane was a slave of Mr. Sherwood Haywood, a prominent citizen of Raleigh, North Carolina. His parents, of pure African descent, were employed as house-servants in the city of Raleigh. In this way, Lunsford had an opportunity to hear the speeches of many prominent men of the day, among others John C. Calhoun. He waited on Lafayette, when he passed through Raleigh in 1824, and was greatly impressed by what he heard this great man say in regard to his hope of ultimate freedom for the slave. Once he heard a Presbyterian minister, Dr. McPheeters, say: "It is impossible to enslave an intelligent people." The words made a great impression upon him. As a matter of fact, he had early learned to read and write, for at that time this privilege was not yet denied slaves in North Carolina.

It was a custom among the coloured boys of the town, to assemble every Sunday afternoon at a mineral spring in the outskirts of Raleigh in order to discuss, in imitation of the white people, the public questions of the day. At these meetings the slaves, who had had the advantages of hearing these questions discussed, would repeat with great exactness the speeches that they had heard during the week. Frequently the white people attended these meetings and a master who owned a particularly bright slave would take great pride in any exhibition of unusual intelligence his slave showed at these meetings, and would encourage him to improve still further. After the Northampton Insurrection, when it was believed that these meetings had the effect of turning the minds of slaves toward freedom, they were very strictly prohibited. Lunsford Lane grew up, however, where he had the benefit of these opportunities.

Lane early began to save with the purpose of purchasing his freedom, the money which was given him from time to time. He was given considerable liberty by his master and was able to employ his leisure time in occupations that increased the sum of his savings. Young Lane's father had, in some way or other, come into possession of a secret method of making a superior kind of smoking tobacco, and, as he grew older, father and son now began to manufacture this kind of tobacco on their own account. In order to have opportunity to carry on this trade Lane hired his time, paying for it from $100 to $120 a year. The demand for his tobacco grew rapidly; he enlarged his plant and made arrangements by which he was able to sell the product in the neighbouring towns of Fayetteville, Salisbury, and Chapel Hill. At the end of eight years he had saved a thousand dollars. With this sum he went to Mr. Benjamin R. Smith, who was the owner of his wife, and, putting his money in his hands, engaged him to negotiate with his mistress for his freedom.

As soon as he had secured his freedom, Lane was able to extend his business. He added to the manufacture of tobacco the making of pipes. He also opened a wood-yard and bought horses and wagons for use in connection with it. In 1839, he bought a house and lot, for which he paid $500. As soon as he had secured his own freedom he made it the one object of his life to buy his wife, and children, of whom there were now six. Mr. Smith offered to sell them for $3,000, but as his wife and her children had been purchased eight years earlier for $560 it seemed that $3,000, an advance of $2,340, was too much to pay. Mr. Smith, after some negotiation, reduced the price to $2,500 and Lunsford Lane gave five notes for $500 each and received in return the latter's obligation to sign a bill of sale for the whole family when the notes were paid.

"His achievement," says Professor Bassett, "had been wonderful, and is an indication of what a policy of gradual emancipation might have done in developing his race, could circumstances have been so shaped that it might have been entered upon. He had paid $1,000 for his freedom, he had paid $1,000 in yearly wages while he was hiring his time; had supported himself and helped support his family in the meantime; and paid $500 for his home, and had a good business in his own name."*

Although he dressed poorly, fared as simply as if he were a slave, and had been careful, as he said, to seem, if possible, to be less intelligent than he actually was, his prosperity had already begun to attract the notice of a certain class of whites and, as several other Negroes in Raleigh were beginning to make progress in the same way, some of the white people thought it was likely to have a bad effect on the slaves. For that reason they determined to run him out of the community.

The circumstances under which he had obtained his freedom enabled them to do this without much

* "Anti-slavery Leaders of North Carolina," John Spencer Bassett, Johns Hopkins Studies, p. 65.

difficulty. Since, under the laws of North Carolina, he was not able to buy his own freedom, he had gone to New York State to have the articles of emancipation executed. As he had, however, returned to North Carolina, he came under the provisions of the law which forbade free Negroes from other states from coming into North Carolina to live. Free Negroes who violated this act and did not remove out of the state within twenty days after notice had been served on them, were liable to a fine of $500, in default of which they could be sold for ten years. About the first of November, 1840, Lane received notification from two justices of the peace that, unless he left the state within the twenty days prescribed by the law, he would be prosecuted under the statute.

At this time Lane was a private messenger and janitor in the office of the Governor of the state. He at once appealed to Mr. C. C. Battle, private secretary to Governor Dudley, who took up the matter with the prosecuting attorney and secured from him a promise that the prosecution would be suspended until January 1. The purpose of this delay was to get a private law through the Legislature allowing him to remain in the state until he had finished paying for his family. Other free Negroes in the town who were buying their families had received similar notices and they, too, petitioned the Legislature. The petitions were referred to a committee which brought in a favourable report. The bill dragged along, Lane and the other free Negroes following its course, as well as they were able, from information they were able to obtain outside the building, since at the time no Negro was allowed to enter the Chamber of either of the Houses when in session. Finally, a member came out and said: "Well, Lunsford, the Negro bill is killed."

This announcement was a great blow to Lane and his companions, but they bowed to the inevitable and made no open complaint against the decision. Nothing was now left for Lane and his companions but to emigrate to the North, leaving their families behind them. Lane had already paid Mr. Smith $620 on his indebtedness, of which amount $250 was in payment for one child, whom he took North with him and left with friends. Mr. Smith now agreed to accept the house and lot in Raleigh for $500, provided the balance of $1,380 should be paid in cash. These arrangements having been completed, he started for the North.

Lane had made some friends in New York during his previous visit there to secure his own freedom. These friends now assisted him to raise the necessary money to secure the freedom of the remaining members of his family. Most of this money he secured by going about the country as a lecturer, telling in simple and straightforward fashion the circumstances under which he had been compelled to leave his home. Early in 1842 he wrote to his friend, Mr. Smith, in Raleigh asking him to obtain from the Government a written permission to return and get his family. The Governor replied that he had no authority to grant such a privilege but thought it would be perfectly safe for him to come to Raleigh, provided he stayed no longer than twenty days. So it was that on Saturday, April 23, 1842, the ex-slave was again in the city of his birth. He remained with his family during Sunday morning and on Monday morning went to the store of Mr. Smith to have a settlement. Before he could transact his business, however, he was arrested and taken before the Mayor on a charge of "delivering abolition lectures in Massachusetts."

In reply to this charge Lunsford Lane made a statement before the Mayor's court which, because it was the only abolition speech, so far as I know, ever made by a coloured man before a Southern audience, I am disposed to quote at some length.

Lunsford Lane's report of the proceedings was as follows:

> He asked me whether I was guilty or not guilty. Retaining my self-possession, I replied that I did not know whether I had given abolition lectures or not; but if it pleased the Court, I would relate the course I had pursued during my absence from Raleigh. He then said I was at liberty to speak for myself. "The circumstances under which I left Raleigh," I said, "are perfectly familiar to you all. It is well known that I had no desire to remove from this city,

but resorted to every lawful means to remain, while in pursuit of an honest calling. Finding that I could not be permitted to stay, I went away, leaving behind everything I held dear, with the exception of one child whom I took with me, after paying two hundred and fifty dollars for her. You are well aware that previous to this I was a slave, the property of Mr. Sherwood Haywood, and after many years of faithful labour purchased my freedom by paying the sum of one thousand dollars. It is also known to you, and to many other persons here present, that I had engaged to purchase my wife and children of their master, Mr. Smith, for the sum of twenty-five hundred dollars, and that I had paid of this sum, including my house and lot, eleven hundred and twenty dollars, leaving a balance to be made up of thirteen hundred and eighty dollars. I could have made up this amount had I been permitted to remain here. But, being driven away for no crime of which I am conscious, no longer permitted to raise the balance due for the liberation of my family, my last resort was to call upon the friends of humanity in other places to assist me. I went to the city of Boston, and there I related the story of my persecutions here, in the same manner that I now state them to you. The people gave a patient hearing to my statements, and one of them, the Reverend Dr. Neale, wrote to Raleigh, unknown to me, to Mr. Smith, inquiring of him whether the statements made by me were correct. After Dr. Neale received Mr. Smith's reply, he sent for me, informed me of his having written and read to me this reply. The letter fully satisfied Dr. Neale and his friends. He placed it in my hands, remarking that it would in a great measure do away with the necessity of using the other documents in my possession. I then, with that letter in my hands, went from house to house, calling upon persons at their places of business, going from church to church, relating, whenever I could gain an ear, the same sad story of my wrongs to which I am now referring you. In pursuing that course, the kind people generously came forward and contributed, the poor as well as the rich, until I had succeeded in raising the whole amount, namely, thirteen hundred and eighty dollars. I may have had contributions from abolitionists; but I did not stop to ask those who assisted me whether they were anti-slavery or pro-slavery. I was too thankful to get the money, and it was immaterial whence it came if it would only accomplish the object I had in view. These are the simple facts as to the manner of my proceeding in the Northern states; and now, sir, I humbly ask whether such a course can be construed into the charge made against me — that I have been giving abolition lectures."

After Lane had made this statement Mr. Loring, the Mayor, held a whispered consultation with some of the leading men of the city who were present, and then remarked that he saw nothing criminal in what had been done. He called upon any one present to make a statement, but no one had anything to say, and Lunsford Lane was therefore discharged.

As Lane was leaving the Mayor's office, however, he was warned that a crowd was waiting outside the building for him and that he had better go directly to the train. He made arrangements with the Mayor to take his money and settle with Mr. Smith and send on the liberated wife and children to Philadelphia. After this was done he started for the train and succeeded in reaching the station as the train was about to leave. The crowd had, however, followed him and refused to allow the train to depart until they had him in their hands. The Mayor was present and appealed in vain to the mob to allow Lane to go. Members of the crowd demanded the Negro's trunk to be searched for abolition literature. While their attention was directed to this task the fugitive was hurried to the jail for protection.

"Looking out from my prison window," said Lane in his account of the affair, "I could see my trunk in the hands of officers Scott and Johnston, and others who were taking it to the city hall for examination. I learned afterward that they broke open my trunk and as the lid flew up, the mob cried out, 'A paper, a paper!' A number seized it at once and set up a yell of wild delight. Among the crowd was a young man of profligate character, a son of one of the most respectable families in the place. When the paper was discovered, he glanced upward toward my prison window and by signs and words expressed his satisfaction.

"The paper proved to be entirely inoffensive, and as nothing further was found in the carpet bag which they searched, the crowd was quiet for a time."

At night, acting upon the advice of his friends, Lane was released from the prison and started for the home of Mr. William Boylan, who was so highly esteemed in Raleigh at that time that it was believed his house would be a safe asylum for the fugitive. It was nine o'clock at night when he left the jail. He had only gone a few yards, however, when he was seized and drawn away to "an old pine field," where a gallows stood. At first he thought they intended to hang him, but finally a bucket of tar and a feather pillow were brought, and then he understood that they intended nothing worse than a coat of tar and feathers. After he had been daubed with tar, and the feathers had been poured over him, his watch and clothes were handed him and he was allowed to go home. Some of the crowd, however, continued to follow him and, as they laughingly watched him remove the tar and feathers, said he might now remain in town as long as he chose.

By this time his friends had become alarmed and appealed to the Governor for protection. He had gone to the home of his friend, Mr. Smith, to pass the night and a detail of soldiers was furnished by the Governor as his guard there. In the morning he settled his business matters and made ready to start with his family for Philadelphia. He went to say farewell to his former mistress, who was then a very old lady. In describing the scene at the home of his former mistress, Lane says:

> My old mistress was affected to tears, as her mind reverted to the past — my faithfulness to her and to her children, my struggles and persecutions. In late years she had been kind to me, and, as I learned, she and her daughter, Mrs. Hogg, then present at her house, had sent a note to the court before which I was tried, representing that, in consequence of my good conduct from my youth up, they could not believe me to be guilty of any offence. And now, with an attachment for me they could not repress, and with tears — the offspring, as I believe, of genuine sympathy — they gave me their parting blessing. My mother was now called in that I might bid her a final farewell. I was her only child, and I had no hope of seeing her again in this world. Our old mistress could not witness this scene of our parting unmoved. Unable to

repress her feelings longer, she decided, to my infinite joy, that my mother should go with me. "Take her, Lunsford, and care for her as I know you will as a dutiful son. Should you ever become able to pay me two hundred dollars, you may; otherwise it shall be my loss."

The story of the treatment which Lane had received had caused the greatest excitement in the city and many of the best citizens in the town now came to his assistance. They gave him food enough to last on his journey; sent a carriage to take him and his family to the station and arranged with the conductor to stop on the edge of the town to take him on, his family having previously been placed on the train at the station. This was accomplished in safety and the whole party started North. A member of the previous day's mob who happened to be on the train made an effort to excite bystanders at the stations at which they stopped to board the train and to drag out the escaping abolitionist, but was unsuccessful.

Lunsford Lane went to live first in Boston, Massachusetts, and after then in Oberlin, Ohio. Two of his children having died there, however, he returned to Boston. He was employed for a time as a lecturer by the Anti-slavery Society but he seems to have had none of the vehemence of the average abolitionist and was never entirely contented with his life in the Northern country. During the War he acted as a hospital nurse, and when the question arose as to what would become of the freedman, he made several public addresses, in which he showed great practical sense and understanding. He emphasised particularly the need of better education and better agriculture in the South. Among other things he said:

> The wishes of the coloured people are much misunderstood by their friends, North and South. We desire, in the first place, freedom in its truest and best sense — not a mere license to do as we please. Having secured this, we wish to be situated so as to be profitably employed, so as to benefit the State as well as ourselves. We have no desire to remain in the Northern states, except as a temporary place of refuge from slavery. This is not our native climate. We love warmer suns and a more productive soil. Here our offspring wither and die. They revive and flourish under the warmer skies of the South. As soon as peace is concluded, and security for life and limb is guaranteed, we would return to a clime so well suiting our constitutions. In North Carolina alone there are thousands of acres of unoccupied lands which might be made to flourish under the diligent culture of the black man. We could occupy these lands as tenants or as owners, adding largely to the annual productions of cotton, rice, wheat, and vegetables. . . . We want more freedom for Northern teachers and religious instructors to visit the South, that they may spread before us the life-giving passages of God's Word. Heretofore, ignorance, and prejudice have almost banished these devoted men from the holy labours to which they were willing to devote their lives. We have no desire to leave the United States for a residence in the British Provinces, under a government with which we are not acquainted; nor to emigrate to Liberia, nor to the West Indies. The South is our home; and we feel that there we can be happy and contribute by our industry to the prosperity of our race, and leave the generation that succeeds us wiser and better. No greater mistake can, therefore, be made than to suppose we desire to come North. We only desire a secure freedom in the South. We hope not only to support ourselves, but to add greatly to the wealth of

the country, in the way of exports of surplus corn, and cotton, rice and sugar. . . . There is no branch of business or of commerce which would not be benefited by our elevation and industry. Millions of acres, now worthless, would be made to bud and blossom as the rose.*

Lunsford Lane remained, to the end, a true son of the South. In spite of the fact that he had been driven out of his native land, he seems to have cherished no bitterness against the people of his native state and city. If he had some enemies there, he had had many friends, the memory of whose kindness he never forgot. Perhaps I can not do better, in concluding what I have to say about this man, than to quote the words of Professor Bassett in regard to him:

The little glimpse that we have of his real self shows what a promise of hope he was for the race he represented. We know enough to be certain that it was a most short-sighted policy in his state that drove him and a number of others out of the community, and made impossible the development of other Negroes like unto him. Since the war we have sadly missed such strong characters in our Negro population. Twenty-five years before the war there were more industrious, ambitious and capable Negroes in the South than there were in 1865. Had the severe laws against emancipation and free Negroes not been passed, the coming of freedom would have found the coloured race with a number of superior individuals who in every locality would have been a core of conservatism for the benefit of both races. Under such conditions Lane would have been of great beneficent influence.†

* "Lunsford Lane," Reverend William S. Hawkins, pp. 204-206.

† "Anti-slavery Leaders of North Carolina," Johns Hopkins University Studies, John Spencer Bassett, p. 74.

CHAPTER XV

THE NEGRO SOLDIER'S FIGHT FOR FREEDOM

NEGRO soldiers have fought in every war, I suspect, that has ever been waged on the American continent. Negroes fought at Bunker Hill and all through the Revolutionary War. Before that time, Negroes are known to have been engaged, in one way or another, in most of the Indian wars. They were conspicuous in the battles of New Orleans and of Lake Erie, in the War of 1812. They fought on both sides in the Civil War, and from that time on they have been an important part of the standing army of the United States. In most of these wars, I may add, the Negro has fought not merely in the interest of the country and of the civilisation with which he has become identified, but also, as in the Revolutionary and Civil wars, to secure and maintain his own freedom.

It is impossible to tell just how many Negro soldiers were engaged in the Revolutionary War. In August, 1778, two months after the battle of Monmouth, the official returns of Washington's army showed that there were 755 Negroes scattered among the different regiments. But this did not include the Connecticut, New York, and New Hampshire troops, in which large numbers of Negroes, who had been slaves, had been allowed to take their masters' places in the ranks. It did not include, either, the regiment of Freedmen, raised in Rhode Island, which fought so courageously at the battle of Rhode Island, in August, 1778.* Three years later, in May, 1781, when Colonel Green, of this regiment, was surprised at Point Bridge, New York, his black soldiers, a detachment of whom accompanied him, defended their leader until every one of them was dead.

As a rule, the Negro soldiers were not organised in the Patriot Army into separate organisations, but were scattered through the different regiments. A Hessian officer, writing under the date of October 23, 1777, in reference to his march through Massachusetts, says: "The Negro can take the field instead of his master; and therefore no regiment is to be seen in which there are not Negroes in abundance; and among them are able-bodied, strong, brave fellows. Here, too," he adds, "there are many families of free Negroes who live in good

* At a meeting of the Congregational and Presbyterian Anti-slavery Society, at Francestown, New Hampshire, Reverend Dr. Harris, a Revolutionary soldier who had fought in the battle of Rhode Island, said of the service of the Negro regiment in that battle: "Had they been unfaithful, or given way before the enemy, all would have been lost. Three times in succession were they attacked, with most desperate valour and fury, by well-disciplined and veteran troops, and three times did they successfully repel the assault, and thus preserved our army from capture." Quoted from "The History of the Negro Race in America," vol. i, p. 369.

houses, have property and live just like the rest of the inhabitants."*

This statement is further confirmed by the official roll of Massachusetts soldiers, which shows that there were Negroes in the regiments of that state from almost every Massachusetts town. Although no Negro regiment was raised in Connecticut, still in Meigs's, afterward Butler's regiment, there was a company made up entirely of coloured men. George W. Williams, in his "History of the Negro Troops in the War of the Rebellion," after a careful study of the rolls of the Continental Army, reached the conclusion that there were no less than 3,000 Negro soldiers in the Continental army during the Revolutionary War.†

Fewer Negroes were allowed to enter the Patriot Army in the Southern colonies, although a strenuous effort was made by Colonel John Laurens, of South Carolina, and other patriots, to carry out the provisions that the Continental Congress had made for raising a Negro regiment. Free Negroes enlisted in considerable numbers in the Virginia regiments, although there was no law by which their service could be accepted. In 1783, however, the General Assembly passed a law directing the emancipation of a certain number

* Quoted from "Schloezer's Briefwechsel," vol. iv, p. 365, in Williams's "History of the Negro Race in America," vol. i, p. 343.

† George W. Williams, "History of the Negro Troops in the War of the Rebellion," p. 35.

of slaves who had served as soldiers in that state, and particularly "of the slave Aberdeen," who had worked for a long time in the state lead mines.

The Revolutionary War contributed, in several ways, toward the emancipation of the slaves. In the struggle of the colonies to secure liberty for themselves the sentiments expressed by Thomas Jefferson in the Declaration of Independence led many people to feel that Negro slavery was wrong. It was partly this sentiment and partly the needs of the Continental Army that led several of the states to pass laws which provided that slaves might serve in the Patriot Army and that, at the end of their service, they should go free. This was the case in New York where, on March 20, 1781, a law providing for two regiments of Negro slaves specified that, after three years of service, these slaves should be free. The Rhode Island law, which provided for a regiment of black men, specified, also, that those who took part in the struggle for freedom of the colonies should have their own freedom. It was, no doubt, largely as a result of the services of the Negro troops during the war that, on February 23, 1784, the General Assembly of Rhode Island passed a law making free all Negroes and mulattoes born in that state after March 1 of that same year.

Negroes not only served in the War of the Revolution, but individual coloured men are still remembered, in the tradition of that time, for the daring exploits in which they engaged. In Trumbull's celebrated historic painting of the battle of Bunker Hill, one of the conspicuous figures is a Negro by the name of Peter Salem, who is said to have been responsible for the death of Major Pitcairn, of the British Marines, who fell just as he mounted the Patriots' redoubt, shouting, "The day is ours!"

Peter Salem was a private in Colonel Nixon's regiment. He was born in Framingham, and was held as a slave until the time he joined the army. Colonel Trumbull, who, at the time of the battle, was stationed with his regiment in Roxbury, and saw the action from that point, has introduced the figures of several other coloured men into his canvas.*

Another coloured man whose name has been preserved in the records of the Revolutionary War was Salem Poor, of Colonel Frye's regiment, Captain Ames's company. He took part in the Battle of Bunker Hill and so distinguished himself that a petition, signed by some of the principal officers who took part in that battle, was drawn up and sent to the General Court of Massachusetts Bay

* A letter written to George Livermore from Aaron White of Thompson, Connecticut, in regard to the death of Major Pitcairn, says: "About the year 1807 I heard a soldier of the Revolution, who was present at the Bunker Hill Battle, relate to my father the story of the death of Major Pitcairn. He said the Major had passed the storm of our fire without, and had mounted the redoubt, when, waving his sword, he commanded, in a loud voice, the rebels to surrender. His sudden appearance and his commanding air at first startled the men immediately before him. They neither answered nor fired, probably not being exactly certain what was next to be done. At this critical moment a Negro soldier stepped forward, and, aiming his musket directly at the Major's bosom, blew him through."

in order to secure recognition for his services. This was less than six months after the battle in which he had taken part had been fought.

Another incident, which illustrates a trait often referred to, namely, the fidelity of Negro soldiers to their officers, has been noticed in the memoir of Major Samuel Lawrence, who took part in the Battle of Bunker Hill. At one time, it is related, Major Lawrence commanded a company, "whose rank and file were all Negroes, of whose courage, military discipline, and fidelity he always spoke with respect." On one occasion, while he and his company were somewhat in advance of the other troops, Major Lawrence was surrounded and on the point of being made prisoner by the enemy. His men, discovering his peril, hurried to his rescue "and fought with the most determined bravery till that rescue was effectually secured." His biographer says that Major Lawrence never forgot that circumstance, and ever after took special pains to show kindness and hospitality to every individual coloured man who came his way. This interest and friendship in the coloured man, which began with Major Lawrence in the way described, was continued to his distinguished grandson, Amos A. Lawrence, who took a prominent part in the struggle for freedom in Kansas, being a member of the Emigrant Aid Society which did so much to make Kansas free.

Negroes played a less conspicuous part in the war in North and South Carolina and Georgia than they did elsewhere. But in White's "Historical Collections of Georgia," there is an account given of a Negro soldier by the name of Austin Dabney, which is so interesting that I am tempted to relate the story here at some length.

Austin Dabney had been born, from all that I can learn, of free parents, but in some way or other, he had fallen into the hands of a man by the name of Aycock, who lived in Wilkes County, Georgia. This man was unable to serve in the Patriot Army himself, and for that reason offered this slave boy as a substitute and, after the circumstances of his birth were explained, he was accepted. Dabney proved himself a good soldier and took part in many a skirmish with British and Tories, in which he acted a conspicuous part. He was with Colonel Elijah Clark at the Battle of Kettle Creek, February 14, 1779, where he was wounded and made a cripple for life. He was unable to do further military duty and was without means to obtain proper medical attention. In this critical condition he was taken into the house of a white man by the name of Harris, where he was kindly cared for until he recovered. So grateful was he to this man, Mr. Harris, for taking him into his home at a time when he was without friends and unable to assist himself, that he afterward devoted a large part of his life to working for and taking care of Mr. Harris and his family.

After the close of the war, Austin Dabney acquired property and became prosperous. He removed to Madison County, carrying with him his benefactor, Mr. Harris, and family. Here he became noted for his great fondness for horses and the turf. He attended all the races in the neighbourhood, and, in the words of Mr. White's chronicle, "his courteous behaviour and good temper always secured him gentleman backers."

Dabney had been freed for his services in the Revolutionary War. He was in receipt of a pension from the Federal Government and in the distribution of public lands by lottery among the people of Georgia, the Legislature gave him a considerable amount of land in the county of Walton. The Representative from Oglethorpe, the Hon. Mr. Upson, was the member who moved this passage of the law.

The granting of this land to a coloured man was strenuously opposed by a number of people and, at the election of members of the Legislature of Madison County, the people were divided into an Austin Dabney and an anti-Austen Dabney party. It was perhaps because he did not enjoy the results of this controversy that Dabney soon after removed to the land given him by the state in Walton County, taking with him the Harris family, for whom he continued to labour. Upon his death he left them all his property. The eldest son of his benefactor Harris sent to Franklin College and afterward supported him while he studied law with Mr. Upson in Lexington. In the account given in White's "Historical Collections," it is stated that Dabney was "one of the best chroniclers of events of the Revolutionary War in Georgia."

As illustrating the character of Austin Dabney and the good repute which he maintained among his neighbours the following anecdote is related in White's "Collections."

> He drew his pension at Savannah, where he went once a year for this purpose. On one occasion he went to Savannah in company with his neighbour, Colonel Wyley Pope. They travelled together on the most familiar terms, until they arrived in the streets of the town. Then the Colonel observed to Austin that he was a man of sense, and knew that it was not suitable for him to be seen riding side by side with a coloured man through the streets of Savannah; to which Austin replied that he understood the matter very well. Accordingly, when they came to the principal street, Austin checked his horse and fell behind. They had not gone very far before Colonel Pope passed by the house of General James Jackson, who was then Governor of the state. Upon looking back he saw the Governor run out of the house, seize Austin's hand, shake it as if he had been his long absent brother, draw him off his horse, and carry him into his house, where he stayed whilst in town. Colonel Pope used to tell this anecdote with much glee, adding that he felt chagrined when he ascertained that whilst he passed his time at the tavern, unknown and uncared for, Austin was the honoured guest of the Governor.

It should not be understood from what has been said here that Negroes were admitted at once and without opposition into the Patriot Army. There was at first considerable opposition to them, particularly from the officers in the army. One incident that hastened their entrance into the army was the proclamation by Lord Dunmore, the Royal Governor of Virginia, in November, 1775, offering freedom to all such Negroes and indentured white servants as might enlist for the purpose "of reducing the colony to the proper sense of its duty." Other proclamations inviting the Negroes to join the King's armies and fight against their masters were issued later by Sir Henry Clinton and Lord Cornwallis. As a matter of fact a great many slaves were carried off by the British troops during the war. It is estimated that no less than thirty thousand of them were taken from the plantations and employed by the British troops in pioneer work and in building fortifications, but the greater part of these slaves died from fever and small-pox in the British camps. The remainder were sent to the West Indies, others to Nova Scotia, and still others to the colony of Sierra Leone. Referring to this matter in a speech in the United States House of Representatives, December 12, 1820, the Hon. Charles Pinckney of South Carolina says:

It is a most remarkable fact that, notwithstanding, in the course of the Revolution, the Southern states were continually overrun by the British, and that every Negro in them had an opportunity of leaving their owners, few did; proving thereby not only a most remarkable attachment to their owners, but the mildness of the treatment, from whence their affection sprang. They then were, as they still are, as valuable a part of our population to the Union as any other equal number of inhabitants. They were in numerous instances the pioneers, and, in all, the labourers, of your armies. To their hands were owing the erection of the greatest part of the fortifications raised for the protection of our country; some of which, particularly Fort Moultrie, gave, at that early period of the inexperience and untried valour of our citizens, immortality to American arms; and, in the Northern states, numerous bodies of them were enrolled into, and fought, by the sides of the whites, the battles of the Revolution.*

Although Negro soldiers had fought in the Revolutionary War and in the War of 1812, it was some time before the Federal Government was prepared to enlist Negro soldiers to fight in the Civil War against the people who were still holding black men as slaves. As a matter of fact, it was in the Confederate armies that the first Negro soldiers were enlisted. During the latter part of April, 1861, a Negro company at Nashville, Tennessee, made up of "free people of colour," offered its services to the Confederate Government. Shortly after, a recruiting office was opened for free Negroes at Memphis, Tennessee. On November 23, 1861, there was a grand review of the Confederate troops at New Orleans, Louisiana, one of the features of which was a regiment of fourteen hundred free coloured men. Some of these coloured troops remained in the service of the Confederacy

* George Livermore: "An Historical Research Respecting the Opinions of the Founders of the Republic on Negroes as Slaves, as Citizens, and as Soldiers," p. 155.

until the close of the war, but in few cases did they have an opportunity to participate in any of the important battles.

In the summer of 1862, General Butler organised a regiment of free coloured people in the city of New Orleans, under the title of the "First Louisiana Native Guard." This was the first coloured regiment to be mustered into the Federal Army. General Butler has related in his autobiography, the circumstances under which this regiment was formed. It seems that two regiments of free Negroes called "Native Guards, Coloured," had been organised in New Orleans, while General Butler was at Ship Island. After the fall of New Orleans, many of these coloured soldiers left the city, but some remained. General Butler learned the names and residences of some twenty of the coloured officers of these regiments and sent for them to call upon him at headquarters. In talking the situation over with them, he called their attention to the fact that if the Federal armies were successful Negro slavery would be abolished, and then asked them if they would be willing to organise two regiments of free coloured people to fight for the freedom of their race. After some further consultation, they readily agreed to do this, and fourteen days later, on August 22, 1862, when General Butler went down to the place where he had ordered the recruits to gather, he says he saw such a sight as he had never seen before: "Two thousand men ready to enlist as recruits and not a man of them who had not a white 'biled shirt' on."

Thus the first regiment of coloured troops was mustered into the service of the United States. A short time after this, three regiments of infantry and two batteries of artillery were equipped and ready for service. General Butler says of these soldiers, "They were intelligent, obedient, highly appreciated their position, and fully maintained its dignity."

Previous to this time, General Hunter, who was located at Beaufort, and the Sea Islands, off the coast of South Carolina, had formed a regiment from the slaves which he had found on the abandoned plantations in that district. When this regiment was first organised the Federal Government was not prepared to accept the Freedmen in the positions of soldiers, so that it was not until January 25, 1863, that the "First South Carolina" regiment was actually mustered into service, though it had been in existence as an organisation for some time before this.

Although these were the first Negro regiments organised by the Federal Government, they were not the first coloured soldiers to engage in battle on the side of the Federal Government. In August, 1862, a coloured regiment, composed partly of fugitive slaves from Missouri, was recruited in

Kansas. Although this regiment was not mustered into the service of the United States until January, 1863, a detachment of it was attacked by Confederate soldiers at Island Mound, Missouri, October, 28, 1862, but after considerable fighting the coloured troops succeeded in beating off their opponents. This was the first action in which Negro troops were engaged in the Civil War.

After the emancipation proclamation was issued on January 1, 1863, the work of enlisting coloured soldiers was taken in hand in more serious fashion. Early in the year 1863, Governor John A. Andrews secured permission to organise a regiment of coloured troops. On April 12, of that year, the Fifty-fourth Massachusetts Volunteer Infantry, composed of "persons of African descent," had completed its quota, and shortly after this two other coloured regiments were organised. These were the first soldiers recruited from among the free coloured people of the North. To complete these regiments, coloured people were summoned from all of the Northern states. Governor Andrews was greatly assisted in the work of recruiting the coloured people to fill these regiments by Frederick Douglass and the coloured abolitionists, William Wells Brown and Charles Lenox Remond. Among the coloured soldiers who sailed for South Carolina with the Massachusetts regiments were two sons of Frederick Douglass, Lewis H. and Charles R. Douglass.

Among the coloured people who enlisted in the Federal army at this time there was a large number who afterward distinguished themselves in some way in public life. Among others I recall two bishops of the African Methodist Episcopal Church and several men who afterward became prominent in politics, among them P. B. S. Pinchback, who was in the First Volunteer Louisiana Infantry, and afterward became Lieutenant, and for a time, Acting Governor of Louisiana during the stormiest days of the Republican rule in that state. Charles E. Nash, who was afterward Representative from Louisiana in the Forty-fourth Congress, enlisted as a private in the United States Chasseurs d' Afrique, and afterward rose to the position of Acting Sergeant-major of his regiment.

Bishop Henry M. Turner is said to have been the first coloured chaplain to receive a commission from the Federal army. Bishop Turner was living at this time, in 1863, in Washington, District of Columbia, where he was serving as pastor of Israel Church. Bishop William B. Derrick, the other A. M. E. bishop who served in the war, was born in the Island of Antigua, British West Indies, July 27, 1843, a decade after England had granted freedom to the slaves in the West Indian colonies. He was educated in a Moravian school at Graceland. It was intended that he should be a blacksmith, but he took to the life of the sea, and became a sailor on vessels travelling between the West Indies and New York. This led him to enlist in the war for the freedom of the coloured people in the United States. He served on the flagship of the North Atlantic Squadron, the *Minnesota*, and at the close of the war became a citizen in the United States.

Among the other coloured men who enlisted in the Civil War was George Washington Williams, who afterward served as an officer of artillery in the Mexican army. Mr. Williams was born in Bedford Springs, Pennsylvania, October 16, 1849. After the Civil War was over he studied law for a time in the office of Judge Alphonso Taft, father of President Taft, and in the Cincinnati Law School. In 1879 and 1881, he was a member of the Ohio Legislature. From 1885 to 1886, he was Minister to Haiti, and in 1888, was a delegate to the World's Conference of Foreign Missions at London. He was a writer and a newspaper man of some note and is the author of a "History of the Negro Race in America," to which I have frequently had occasion to refer, in the preparation of this book.

Joseph H. Rainey, who was a member of the Forty-second, Forty-third, the Forty-fourth, and the Forty-fifth Congress, as Representative from South Carolina, served for a time in the Confederate Army. Joseph Rainey was born in Georgetown, South Carolina, June 21, 1832. His father and mother had been slaves, but had purchased their freedom. When the war broke out Mr. Rainey was working at his father's trade of barber. Being a free man he was drafted into the service of the Confederate Army and compelled to work upon the fortifications, until he succeeded in escaping to the West Indies, where he remained till the close of the war.

A small number of coloured men, probably as many as seventy-five, were granted commissions as officers in the latter part of the war. Major Martin R. Delany, and Captain O. S. B. Wall, both of whom were detailed in the Quartermaster's Department, attained the highest rank of any of the coloured officers in the Army. Dr. A. T. Augusta, who afterward became one of the leading coloured physicians of Washington, District of Columbia, and Dr. Charles B. Purvis, a son of Robert Purvis, the coloured abolitionist of Philadelphia, were the best known of the coloured army surgeons during the Civil War. Dr. Purvis has been for many years a teacher and officer in the School of Medicine at Howard University.

From first to last no less than 178,975 Negro soldiers were mustered into the United States Volunteer Army during the course of the Civil War. Of this number, 36,847 were reported killed, wounded, or missing. The coloured troops did not have an opportunity to participate in many of the great battles of the war. They did, however, serve in nearly every military department in the United States and took part in four hundred and forty-nine battles. In addition to the large military force mentioned there were at least 150,000 Negro labourers employed in the Quartermasters' and Engineering Department. They were employed as teamsters and as cooks or in the building of fortifications.

The first general engagement in which coloured soldiers took part was the assault upon Port Hudson, Louisiana, made by the troops under General Banks, May 27, 1863. There were eight regiments of coloured troops among the forces that took part in this assault, and among them was the first Louisiana Native Guard, organised by General Butler. This regiment is said to have suffered heavier losses than any other regiment engaged in the assault, losing in all one hundred and twenty-nine officers and men.

The soldiers in this same Department did some desperate fighting a few days after, June 6 and 7, 1863, at Milliken's Bend. This post was defended by about fourteen hundred men, all of them newly organised and undisciplined black soldiers, with the exception of one hundred and sixty men of an Iowa regiment which chanced to be there. The battle lasted for eight hours, during which the soldiers came to close quarters and fought hand to hand with bayonets and clubbed muskets. Although the attacking force was said to have been considerably superior to that of the black troops, the latter succeeded in repelling the attack and in driving off the enemy.

Two of the most desperate battles of the war in which coloured troops were engaged were the assault of Fort Wagner, July 18, 1863, in which the Fifty-fourth Massachusetts, the first regiment of coloured soldiers to be recruited in the North, was engaged, and the battle of Honey Hill, South Carolina, November 30, 1864, in which the Fifty-fifth Massachusetts, the second coloured regiment raised in the North, was engaged. It was in the assault of Fort Wagner that the gallant Colonel Robert G. Shaw fell dead at the head of his Negro regiment and mingled some of the best blood of New England with that of these black men whom he had volunteered to lead in the fight for the freedom of their race. It was in this same battle that Sergeant William H. Carney of the Fifty-fourth Massachusetts, though wounded in the head and in the shoulder and in both legs, carried the National flag of his regiment across the open field which separated him from safety, where he handed it over with the words which made him famous: "Dey got me boys, but de old flag neber touched de groun!"

After the war, Sergeant Carney returned to

Massachusetts, and for a number of years, up to the time of his death, in the early part of December, 1908, was employed at the Massachusetts State House in Boston, where the torn flag that he had kept flying upon the battlefield at Fort Wagner is still preserved among the other colours of the Massachusetts regiments.

Following the death of Sergeant Carney, in Boston, Mr. N. P. Hallowell wrote a communication to the Boston *Transcript* in which he gave so accurate and concise a description of this battle and the part that Sergeant Carney had in it that I have ventured to reproduce it here. Mr. Hallowell wrote:

Sergeant William H. Carney was one of the colour-bearers of the Fifty-fourth Regiment, Massachusetts Volunteers, when the famous assault upon Fort Wagner, South Carolina, was made at twilight on the evening of July 18, 1863. In that assault Colonel Robert Gould Shaw fell dead upon the parapet. Captains Russell and Simpkins and other brave men fell while keeping the embrasures free from the enemy's gunners and sweeping the crest of the parapet with their fire. Lieutenant-colonel Edward H. Hallowell reached the parapet. Desperately wounded, he rolled into the ditch, was again hit, and with great difficulty managed to crawl to our lines. An unknown number of enlisted men were killed within the fort. Forty enlisted men, including twenty wounded, were captured within the fort. The State flag, tied, unfortunately, to the staff with ribbons, was lost. The staff itself was brought off. The national colours planted upon the parapet were upheld and eventually borne off by Sergeant William H. Carney, whose wounds in both legs, in the breast and right arm attest his devotion to his trust. His words, "The old flag never touched the ground, boys!" are immortalised in the pages of history and the verses of poetry. The regiment went into action with twenty-two officers and six hundred and fifty enlisted men. Fourteen officers were killed or wounded. Two hundred and fifty-five enlisted men were killed or wounded. Prisoners, not wounded twenty. Total casualties, officers and men, two hundred and sixty-nine, or 40 per cent. The character of the wounds attests the nature of the contest. There were wounds from bayonet thrusts, sword cuts, pike thrusts and hand grenades; and there were heads and arms broken and smashed by the butt-ends of muskets.

It is fit that the last act, the act which cost his life, should be one of courtesy. In stepping aside to make room for another his leg was caught and crushed. Sergeant William H. Carney was a gentleman. Peace to him.

Coloured troops took part February 20, 1864, in the disastrous battle of Olustee, Florida, in which the losses were quite as severe, it is said, as in any other battle of the Civil War. Speaking of this battle, Colonel J. R. Hawley, who commanded the First Brigade in this engagement, says: "Old troops finding themselves so overmatched would have run a little and reformed with or without order. The black men stood to be killed or wounded, losing more than three hundred out of five hundred and fifty." In the battle of Nashville, the coloured troops were under a life-long Democrat, General James B. Steedman, who was one of the delegates in 1860 to the Charleston Convention which nominated Breckenridge for president. It is related that as he rode over the field immediately after the battle, he said with a grim smile: "I wonder what my Democratic friends over there would think if they knew I were fighting them with 'nigger troops.'"

Coloured troops took part in the campaign which resulted in the fall of Richmond. June 15, 1864, they captured seven guns in front of Petersburg and, on July 30, they took part in the disastrous attack at the "crater" in which 4,000 men were lost, wounded or captured in a fruitless and hopeless assault.

Finally, when General Weitzel took possession of Richmond on April 3, 1865, he was in command of a corps made up entirely of Negro soldiers. It was a Negro soldier who hauled down the Confederate flag and it was Negro soldiers who assisted in quenching the fires which had been started, when the Confederate soldiers evacuated the city, thus saving the helpless citizens who were left behind much loss and suffering. It illustrates to what extent the Negro soldiers had won the favour of the Federal officers who commanded them that black troops were called upon to maintain order in the confusion and anarchy which reigned at this time in the abandoned capital of the Confederacy. Two years before, the same General Weitzel, who was in command of the Negro troops, who at this time took possession of Richmond, had written to General Butler to be relieved of his command in Louisiana because, as he said, he "could not command Negro regiments." At that time he believed that to employ Negroes in the army was to bring about a servile insurrection for which he did not care to be responsible.

The services which the Negro troops performed in the Civil War in fighting for the freedom of their race not only convinced the officers who commanded them and the white soldiers who fought by their side that the Negro race deserved to be free, but it served to convince the great mass of the people in the North that the Negroes were fit for freedom. It did, perhaps, more than any other one thing to gain for them, as a result of the war, the passage of those amendments to the Constitution which secured to the Negro race the same rights in the United States that are granted to white men.